JUNIPERO SERRA

Fray Junipero Serra
Detail from a 1785 painting by Mariano Guerrero.
The painting is in the Museo de Historia, Castillo de
Chapultepec, Mexico City.

JUNIPERO SERRA

The Illustrated Story of the
Franciscan Founder of California's Missions

DON DeNEVI
NOEL FRANCIS MOHOLY

HARPER & ROW PUBLISHERS, San Francisco
Cambridge, Hagerstown, New York, Philadelphia, Washington
London, Mexico City, São Paulo, Singapore, Sydney

JUNIPERO SERRA.
Copyright © 1985 by Donald DeNevi and Noel Francis Moholy. All rights reserved. Printed in the United States of America. No part of this book may be used or reproduced in any manner whatsoever without written permission except in the case of brief quotations embodied in critical articles and reviews. For information address Harper & Row, Publishers, Inc., 10 East 53rd Street, New York, NY 10022. Published simultaneously in Canada by Fitzhenry & Whiteside, Limited, Toronto.

First Harper & Row paperback edition published in 1987.

Designed by Leigh McLellan

Library of Congress Cataloging in Publication Data
DeNevi, Don
  Junípero, Serra : the illustrated story of the
Franciscan founder of California's missions.

  Bibliography: p.
  Includes index.
  1. Serra, Junipero, 1713–1784. 2. Explorers—
California—Biography. 3. Explorers—Spain—Biography.
4. Franciscans—California—Biography. 5. California—
History—To 1846. I. Moholy, Noel Francis. II. Title.
F864.S44D46 1985   979.4′02′0924 [B]   84-47718
ISBN 0-06-061876-0
ISBN 0-06-250228-X (pbk)

87 88 89 90 91 RRD 10 9 8 7 6 5 4 3

To Adele Firpo DeNevi and Aldo DeNevi,
who was still with us when this project began;

and John Joseph and Eva Gertrude Moholy,
whose prayerful, unobtrusive collaboration yet
perdures effectively, supernaturally.

"What is your name, my Brother?"
"Juniper," I answered.
"Juniper, so please it God that upon your branches
thousands of souls shall build their nests!"
—Nikos Kazantzakis

CONTENTS

ILLUSTRATIONS

PHOTOGRAPHS AND DRAWINGS

MAPS

SIERRA GORDA MISSIONS

TO RIO VERDE

Conca

Tancoyol

TO JACALA

Jalpan   Landa

Tilaco

TO MEXICO CITY

TO GUADALAJARA

San Miguel

San Fernando

Santa Gertrudis

San Ignacio

La Purisma
Loreto

RIO GRANDE

GULF
OF
CALIFORNIA

San Blas

SIERRA
GORDA
MOUNTAINS

Mexico City

Vera Cruz

PACIFIC OCEAN

Loreto

MOTHER OF ALL THE MISSIONS
OF UPPER AND LOWER CALIFORNIA

Mexico, with Sierra Gorda region and Lower California.

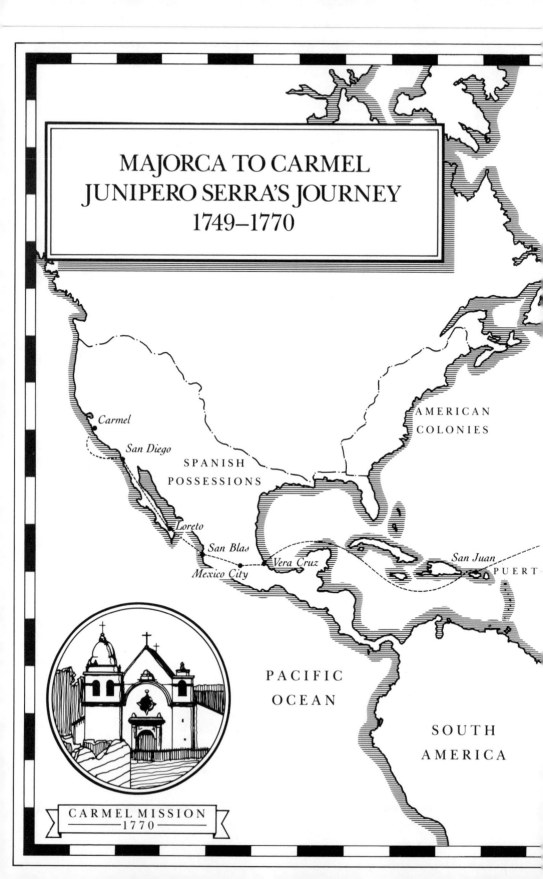

MAJORCA TO CARMEL
JUNIPERO SERRA'S JOURNEY
1749–1770

Carmel

San Diego

SPANISH
POSSESSIONS

AMERICAN
COLONIES

Loreto

San Blas

Vera Cruz

Mexico City

San Juan

PUERT

PACIFIC
OCEAN

SOUTH
AMERICA

CARMEL MISSION
—1770—

SAN FRANCISCO DE ASIS
October 9, 1776

San Francisco Bay

SANTA CLARA DE ASIS
January 12, 1777

Monterey Bay

SAN CARLOS BORROMEO DE CARMELO
June 3, 1770

SAN ANTONIO DE PADUA
July 14, 1771

SAN LUIS OBISPO DE TOLOSA
September 1, 1772

PACIFIC

SAN BUENAVENTURA
March 31, 1782

SAN GABRIEL ARCANGEL
September 8, 1771

SAN JUAN CAPISTRANO
November 1, 1776

OCEAN

SAN DIEGO DE ACALA
July 16, 1769

Upper California, showing the missions founded by Junipero Serra.

PREFACE

Junípero Serra played a decisive role in the European settlement of the New World, particularly on the American West Coast. His name belongs in the familiar litany of heros that everyone knows: the conquistador Cortes, the American Founding Fathers, the explorers Lewis and Clark, and, perhaps most appropriately, the thousands of nameless pioneer families that truly settled the West.

A Franciscan monk from the Mediterranean island of Majorca, Serra is well known by secular and church scholars alike as the tireless and devout padre presidente who first established a system of nine missions in what is now the state of California. The pivotal role, however, that this network of missions played in the West Coast's formative history is less familiar to the general public. Nor is the human side of this saintly monk widely known. Serra's story is that of a stubborn, visionary man who persevered in his mission in spite of great adversity, and some controversy, and in so doing helped lay the foundation for the future settlement and prosperity of the western United States. The present volume draws on previous sources to retell Serra's story so that it is accessible to everyone.

The first biography of Serra was written just after his death by his lifelong friend and closest companion Francisco Palóu, who was also a Franciscan monk from Majorca. His *Life of Serra*, an eyewitness account drawn from the diaries that Palóu kept during Serra's lifetime, is in a sense a panegyric work, yet its basic accuracy is unchallenged after two centuries and it remains the primary account from which subsequent biographies derive.

The picture that Serra's protege painted so painstakingly has been placed upon a broader canvas with colorful background filled in by the late Maynard J. Geiger, O.F.M., in *The Life and Times of Junípero*

Serra, the source on which we are most dependent. Geiger spent the years between 1941 and 1955 reviewing archival records from Majorca to Vera Cruz to Monterey, and even traveled Serra's route along El Camino Real, photographing as he went, to locate and assemble the documentation for his definitive and "magesterial," as it has been called, thousand page tome. The biography won the prestigious John Gilmary Shea Award from the California Historical Society. Unfortunately only two thousand copies were published by the Academy of American Franciscan History. It should also be noted that, while some of the pictures taken by Geiger for his biography are reproduced here, the majority of photographs in the present book have been culled from unpublished material in the Santa Barbara Mission Archives-Library.

Since 1934 Junípero Serra has been a candidate for canonization as a saint by the Roman Catholic church, and the most recent account of his life and accomplishments is the *Summarium,* which was written to present Serra to the Sacred Congregation for the Cause of Saints. Compiled under the direction of the Realtor Generalis of that ecclesiastical tribunal, it is the work of Jacinto Fernandez, O.F.M. While this account is written from a hagiographical point of view to demonstrate that Serra practiced virtue to a heroic degree, it is nevertheless a critical, historical account and complements the authoritative work of Geiger.

The present collaboration endeavors to embody the fruits of all three of these distinctive biographies of Junípero Serra and present to a larger audience the critical insights of their authors in a biography that is both accessible and reliably accurate. In particular, we acknowledge our reliance and dependence upon Geiger's *The Life and Times of Junípero Serra.*

We wish likewise to express our gratitude for the kindness and cooperation of the many who have assisted the authors. The Franciscan Fathers of California and the Academy of American Franciscan History have graciously accorded permission to quote from their publications. In special manner, we are indebted to the Reverend Virgilio Biasiol, O.F.M., Director of the Santa Barbara Mission Archives-Library, for his wholehearted cooperation and invaluable assistance in the preparation of this book.

I

FRAY JUNIPERO SERRA: BEGINNINGS

*In the last analysis, the essential thing is the life of the
individual. This alone makes history; here alone do
the great transformations first take place; and the
whole future, the whole history of the world, ultimate-
ly springs as a gigantic summation from the hidden
sources in that individual. In our most private and
most subjective lives we are not only the passive wit-
nesses of our age, and its sufferers, but also its mak-
ers.*

—C. G. Jung
The Meaning of Psychology for Modern Man

CHAPTER ONE

SPAIN IN QUEST
OF AN EMPIRE

Never had men struggled so hard to achieve martyrdom. They came from great distances, these Franciscans, Dominicans, Carmelites, and Jesuits. "Union with God, to seek and to save" was their charge, given by Christ himself. They came in spite of danger, risking torture at the hands of hostile natives, suffering in the rugged mountains, freezing in snowstorms, enduring hunger and thirst in the barren deserts and boundless forests.

No greater reward could come to them than the crown of martyrdom, inspiring their fearlessness, resolution, and energy. Men of the cross, no matter what order, have always made brave and adventurous explorers. Now, inspired by Christopher Columbus, the first of a long line of explorers and conquerors who set out from Spain for the New World, the Catholic church burned with fiery zeal to convert the native populations there.

All Europe was in ferment. The activity in Spain was especially noteworthy. After fighting among themselves for several hundred years, the Christian peoples of the Iberian peninsula, driven together by the invasion of the Muslim Moors in the eighth century, had become the Spanish people. After Moorish power had been broken by Ferdinand and Isabella in 1492, then came the conquistadores. Spain's great years had arrived, and the influence of the Spanish spread all over the world. Under the guidance of Queen Isabella (who deserves as much credit as Columbus for discovering the Americas), expedition after expedition departed westward to claim for the crown these newly discovered lands. For these bold forays into the unknown, Spain sent its best. None meant to stay. They found nothing in the isolation to their liking, and their initial reports were discouraging.

Over a period of almost three centuries, Spanish explorers blazed awe-inspiring trails across the New World, opening a wilderness over four times the size of their homeland. Although their avowed goal was the conversion of the natives to Christianity, many, such as the hot-blooded Juan Pizarro and Francisco Vásquez de Coronado, proved unscrupulous and ambitious. With gunpowder and sword, instead of pilgrim's staff and pastor's cross, the conquistadores, lusting for power and riches, explored the New World in search of gold and precious stones. Most had read or heard of *Las Sergas de Esplandian (The Exploits of Esplandian)*, a romantic novel written by Count Ordóñes de Montalvo in 1506 dealing with an attack by pagan forces on the medieval Christians occupying Constantinople. During the battle, the pagans were aided by Calafia, a warrior queen who came from a place "at the right hand of the Indies, an island named California, very close to that part of the Terrestrial Paradise which is inhabited by black women, without a single man among them, who live in the manner of Amazons. . . . Their weapons were all made of gold. The island everywhere abounds with gold and precious stones, and upon it no other metal is found." Also, upon this island, "there are many griffins. In no other part of the world can they be found." From Biscay to Cádiz, "California," the lilting name for Queen Calafia's land, was on everyone's mind.

The gleam of gold haunted the vision of Hernán Cortes, the conqueror of Mexico, who earlier had invested two hundred thousand ducats of his own to explore islands in uncharted Caribbean seas. In 1533, following the directive of Spain's Charles V, who ordered "Explore. Find gold. Find the island of Queen Califia," he dispatched his blue and red-clad warriors from the west coast of Mexico to the ovenlike deserts of the long, narrow peninsula separating the Gulf of California from the Pacific Ocean. Cortes suspected that Lower, or Baja, California, unpromising as it looked, might be the home of the Amazons and the griffins, where treasure lay everywhere in abundance. Two years later, he went himself with a large expedition that included a few padres and established a short-lived colony in the southeast, where La Paz is now located. But Cortes found that Baja California was a very poor land indeed, in both population and resources. There was certainly no evidence of Amazons, griffins, pearls, or gold.

The name California remained, because, not only was Queen Califia's land believed to be an island separated from Asia somewhere to the north by the legendary Strait of Anián, but it was also said to be by Juan Crespí "sterile, arid, lacking grass and water, and abounding in stones and thorns."

Knowledge of California advanced so slowly that not until 1705 did there appear a map depicting California not as an island but as a peninsula directly attached to the land mass above, called Alta, or Upper, California.

Seafarers such as Balboa, Cabrillo, and Vizcaíno, were just as active as the conquistadores. Braving storms, exposure, disease, and famine, they were the first Europeans to sail in the treacherous waters of the mighty Pacific off the American west coast. Yet none of these early mariners who battled adverse winds up and down the west coast looked upon the interior as suitable habitat for man or beast and an astonishing 227 years would elapse between the discovery of the region and its first European settlement.

However, such coastal probes did pave the way for occupation. Soon a number of small outposts in the southwest of North America asserted Spain's title against foreign interlopers. The brunt of colonizing these untamed and inhospitable regions was borne by the Flemish Franciscans, who arrived in Mexico in 1523, followed by the Spanish Franciscans in 1524. At their heels were the Dominicans and the Jesuits. Each missionary, it was said from the civil authorities' point of view, was worth a thousand soldiers in "subduing" the natives.

Chief among these men of piety were the "twelve apostles of Mexico" and others, including Juan Pérez, Eusebio Francisco Kino, Antonio Llinás, Juan Maria Salvatierras, Bartolomé de Las Casas, and Francisco Garcés. With fervent enthusiasm and compassion, they brought the gospel to the Indians who lived between the rugged mountains and the seas. Each of their orders had its own work, and there was considerable rivalry, if not jealously, between them.

Although the energy and boldness of the conquistadores and the padres were developing a great empire for Spain, little effort was being made to colonize the California coastal regions charted in 1542 by the Portuguese-born Juan Rodríguez Cabrillo. In 1579, a navigator even more renowned than Cabrillo appeared in the dim, foggy mists off the California coast. Sir Francis Drake, "master thief of the unknown world," having freighted the *Golden Hind* with looted treasure, sailed beyond the reach of Spanish vengeance and found refuge in what he described as a "conveynient harborough," which most historians identify as the modern Drake's Bay, north of the Golden Gate. Upon departing to complete his "voyage around the whole globe of the earth" during the summer of 1579, Drake claimed the unexplored interior for Queen Elizabeth of England, naming it New Albion.

A generation later (1602–3), Sebastián Vizcaíno, a seafaring merchant, sailed from the tiny port of Navidad on the western shore of Mexico, following the route taken by Cabrillo. He explored the coast of California, renamed San Miguel, San Diego, discovered the bay of Monterey, and further charted and named the prominent landmarks along the coast.

After the Vizcaíno expedition, more than 160 years went by before the Spanish crown concerned itself again with California. With churches springing up by the hundreds throughout Mexico and missions established in every province, Spain, fearful that California was becoming irresistible to other nations, once again began to carry out a colonization program. Already in possession of all Hispanic America from the tip of South America stretching into present day Texas, and across to Florida, as well as the long peninsula of Baja, Spain had remained apathetic while Russia, England, France, and Prussia were drawn to the Pacific west coast as if by an enormous magnet. Spanish armies were fighting all over Europe and Africa, preventing the monarchy from realizing its ambition to extend its Mexican dominions northward. Now, with Russia already established in Alaska and slowly reaching southward toward Point Reyes, just north of San Francisco Bay, Carlos III of Spain had little difficulty imagining the problems maintaining Spain's thousand-mile Mexican frontier if the czar were to occupy what is now California, Arizona, and New Mexico. Once entrenched, the newcomers would have a strategic position within the new world which they would never relinquish.

To meet the challenge of the encroaching Russians, Carlos III dispatched additional missionaries and colonizers to the lonely, isolated region. Two promising bays were their goals: San Diego, discovered in 1542, and Monterey to the North, named in 1602. The founding of mission colonies in these and adjacent areas would presumably discourage foreign intruders.

Meanwhile, there was another development that would affect the destiny of Alta California. In 1767, an angry and apprehensive King Carlos III decided to banish the Jesuit order from Spain and its colonies in the Americas and the Philippines. For seventy years, many Jesuits had toiled zealously in Baja California, steadily moving northward, evangelizing everyone in their path, never abandoning a mission. With patience and devoted zeal, they had accomplished what Cortes had been unable to do with the sword—Spanish dominion over the native populations. The banishment edict is one of the enigmas of history, and no attempt to explain it has yet provided a satisfactory cause. At the heart of the intrigue, apparently, was that the Jesuits were perceived by the court to covet political and ecclesiastical power. Most of the order's members were clearly simple-hearted, honest toilers of God, but others, especially the leaders, were accused of corruption. When an attempted assassination of Carlos III failed, he blamed the Jesuit leaders for the crime.

On the evening of June 24, 1767, Marqués de Croix, viceroy of New Spain, read the king's decree to the archbishop of Mexico and his assembled church officials:

> Repair with an armed force to the houses of the Jesuits. Seize the persons of all of them and within twenty-four hours transport them as prisoners to

6

the port of Vera Cruz. Cause to be sealed the records of said houses and records of such persons without allowing them to remove anything but their breviaries and such garments as are absolutely necessary for their journey. If after the embarkation there should be found one Jesuit in that district, even if ill or dying, you shall suffer the penalty of death.

(Signed)
Yo, el Rey
(I, The King)

Within days, all the black-cassocked brothers were expelled from their sixteen missions and thirty-two stations in such haste and under such circumstances that a great deal of suffering occurred. Neither age nor illness was considered. Many died hobbling along the cactus-tangled trail to Vera Cruz, on the east coast of Mexico. Each and every one obeyed the edict without protest. The people of Mexico, rich and poor alike, thronged the paths, watching with tears and lamentations as the Jesuits made their way to embark on overladen ships. Later, when the king's representatives sought to uncover the hidden mines and accumulated treasures, they found only well-kept accounts and well-furnished chapels. The missionaries, who had spent the greater part of their lives persuading the Indians within their reach to gather and adopt an agricultural way of life, neither took wealth with them nor left any behind.

The same royal edict that banished the Jesuits from the New World also charged the Franciscan College of San Fernando in Mexico City to replace them with missionaries from its order. The papacy in Rome had virtually no voice in the spread of Christianity through such Flemish and Spanish missionaries as the Franciscans, since the king of Spain authorized all missionary recruitment and expeditions, as well as paid all the bills for their undertakings. Now, Carlos III ordered the gray-cowled, rope-girdled Little Brothers of Saint Francis of Assisi to attend to the Indians on the Baja peninsula, who had been told by the departing Jesuits to await their new fathers. Of course, the Indians did not wait. Fearing with good reason the Spanish soldiers left behind, they fled into the wilderness. The first Franciscans had reached Mexico in 1523. At that time, Cortes, perhaps the most devout of all the conquistadores, knelt and kissed the hem of their robes with reverence.

In casting about for a missionary leader, a padre presidente, to rekindle the religious spirit of the Indians, as well as guide the Franciscans, the authorities at the College of San Fernando unanimously selected 54-year-old Fray Junípero Serra, a former professor of theology with two decades as a missionary in the New World.

With the choice of Serra, a figure of destiny stepped upon the stage

—not a general in crimson uniform with a great army and banners flying, but a humble padre in robe and sandals intent only upon saving souls. In less than twenty years, he would provide the enduring foundation for the development of the west coast of the United States.

CHAPTER TWO

GENTLE GIANT OF
THE CONQUISTADORES

Now in 1768, with the expelled Jesuits gathering in Vera Cruz for their return to Spain, the Franciscans faced a task that would call for all the courage and determination they could muster. They must not only re-establish the Jesuit missions, but push on quickly into Alta California to build a chain of Franciscan missions stretching from Cabo San Lucas at the southern tip of Baja California all the way to the Golden Gate.

The long struggle among Spain, England, and France for eastern North America had produced five costly European wars, leaving Spain drained and exhausted and its American colonies sinking into stagnation. But although Spain had managed to retain its hold on Texas and to occupy half of what is now Louisiana as a buffer for its colonies in New Spain, Alta California was rapidly becoming a potential scene for new struggle.

Stimulated mostly by the threat of Russian influence beginning to be felt along the west coast of North America, King Carlos III experienced a resurgence of interest in the area. Well aware of previous neglect and failure, the Spanish appointed their ablest colonial administrator, José de la Sonora Gálvez, the inspector general of Mexico, to reform the administration of New Spain. Once there he realized the strategic importance of California and planned an expedition with the goal of occupying Monterey and San Diego. San Diego would serve as a base between Monterey on the Pacific coast and Loreto (a port in Baja on the Gulf of California). Soldiers, and eventually settlers, were to hold the country; missionaries were to convert the Indians to Christianity.

Summoned from the province of Mesquital, Fray Junípero Serra was told he had been appointed president of the Baja missions. Four decades of prayer and service had prepared him for what lay ahead; the spirit of the new effort would be kindled by his own.

Junípero Serra lived his life for the truth of Christ, which he taught, following the example of Saint Francis. It is the individual Christian who is the carrier of goodness and upon whom depends the welfare of the world. Dangers to civilization emanate from satanic influences on human nature, and to combat such evil, humankind must believe in God with courage and compassion, and commit itself with conviction. Humanity alone can save or destroy the world and itself. Writing of threats to the growth and development of his missions and his conversion efforts during the 1770s, Serra stated that the un-Christian side of the individual containing unrecognized, often barbarous and uncivilized impulses, must be brought into consciousness. Only then can God, and his Son, Jesus Christ, eradicate human perniciousness. Fully realizing that the supernatural transformation of humankind follows the slow tread of centuries and cannot be brought to fruition in one generation, Serra preached to his Franciscan brethren and his Christian Indians that to achieve that end, "We must teach with all we have in us about domestic animals, economic development, trade and commerce, cultural values and artistic endeavors, and, above all, about God. Unless our Catholic philosophy and way of life are taught religiously, our civilization will be founded on sand." Later, expressing how profoundly he wished to be understood, he added, "As long as life lasts in me, I shall do all I can to propagate our Holy Faith. In California is my way of life and please God, there I hope to die."

In his burning missionary zeal were combined to an extraordinary degree idealism with the capacity for simple manual labor—sowing crops, planting rosebushes and grapevines. He preferred missionary work in the field to teaching, preaching, or writing, however great the recognition he had received for all of these. To him, each individual soul, all God's creation, was important. In his writings, he often seems to be bursting with happiness as he describes whatever attracts him using simple, colloquial language spiced with humorous stories.

His love was for his "dear children"—the 6,736 Indians baptized and the more than five thousand he confirmed. During his time, the health and living standards of the California Indians were improved and an economic entity created possessing 5,384 head of cattle, 5,629 sheep, and 4,294 goats, unprecedented prosperity for the natives of the Pacific coast. In all the mission workshops and fields, Indians were trained in agriculture, crafts, letters, and music. And in his love for his converts he did not shrink from applying punishment, corporal punishment for those who abandoned their work or killed cattle and sheep needlessly and thus put the whole community at risk of starvation. But the Indians understood and respected his motives; they especially admired his Franciscan vow of poverty. Never did they see him eat more than they did, or own anything. Serra believed that colonizing California was only secondary to converting the Indians to Christianity, and that the land rightfully belonged to the Indians. Everything they accomplished, the missions, farms, sheep and cattle ranches, were held in trust by the Franciscans. Thus, as Father Serra threaded his way through the paradoxes of a church-run state and a state-run church, he never hesitated to emphatically express what he felt was best for his "dear children," bringing him into conflict with the civil and military authorities and earning him a reputation as single-minded and quarrelsome.

He was a man with many of the traits of medieval piety, some strange to us today. Like Saint Francis of Assisi, he thought the body an enemy of the soul and spent his life in an intense battle between spirit and flesh. His garments were flimsy, and his bed was a single blanket on the damp earth or a simple wooden frame. His food was of the simplest and only enough to sustain life. Accustomed by the routine of his order to only three or four hours of sleep each night, he spent long hours in prayer. He awed congregations with his flagellation in the pulpit; this was done as an act of public penance for his sins and to encourage others to repent.

This physical discipline, so alien to us today, served him well in his missionary expeditions, which eventually covered, all told, an incredible twenty-four thousand miles—more than Marco Polo or Lewis and Clark.

His story played out in a setting marked by Spain's ambitious drive to defend and broaden its colonial dominions, Serra believed with an unshakable assurance and indomitable will that, by the single-mindedness of his devotion and his willingness to allow every thought for his person and comfort to be fuel for the fire of his zeal, he could be the instrument for bringing miracles to earth.

His influence extends to today. The missions he and his padres established introduced crops that are part of the economic foundation for the agricultural wealth of the state of California. Railroads and freeways follow El Camino Real along which he traveled. Some of the largest and most important cities on the West Coast—San Diego, Los Angeles, Santa Clara, and San Francisco—were founded as missions or presidios under Serra. And though not widely known, his heritage is not silent—Serra is memorialized from local place names on the West Coast to Statuary Hall in the national capitol.

CHAPTER THREE

A FRANCISCAN FOREVER

In the village of Petra, the "nest of Majorca," a fledgling stirred on the morning of November 24, 1713, gladdening the hearts of Antonio and Margarita Serra. Immediately, the father nailed a laurel branch to the door of their simple home, announcing to the world that the gift God had granted them was a baby boy.

A few hours later, relatives and friars formed a procession to the village Church of San Pedro. Led by the midwife bearing the newborn infant, the procession consisted of the godmother and godfather, the child's father, Antonio Serra, and the other men who would figure in the boy's life. As the procession entered the massive parish church, the chatter hushed as everyone assembled around the baptismal font to observe the baptism of the tiny infant. He was christened Miguel José.

Returning from the ceremony, the midwife rushed to the bedroom loft and joyously informed Margarita, "We return your son to you a Christian." Receiving her son in her arms, the mother responded with the prayerful wish, "Lord, may this child survive." She and Antonio remembered with pain their suffering at the deaths of their previous two infants.

Friends and neighbors gathered in the main room of the modest two-storied stone house, and the baby's sponsors, the godmother and godfather, dispensed the traditional brandy and sweets. Margarita and Antonio later followed their native tradition by carrying their delicate infant to the hillside shrine of Nuestra Señora del Bon Any, overlooking the plain of Petra. There, in a brief ceremony, they entrusted their precious son to the Mother of God, who from this sanctuary guarded their village and protected its crops as Our Lady of the Good Year.

From his earliest moments, Miguel accompanied his parents, and later his younger sister, Juana Maria, down the narrow Calle Mayor to

General view of Petra. Near Serra's birthplace the churches San Bernardino (left) and San Pedro (right), with their Moorish and Gothic towers, respectively, recall Majorca's Muslim and Christian past. San Bernardino was the convent church attached to the former Franciscan monastery. San Pedro was and remains the parish church.

that same village church in which he had been baptized. It was the custom in Petra for mothers to take their children who were just beginning to walk to the Franciscan convent of San Bernardino. There, before the beautiful white and gold image of Nuestra Señora de los Angeles, Miguel was coaxed to take his first steps, accompanied by Margarita's prayers that he walk in life under the protection of Our Lady, Queen of the Angels.

Amid a life of almost biblical simplicity, Miguel grew and developed, learning his native Majorcan dialect from his mother and father. For Miguel, pride of his parents, memorizing his catechism, reciting his prayers, and talking to God was as natural as taking the livestock to pasture or carrrying the heavy water bucket from the town cistern. The living quarters, consisting of rough floors, plain furniture, and dim light furnished by a wick burning in oil, radiated religion and piety. Antonio and Margarita provided him the simple farmers' fare of wheaten bread, beans, cheese, fruits and vegetables, and the Majorcan *enseimada,* or sweetcake. Raised in simple frugality, Miguel never expected material luxury. "What more do we want," he would ask in later years, "than a little tortilla and the wild herbs of the field?"

Even by the age of seven, Miguel was becoming knowledgeable

about produce, livestock, and farming. Joining his parents in the fields they farmed some distance from their home, he spent long hours hoeing and tilling, learning both the secrets of nature and the dignity of labor. Like the other devout people of Petra, the Serras had little interest in anything beyond their neighbors and happenings on the island. But although he was growing up in an atmosphere reminiscent of the isolation of medieval times, Miguel's dreams reached beyond the sea to faraway lands. The sea had always played the dominant role in his culture, and it is not surprising that an inquisitive boy would find the islanders' twenty centuries of history fascinating. Majorca could boast that all had visited it—Phoenicians, Egyptians, Greeks, Romans, Moors, Sicilians, Frenchmen and Spaniards.

The friary and church of San Bernardino, only a few hundred yards away from the Serra home, to Antonio and Margarita, was a spiritual haven and an intellectual oasis in the agricultural plain of Majorca that comprised their world; it was also their son's only boyhood school. Unaccompanied, Miguel would visit the friary, where he was always welcomed with delight by the friars, who admired his quick intellect and insatiable curiosity. The brethren of Saint Francis of Assisi had been in Petra since 1607, and the youngster enjoyed nothing more than to hear about their founder.

These same friars were his earliest teachers, introducing Miguel to reading and writing. The young boy also eagerly learned mathematics and religion and asked permission to study music, particularly Gregorian chant. When Miguel José was eight years old, one of the friars, a professor of grammar, would take him to chant with the other Franciscans on feast days. One occasion was the consecration of the statue of La Purísima, the image of the Immaculate Conception that was the central figure of the high altar, and it left a lifelong impression on the child. Dwelling in the shadow of the altar and participating in the canonical hours and other liturgical functions, the lad's vocation gradually, almost imperceptibly, began to emerge.

On the right of La Purísima was the statue of San Juan Capistrano, banner in hand and foot upon the Turk's head. On both sides of the Renaissance church were richly decorated baroque chapels dedicated to saints: Santa Clara, San Antonio de Padua, San Juan Bautista, Nuestra Señora de los Angeles, San Francisco Solano, San Buenaventura, San Miguel, Santa Rosa, San Gabriel, San Rafael, Santa Ana, San Diego de Alcalá, and San Francisco. The young Serra attended mass in the convento, and his love for the saints to whom, the convento was dedicated, would one day bring him to select their names for the missions in California.

Delighted and perhaps slightly surprised to find in their young son such a devout nature and avid thirst for knowledge, and presuming that he dreamed of one day wearing the habit of the Franciscan order, his parents took him to the capital city of Palma, twenty-five miles away. Descending the plateau, they arrived before a walled city of sixty churches and thirty thousand people. Antonio and Margarita sought out for a tutor a canon of the cathedral to whom they could entrust their fifteen-year-old son. Having selected this priest, who was to supervise Miguel's religious and intellectual development, the Serras returned home to Petra to cultivate their fields. The canon taught Miguel to pray and supervised his daily studies and responsibilities, and soon the young man rewarded his teacher's efforts. Thus began a new way of life that would hold Serra in Palma for the next twenty years.

After a year of tutoring, Serra enrolled as a student of philosophy in the classes conducted by the Franciscans at the Convent of San Francisco. There, they prepared students for the priesthood, as well as secular students for the various professions. Too young to enter the Franciscan order, Miguel spent a year in study. At the age of 16 he formally applied for admission to the Franciscan order. The brief interview ended with a denial of admission. Because he was short of stature and frail-looking, Miguel was told to wait until he was a little older. It was not until the canon and other Franciscan friends earnestly presented his cause before the Very Reverend Fray Antonio Perelló Moragues that the young man was permitted to enter the Convent of Jesus, located outside Palma's city walls. For the remaining fifty-four years of his life, Serra would wear the habit of the Franciscan order.

The novitiate, required by canon law before a novice takes his vows and becomes a full member of the order, was a year of strict seclusion and rigorous discipline. An unvarying round of prayers, silence, meditation, choir attendance, spiritual readings, daily instruction and physical chores around the convent made up each day. Even sleep was interrupted by chanting of office at midnight. Visits and letters were discouraged. During this period a novice was free to leave at any time, yet, undistracted for a year, he could make great strides forward.

Although most of the personal details of Serra's novitiate have long since been lost, a few incidents were recorded. For instance, it is known that Miguel's lack of height and physical frailty prevented him from carrying out certain assignments. One of his daily responsibilities was to turn the large, musically notated sheepskin pages of the hymn book for those who chanted or sang from it. Serra was so short that he could not easily turn the pages of the book, which was slightly inclined on a large, ornamented lectern. As a result, the novice-master excused him from the task, assigning him to serve mass instead.

It is also known that the young man devoted much of his free time to reading historical accounts of the Franciscans. The order of Saint

Francis's spiritual sons was founded in Italy in the thirteenth century and was called "Order of Lesser Brothers," in Latin, *Ordo Fratrum Minorum,* or "Order of Friars Minor" (O.F.M.). Its priests came to be known as gray friars from their habits, simple robes woven from undyed wool. Recruited mostly from the humble classes, they eventually served all over Europe, Palestine, North Africa, Persia, India, and parts of eastern Russia. They were always to walk in imitation of Christ and the apostles, practicing humility, poverty, and austerity, and avoiding signs of pride and ostentation.

The chronicles Serra read contained the early history of the Franciscan movement in the provinces in Spain and the history of its missionary activities in far-off lands. It was of the missionaries that Miguel read with special interest, igniting in him the desire to "serve God better and to save my soul."

During that novitiate year, Serra followed closely the accounts of the beatification of Peter Duenas and John of Cetinas, who had been martyred in 1397. Fresh in his memory was the canonization of Saint Francis Solano the Franciscan Apostle of Peru, in 1726. As avidly as a youth fascinated by technology reads about computers today, Miguel studied the achievements of the order's venerable men. Francisco Palóu, his close friend and biographer, recorded how well Serra could recount with freshness what he had read in his youth. Later in his life, Serra would thank God for his facile memory.

There is little question that these early readings inspired in the young man a strong desire to serve as a missionary, although he would not realize his dream for another nineteen years. For the time being, Miguel's enthusiasm for an active missionary life would be buried under a mass of professional studies leading to ordination.

It was the option of Franciscans in the province of Majorca to choose a new name to replace their baptismal name when they made their profession, and Serra decided to do so, taking Junípero.

Naturally, every Franciscan novice becomes intimately acquainted with the life of Saint Francis of Assisi, as well as with the inspirational literature about him and his associates that has accumulated through the centuries. *The Little Flowers of Saint Francis* was by far the most popular of these writings, and it became Miguel's favorite. Written anonymously in the fourteenth century, it is a collection of stories about Saint Francis and his companions told in the Italian countryside where he lived. Without footnotes or criticism, the author simply wrote down the tales, infusing them with life out of his own creativity and style. A variety of interesting characters such as Brothers Masseo, Leo, Giles, and Juniper, are vividly portrayed in all their humanity. Miguel chose Brother Juniper, renowned for his guileless simplicity and celestial mirth. Saint Francis loved and understood Brother Juni-

Serra's cell, Mission San Carlos de Borromeo (Carmel Mission). The room where Serra lived in California reflects the vows of poverty taken by all Franciscan friars at the time of their profession. © Piggot, 1938.

per, who was known as the "jester of the Lord." Here was a kindred spirit, someone unhampered by deviousness, a personality with the humor and common sense of Miguel himself. Juniper followed Saint Francis wherever he went with warmth and happiness. He "longed to be his equal in humility," and was so zealous in the service of the others that he utterly disregarded himself. It was Saint Francis who said, after complaints from the others about Brother Juniper's whimsical antics, "Would to God, my brethren, that I had a whole forest of such Junipers!"

Miguel decided he not only would make Brother Juniper his patron but would also take his name for his own. From the day of his profession, he would be known to the world as Fray Junípero Serra.

With the long months of his probation coming to an end, Serra was ready to bind himself irrevocably to God. Before taking his vows, he promised to renounce the right of ownership to everything he had. For the rest of his life he would depend upon the "table of the Lord," the Franciscan designation for the providence of God.

On the morning of September 15, 1731, Serra and his fellow novices knelt before the Very Reverend Antonio Perelló Moragues in the sanctuary of the Convent of Jesus. To the kneeling youths, the provincial addressed the following question: "My sons, what is your petition?" In unison, they responded, "I desire to profess the rule of our Blessed Father Francis, confirmed by the Lord Pope, Honorius III, by living in obedience, without property, and in chastity, in order to serve God better and to save my soul." Then, one by one, the novices knelt before him and placed their hands within his. Miguel, now eighteen, said in his Majorcan dialect: "I, Fray Junípero Serra, vow and promise to Almighty God, to the ever blessed Virgin Mary, to Blessed Father Francis, to all the saints, and to you, Father, to observe for the whole span of my life the rule of the Friars Minor confirmed by His Holiness, Pope Honorius III, by living in obedience, without property, and in chastity."

With the pronouncement of these words, Serra was a Franciscan forever. He vowed to be one of the trees in the forest of Saint Francis, striving for the hardiness and resilience of the juniper tree, undaunted by the worldly winds of adversity.

Junípero never forgot the day when he had bound himself to God. It is customary for Franciscans to renew their vows each year on April 16, the traditional date when Saint Francis received the verbal approval of the pope for his rule. If held in a church with a large community, it can be an imposing ceremony. But many friars are not so conveniently situated, especially those doing missionary work. For the rest of his life, wherever he was on that date, even at sea or on the trail with no other Franciscans to help him mark the day, Serra never failed to renew his vows. April 16 was the most meaningful day of his year. During his later years, whenever Serra was present at the profession of a novice, he would recall his own jubilation, *"Venerunt mihi omnia bona pariter cum illa"* ("All good things came to me with this profession") even crediting his physical growth and the improvement of his health to the blessings received.

> In the novitiate, I was almost always ill and so small of stature that I was unable to reach the lectern, nor could I help my fellow novices in the necessary chores of the novitiate. Therefore, the Father Master of Novices employed me solely in serving Mass daily. However, with my profession I gained health and strength and grew to medium size. I attribute all this to my profession, for which I gave infinite thanks to God.

Without doubt, his acceptance as a friar in the Order of Saint Francis proved to be influential in his personal development. But it would have importance in the larger world as well, as his missionary zeal added California to the church and the Spanish Empire.

San Francisco Church exterior. The facade of the cathedralesque church of San Francisco in Palma, founded in 1281, adjoins the monastery where Serra studied as student and priest between 1731 and 1749. The courtyard reflects Majorca's pre-13th century Islamic heritage.

Monastery courtyard.

CHAPTER FOUR

A QUIET, SCHOLARLY LIFE

Leaving the novitiate house at the Convent of Jesus, Junípero moved to the Convent of San Francisco within the city walls. Here, in the center of medieval Palma close to cathedral and sea, he would spend the next eighteen years, first as a student and then as a professor of philosophy and theology. Ahead of him now were six years of study, three in philosophy and three in theology, before he could become a priest.

The church of San Francisco, constructed over two hundred years before Columbus sailed for the Americas, was the second largest church on the island, with twenty-three side chapels and two cloisters, and wide ambulatories marked by graceful arches. In the center of the patio was a well, bearing the date 1658, which supplied the community with cool, fresh water. Here, in this tranquil setting, Junípero and his fellow Franciscans prayed and meditated, as patterns of sunlight played on the Gothic arcade and cast shadows on the monastery walls. Later in his life, Serra vividly recalled this beautiful edifice that had been his first home as a Franciscan.

Classes in philosophy began in early October. Now, in 1731, Junípero would begin a severe training of his intellect. Logic, dialectics, metaphysics, and cosmology followed one after the other, in order to train his mind to grapple with the essence of things. Between 1734 and 1737, he studied theology. Books and study would be his passion until middle life. His recently discovered lecture notes show that on June 23, 1737, he concluded one course on a note of truimph and satisfaction: "Today I finished my studies." But he was mistaken, not realizing what was yet in store for him.

During his years of studying theology, Serra, along with thirty-three other Franciscans, was ordained subdeacon on December 18, 1734, and, with twenty-seven others, deacon, on March 17, 1736. As yet, the date of his ordination to the priesthood has not been discovered. The same friars who were ordained deacons with him received the order of priesthood on May 31, 1737. Serra's name does not appear on that date in the official ordination book, because he had not reached the canonical age; he was still not yet twenty-four.

Even before he was ordained, his superiors recognized his intellectual accomplishments by singling him out to be a professor within the order. Along with five already ordained priests, he was told to prepare for the competitive examinations leading to the position of lector of philosophy. Those who were successful formed a standing body from which professors would be chosen as openings occurred. On November 29, 1737, after several days of punishingly difficult examinations, Serra passed and was unanimously declared lector of philosophy by the provincial and the members of his council. However, the actual call to teach would not come until nearly three years later, in the fall of 1740.

Meanwhile, Serra was ordained a priest in 1737, probably during Advent, the traditional days of ordination. He received permission to preach on March 19, 1737, and jurisdiction to hear confessions in the diocese nearly two years later, on February 21, 1739. Junípero received his first appointment to office, that of librarian of the convent, in 1739.

On January 9, 1740, Serra was officially commissioned to teach philosophy for the next three years in the Convent of San Francisco. Facing him in that initial lecture were twenty-eight students. Two of these, no less than their more celebrated professor, were destined to become famous figures in North American history. They were Francisco Palóu and Juan Crespí, both natives of Palma who chose to retain their baptismal names in the order. From that first session, Serra, as their professor, would keep his eyes on them.

Crespí had a poor memory, making up in industry what he lacked in retentiveness. All through his life he worked hard and would one day become known as a diarist, explorer, and naturalist with the Portolá expedition in California. As a youth, he had been extremely pious; his playmates nicknamed him *Beato*, "Blessed."

But it was Palóu that Serra looked upon with particular favor, and the esteem was mutual. From the beginning, they saw eye to eye, as they would for the rest of their lives. In later years, after serving with Serra faithfully and devotedly, Palóu would become his chronicler, writing his venerable teacher's biography in 1787. That effort is the source all serious researchers turn to first when beginning the study of Serra's life. After Serra's death, Palóu wrote:

From the year 1740 when he received me as one of his students, until the year 1784 when death separated us, I was the object of his very special affection, an affection we always mutually shared, more than if we had been brothers in the flesh.

Although Serra, Palóu, and Crespí were familiar with the history of the great Majorcan philosopher-missionary Ramón Lull, whose sarcophagus they saw daily in the church of the friary, and well informed about the dangers he and other missionaries had survived or succumbed to, the hardships they would encounter themselves could scarcely have been imagined as they wrestled with philosophical questions in the peaceful gardens of the convent.

Serra realized that his calling as a professor of philosophy carried with it high privilege and heavy responsibility. For three years, he was concerned with fostering the critical and creative thinking so necessary for friars—the ability to wrestle with the great moral, intellectual and spiritual questions of the era. Philosophy, he told his students, possessed a nobility in the realm of knowledge beyond compare. It was the fountainhead of mental disciplines and the science of sciences, the study of "mental light." Serra exhorted his students to "Walk in that light worthily that you may be sons of Him who is Light itself and in Whom there is no darkness."

Intellectual philosophy for Serra was not to be divorced from faith or from moral living. In an equally spiritual vein, he would instruct: "Seek wisdom and diligently cultivate the fear of the Lord, which fear is the beginning of wisdom, as we are told by the Royal Psalmist. We know furthermore that wisdom will not enter into a malevolent soul nor into a body subject to sin." Truth is one.

During the three years of the philosophy course, over sixty students had been enrolled, absorbing the wisdom of their young professor. In the final class session, held on June 23, 1743, Serra concluded his lectures by declaring:

> My dear students. Today we have the greatest reason for rejoicing. After three years we have reached the final goal of our laborious philosophical exercises. On looking back upon our labors, and on congratulating one another, we can sing out in the lines of Virgil:
> Jove will soon dispose to future good
> Our past and present woes.

Throughout the years, as their son lectured within the walled monastery of San Francisco, Antonio, and Margarita continued their lives in the home and fields with the same regularity as when Miguel was a boy. Although parents and child had taken different paths during the years that separated them, their bonds of love, affection, and memory remained. From time to time, Junípero went home for brief visits. His arrival always caused a stir and excitement in tranquil Petra, where the townspeople who remembered him as a boy knew him now, as friar, priest, and professor.

On a few occasions, Serra was able to help his parents economically. During his last five years on Majorca, drought and plague harassed the Serra family, as well as the other folk of Petra. On one of his visits, probably early in 1749, Junípero found his younger sister near death. On another occasion, he was called home to anoint his father, seriously ill, with the sacrament of the dying. From his sick bed, Antonio said, "My son, let me charge you to be a good religious of your Father, Saint Francis." Junípero would remember and quote those words back to him when he lost his son forever to the New World.

While he instructed Palóu, Crespí, and the others, Serra was himself pursuing graduate studies in sacred theology at the University of Blessed Ramón Lull, which was founded in Palma during the late fifteenth century and located in the medieval quarter near the convent. Serra was awarded the doctorate in sacred theology in 1742. He pursued his studies in theology while teaching undergraduate philosophy courses. The surviving records of the Lullian University do not indicate the topics of his graduate studies or the exact day upon which he received his degree, although university rolls refer to "Doctor Junípero" and "Doctor Serra" assisting at hundreds of baccalaureate and doctoral examinations in theology.

Not much has come to light concerning Serra's activities during his academic career; no personal recollections by him survive. It is known, however, that Junípero's life was centered at the Convent of San Francisco, and that he preached all over the island.

In June of 1743, Serra was accorded the singular honor of being invited to preach the sermon in Palma's cathedral on the Feast of Corpus Christi, an important festival celebrated on the Thursday after Trinity Sunday in honor of Jesus Christ present in the Eucharist, to which only the better known preachers were invited.

On October 16, 1743, Serra was unanimously chosen by the provincial and his council at the Convent of San Francisco to fill the *de prima* Duns Scotus chair of sacred theology within the Lullian University. The designation *de prima* indicated the principal Franciscan professor of theology at the university who taught the morning seminars; the secondary professor, called *de visperas*, conducted the afternoon courses. Once again, as when he was appointed lector of philosophy at the Convent of Palma, he was being accorded a singular distinction based upon his intellectual ability.

Serra's preaching was important to him. The young professor, preached with a sonorous voice surprising in so frail a man. According to Palóu, Serra preached "with such fervent zeal . . . that sinners were awakened from the heavy slumber of sin and converted to God in spite of their mortal enemy." Palóu tells us that Serra's sermons were applauded by the learned and the unlettered alike. Sprung from the country soil of Petra, Junípero never lost the ability to touch his hearers, simplifying difficult theological concepts to make them understandable to all. During those evangelizing efforts, which lasted until 1749, Serra toured most of the island. He preached in the cities and the towns, to the religious and the laity, to the wealthy and the poor.

The most prestigious sermon of the year was given at the feast of the patron of the university, Ramón Lull, an occasion for one of Palma's most important celebrations. A committee of professors and benefactors bestowed on Fray Junípero Serra the great honor of being chosen to preach the sermon on January 25, 1749.

That morning, the faculties of theology, philosophy, jurisprudence, and medicine were assembled at the university, members richly capped and gowned in the colors of their faculties. Hats, tassels, hoods, and capes, along with the banners and flowers decorating the church, provided a magnificent display of color. With trumpets and drums playing, the viceroy, the bishop, the mayor, the aldermen, professors, students, and their hundreds of guests took their seats. Serra had been wrestling privately with certain decisions and now believed this sermon might well be his final lecture in Palma. He devoted a great deal of time to its preparation; he wanted to honor the patron saint of the university with the most noteworthy sermon he could achieve.

After mass had been sung, Serra stepped into the pulpit. Gazing up at the tilted sarcophagus and the reclining sculptured figure of Lull, he began his oration. Although his sermon was printed at the time, it has not come to light. Palóu tells us that one professor was heard to say, "This sermon is worthy of being printed in letters of gold."

Despite the acclaim he was receiving as a noted lecturer, as well as the joy he gained from preaching, Serra once again began to feel the longings he had had as a novice to become a missionary. The young priest-professor from Petra, now in his mid-thirties, dreamed of following in the footsteps of Saint Francis Solano, the gentle missionary who had walked alone throughout Peru, Chile, and northern Argentina, playing his violin and singlehandedly converting several hundred thousand people.

During the previous fall (1748), even amid the secure routine of university life, he heard much exciting talk about the Americas, where it seemed gold and precious gems were to be had for the taking. Junípero, little concerned, of course, about the wealth of faraway lands, worried about the people of those lands. A flock without a shepherd, they worshiped strange idols and had never been told of the true God.

Serra did not dismiss his renewed surge of enthusiasm as something childish or impulsive. Instead, he quietly prayed for counsel. Should he venture out to the New World and preach Christ to the Indians? If it was to be so, Junípero was human enough to want a friend from his own province to accompany him, and from the first he seems to have had Palóu in mind. But just what finally led to his decision to become a missionary does not seem to have been known even to Palóu, his closest confidant. Although Serra kept his newly arisen desire secret, continuing his teaching at the university and leaving developments in the hands of God and the workings of time, he told his friend on one occasion, "I have had no other motive but to revive in my soul those intense longings which I have had since my novitiate when I read the lives of the saints. These longings have become somewhat deadened because of the preoccupation I had with studies." Recapturing the fervor he had known in the novitiate could be achieved, he felt, only through some heroic or self-sacrificing act. Had Junípero remained a professor living in the friary under Franciscan rule, he might eventually have become the rector of the university and, much later, perhaps the bishop of Majorca. Perhaps he wished to avoid the temptation to remain in such secure surroundings and that is why he focused instead upon distant horizons.

Soon after Serra's longings had taken definite shape, Father Mezquía, a special representative of the Apostolic College of San Fernando, arrived in Spain. The apostolic college was a Franciscan institution whose purpose was to train an elite band of missionaries for the Indian missions of the New World. The College of San Fernando in Mexico City was founded in 1734, the second of four such colleges, the first of which had been established at Santa Cruz de Querétaro in 1683. Father Mezquía had arrived in Spain to recruit new missionaries for the perilous work of converting the Indians of northeastern Mexico to Christianity. Within a month, he sent word to the Lullian University officials that he had been informed that one of their professors wished to join him and the other thirty-three missionaries sailing for Hispanic America.

Serra had apparently revealed his dream, at least to his father provincial. The provincial, who in the event of Serra's leaving would be responsible for filling the vacant Duns Scotus chair, undoubtedly mentioned to someone else that one of their professors wished to become an apostolic missionary. Soon, rumors were rampant. Fray Rafael Verger, also a professor of philosophy (and years later, Serra's superior at the College of San Fernando), told Palóu of his own desire to become a missionary. Palóu confided that he, too, would like to go.

As missionary enthusiasm began to manifest itself, Serra continued to keep his own counsel and to pray for guidance, choosing for his patrons the Immaculate Conception and Saint Francis Solano.

One day, Serra visited Palóu in his monastic cell, and Francisco confided to his former professor his ardent wish to become a missionary to the Indians at the farthest reaches of the world.

"What do you think?" Palóu asked, hesitantly.

There was no answer, but tears welled up in the eyes of his mentor. Palóu misinterpreted the tears as an expression of sorrow over their parting. For Junípero, it was now time to reveal his own secret.

> You heard a rumor, Francisco, and you could not find out the identity of the friar. The rumor is true. I am the one who intends to make this long journey, and I have been sorrowful because I would have no companion for so long a journey; but I would not on that account turn back from my purpose. I have just finished making two novenas to the Most Pure Conception of Mary, Most Holy, and to Saint Francis Solano, asking them to bestir the heart of someone to go with me, if it were the will of God. . . . In my heart I felt that inclination to speak to you as I was led to believe Your Reverence would be interested. And since what I have guarded in my heart with such secrecy has become known to Your Reverence by the means you narrated, you being unaware of my intentions, and this while I was beseeching God to touch someone's heart, it is without doubt, God's will, since I was most inclined to have Your Reverence go with me. Nevertheless let us commend the matter to the Lord and do as I did in regard to the two novenas, and let us both keep this secret.

Then, the two embraced each other, shedding tears of joy and agreeing to press forward their plans.

However, it was one thing to decide to be a missionary and quite another to bring that dream to fruition. Forgetting for a moment the need for obtaining the permission from the various secular authorities, there was considerable reluctance to appoint missionaries from the Lullian University since that institution had not been established as an apostolic college.

Now that Palóu had made his decision, Serra wrote to the commissary general of the Indies, Fray Matías de Velasco, in Madrid, asking permission for Palóu and himself to become missionaries. All matters pertaining to the New World were handled through one central agency located in the capital, close to the king's court. The commissary general dealt directly with the Council of the Indies, and the council with the Board of Trade in Cádiz. The whole matter was under the control of the state; accordingly, Franciscan volunteers processed their petitions through this governmental body.

The response Serra received from Velasco a few weeks later was discouraging: Father Mezquía, recruiting for the Apostolic College of San Fernando, had already filled his contingent of thirty-three. Nevertheless, the commissary general promised he would keep Junípero's letter of inquiry on file in case any of the applicants failed to make the trip. But, in truth, the missionaries destined for Mexico were already in Cádiz awaiting embarkation. Serra, in a response to Velasco, next requested permission to join one of the apostolic colleges in Spain; if he were to become a member of such a college, his name would more easily find its way onto a missionary list.

Meanwhile, Serra continued his lectures, taking part in his last examination of a student on February 5, 1749. Lent that year began on February 19, and he had been invited by the town council of his native Petra to deliver the Lenten sermons in the parish church of San Pedro, where he had been baptized and confirmed. Among his listeners were relatives, friends, and former schoolmates now married with children. During these quiet days, Junípero had ample time to visit with Antonio and Margarita, as well as his sister Juana María, his nephew, Miquel Ribot, and his two nieces. But all the while, through the busy hours and pleasant days, he hoped good news would arrive from Madrid.

Fortune favored Serra and Palóu. After observing the high, frigid waves of the Atlantic, five of the thirty-three recuits awaiting embarkation in Cádiz decided that discretion was the better part of valor and returned home. The head of the delegation hurriedly sent Palóu the two authorizations requested. But the missionary appointments arrived by ordinary mail, which apparently suffered interference. Palóu noted, "The patents were lost somewhere between the friary's portal and the cell I inhabited." Someone who did not want the two to leave had intercepted the letter, although such action was punishable by excommunication.

When no response was received from Serra and Palóu, a second letter was dispatched by special envoy to ensure delivery.

On the morning of Palm Sunday, as Palóu was about to join in the blessing of the palms, the envoy arrived at the Convent of San Francisco with the urgent letter from Velasco containing the patents; the commissary general awaited a reply in Cádiz. Palóu immediately asked permission to leave for Petra to inform Serra. That evening, Palóu handed his mentor the documents that would allow the two to proceed to Cádiz to join the missionaries bound for the New World.

"The fact was for him a source of greater joy and happiness," wrote Palóu, "than if he had received a royal decree naming him to some bishopric." Palóu remained in Petra overnight, and the two planned their departure. Maintaining their secret for a while longer, Serra decided to complete his mission in Petra and return to Palma after Easter. The next morning, Palóu returned to the capital to begin final preparations.

Serra braced himself for one of the most difficult tasks of his life: saying good-bye forever to his parents. Of course, he had left "the world," including his parents, upon entering the Franciscan order and taking his vows and was completely at the disposal of his superiors. Normally, however, they could have expected him to remain on Majorca, never more than twenty-five miles away.

Antonio, now seventy-three, and Margarita, seventy-one, were old. Had they learned of Junípero's intended departure, they may have pleaded with him not to go. They had already lived beyond the usual life span of the eighteenth century and could not have expected to live much longer. His farewell would have to be a final one. Junípero may have feared that their pleas would break his resolve.

Two traditions were dear to the hearts of the people of Petra. One was to go on a *romería* (pilgrimage) to the Sanctuary of Bon Any every year on Easter Tuesday to pray for an abundant harvest. The other was not to leave Majorca on a journey, long or short, without climbing the hill to ask for the blessing and protection of Nuestra Señora del Bon Any. Serra's presence in Petra this last Easter before leaving for the New World made it possible for him to observe both of these ancient traditions.

Early in the morning of third day of Easter, Serra and his family joined the other villagers of Petra. With flags flying, banners waving, and the venerated statue of Saint Joseph borne on the shoulders of four men, the assemblage formed a procession that made its way up the wooded slopes.

As they reached the top of the holy hill, Serra, accompanied by those he loved most, had a last view of the beauty of Majorca and of Petra in the fields below with the blue Mediterranean and the the Bay of Alcudia in the distant north. There he partook of a midday meal of *empanadas*, savory small pies filled with lamb, and, without revealing his secret, bid farewell to his family and friends. Then, after one last look at Nuestra Señora del Bon Any, and a prayer asking for her protection, Serra fell in line with his parents and slowly walked back down the slopes in prayer. Though he traveled from home and never returned—and though he lived for another thirty-five years—the hilltop shrine of Bon Any would remain with him as close as his heartbeat, or the ceaseless pounding of the Pacific surf at Carmel Bay.

Pain was inevitable. Serra, who knew the Scriptures well, recalled the words of Christ: "He who loves father or mother more than I is not worthy of me." It was not that Junípero loved his father or mother less, but that he loved his Heavenly Father's business more. The primacy of God's will he would explain in a farewell letter after he left Petra. Four years later, on May 5, 1753, Antonio died. Margarita died the following year. Junípero's sister lived until 1783. All three are buried in the crypt of La Purísima in the Franciscan Church of San Bernardino.

Bon Any hill and shrine. Shortly before leaving Majorca, Serra paid a devotional visit to this shrine. The statue, inside the shrine, is judged to be of the 16th century and continues today as the center of Marian devotion for Petrans.

Statue of Nuestra Señora de Bon Any

It was now midafternoon as Serra walked west. A seven-hour journey lay before him. On both sides of the dirt road, he saw fig orchards, vineyards, and wheat fields. Herds of sheep grazed in the pasture lands. Sturdy stone houses and windmills appeared occasionally amid the fields, and ancient towns dotted Majorca's hillsides. Every rock and tree reminded him that this was home. Yet he was leaving it with joy in his heart. The twenty-five-mile walk to Palma was but the first lap of a journey to the western lands where he would aid the bodies and bless the souls of the American Indians.

Once back in the convent, Serra conferred with Palóu, then resigned from the university. After filling his small trunk with the articles a Franciscan missionary needs, his sermons and the books of his choice, he was ready to leave the Palma he had known for over twenty years.

On Sunday, April 13, 1749, Serra and Palóu, and the friars of the community of San Francisco assembled in the refectory to make their formal farewells. Serra made a public confession of his faults and asked forgiveness for any offense inadvertently given during the years of dwelling under the same roof. He received the blessing of his superior, or father guardian, Fray Juan Pol, who had been his first professor of philosophy and had watched him rise to fame and distinction. Junípero then touched everyone's heart by rising and walking around the refectory, kneeling to kiss the sandaled feet of each friar present, including those of the humble novices. It was his token of humility and affection for the brethren he was leaving.

Serra and Palóu, perhaps accompanied by some of their brethren, hurried straight down to the harbor, where they boarded an English cargo ship headed for Málaga. The two Franciscans watched Majorca gradually fade from view, as they picked out familiar landmarks. They were looking upon their island home for the last time. Their last sight would have been Palma's thirteenth-century cathedral, standing against the sea wall just behind the fortifications.

With the hazards of the future unknown, Doctor Serra turned to Professor Palóu and said, "From now on let us stop using all these titles of respect and superiority in regard to each other; no longer will we use the titles 'Master' and 'Your Reverence,' for we are now in every respect equals. Call me Junípero and I shall call you Francisco." Serra thus broke completely with the past. The age-long courtesies of the classroom and cloister were exchanged for the more familiar, more brotherly, relationship of the frontier.

The voyage to Málaga, from where they would take another boat to Cádiz, lasted fifteen days. For the two Majorcans, it was their first time on the open sea. Their hours on board were their own, and they could arrange their daily religious program as they saw fit. Normally, it would have been a pleasurable trip, but the vessel's skipper created such storms that the voyage turned into one of the unhappiest in Serra's life.

According to Palóu, the Englishman was "an obstinate heretic" who had dabbled in theology. Despite the language barrier, he continually insisted upon arguing religion; the two Franciscans scarcely had time alone enough to recite the Divine Office. Musty Bible in hand, the provocative sea captain argued his views, never realizing that Serra was an expert in sacred theology with five years of experience in examining doctoral candidates. Palóu implies, and Serra supports him, that the two never sought debate but were provoked into replies. In response to the captain's passion for argument, Serra would quote chapter and verse from memory, suggesting the man look up the corresponding pages in the Bible. When this became too embarrassing for the captain, he replied that the pages must be missing. The captain became so irate that he threatened to throw Junípero and Francisco overboard and proceed directly to London. Palóu considered the threat serious. Serra had to remind the sour, cantankerous fellow that if he did not deliver the friars safely to Málaga, there would be international repercussions. "Our king will demand indemnity from your king, and you will pay with your head."

One evening, the man became so furious he pulled his dagger and placed it at Serra's throat, "apparently with the intention of taking his life." But the anger subsided, and the bully withdrew the knife and stalked off, leaving a torrent of abuse in his wake. However, it was to be a sleepless night of vigil, Palóu admitting that he was the more fearful of the two. Fortunately, it was the last night they would spend aboard the vessel. The next morning, Sunday, April 27, Málaga was at last in view. On this day, the feast of the Patronage of Saint Joseph, the two Majorcans disembarked. What parting words, if any, passed between them and the captain will never be learned. The bullying captain may well have had a great hatred for all things Spanish, since the Spaniards were rivals of the English in trade, commerce, and overseas expansion. Having overindulged in grog, the man may have decided to wreak a little vengeance on these particular Spaniards, who so easily routed him in theological debate. However, it is also possible that the difficulties may have stemmed largely from the language barrier.

The city of Málaga lies on a plain in the form of an amphitheater surrounded by the mountains of Andalusia. An exotic castle and fortress dating to Moorish times crowns one of the eastern hills. In the city's center in Serra's day was the large unfinished cathedral. The two missionaries, relieved to be on land again after two unusual weeks at sea, immediately proceeded to the Franciscan convent of San Luis.

Fray Juan Jurado, the superior of San Luis and a former professor, received them warmly. Palóu describes Serra joining the community in their evening prayers within half an hour of arriving at the convent, demonstrating his love of and devotion to monastic regularity. "Thus he followed the community exercises during the five days we remained there." Yet, "when the humble Father realized the excessive regard in which he was held by that superior, he decided immediately that we should leave the friary and go aboard a small Spanish vessel which was to take us as far as Cádiz." They sailed on May 2nd or 3rd.

CHAPTER FIVE

ALWAYS GO FORWARD
AND NEVER TURN BACK

Skirting the hill-fringed coast of southern Spain and the formidable Rock of Gibraltar, the small Spanish craft carrying Serra and Palóu sailed northwest and soon entered the ancient seaport of Cádiz—with Seville, one of the two centers for Spanish trade with the Americas.

On board, Junípero reflected on his success in overcoming all the obstacles so far set in his path. He had sidestepped the inducements of his superiors in Palma (despite his youth, he had been offered the position of *custos* in his province—second in charge after the provincial —if he remained), defeated the purpose of those who had intercepted the letter, and ignored all the honors and advancements that most likely would have come his way. His mental discipline had come from his years of reading and reflection on the Sacred Scriptures, the Church Fathers, Aristotle, and Scotus. But to win the hearts of the people of the faraway Americas, Serra would rely upon the spirit of Saint Francis of Assisi and Saint Francis Solano, and above all upon the grace of Jesus Christ. Patience and self-sacrifice, he realized, would now be more important than scholarship.

Serra and Palóu disembarked at Cádiz into a scene of ceaseless activity, a busy seaport full of mariners, merchants, and missionaries. The two friars walked to the Convent of San Francisco, where they would rest until departure for the New World. Here, they met Fray Pedro Pérez de Mezquía from the College of San Fernando in Mexico City, a veteran of the missionary effort in Texas and in Mexico's rugged Sierra Gorda. Embraces and introductions followed as the two Majorcans met the volunteers from the other parts of Spain, who had arrived before them. Eleven had come from the north, four from the region of Madrid, six from the eastern coast, and five from western Andalusia, leaving five vacancies. Serra immediately reported that there were certainly more volunteers in Majorca and suggested that if time permitted, they should be notified. Following his advice, Mezquía dispatched letters patent to Palma inviting three more missionaries to join the group. Fathers Juan Crespí, Rafael Verger, and Guillermo Vicens accepted.

For four long months, the impatient contingent remained in Cádiz before sailing for the Americas. While church and state officials prepared provisions for their departure, the friars followed their daily routine of relogous exercises.

Meanwhile, officials of the Board of Trade were busy documenting the vital statistics, titles, and physical characteristics of the missionaries. In the Archive of the Indies in Seville, there is a bulky 196-page folio covering the history of the Mezquía mission. In it are described as follows the four men who would be bound so closely to the history of the two Californias:

Father Junípero Serra, lector of theology, native of Petra in the province of Majorca, thirty-five years old, of medium height, swarthy, dark eyes and hair, scant beard.

Father Francisco Palóu, lector of philosophy, native of Palma, twenty-six years old, of medium height, swarthy, dark eyes and hair.

Father Juan Crespí, native of Palma, twenty-eight years old, short of stature, sallow skin but somewhat florid complexion, blue eyes, and dark hair.

Father Rafael Verger, lector of philosophy, native of Santañyi, twenty-six years old, of regular stature, fair complexion, face pock-marked, somewhat florid, with a scant beard.

During the long wait at Cádiz, Serra wrote a farewell letter to his parents. By now they had learned of their son's intentions, and they were full of grief. Francisco Serra, not a relative but Junípero's confrere at San Bernardino, was assigned the sensitive task of visiting Antonio and Margarita and reading them Junípero's farewell letter in the intimacy of Serra's family circle. It is a letter written by a man at the crossroads of his life, filled with enthusiasm for the work ahead, but keenly aware that in undertaking it, he is unlikely to see his family or his home again. In it we see expressed his deep faith in God and his belief in the importance of a "tranquil death in His holy grace."

Most Dear Friend in Jesus Christ, Father Francisco Serra:

Words cannot express the feelings of my heart as I bid you farewell nor can I properly repeat to you my request that you be the consolation of my parents to sustain them in their sorrow. I wish I could communicate to them the great joy that fills my heart. If I could do this, then surely they would always encourage me to go forward and never to turn back. Let them remember that the office of an apostolic preacher, especially in its actual exercise, is the greatest calling to which they could wish me to be chosen.

Since they are advanced in years, let them recall that life is uncertain and, in fact, may be very brief. If they compare it with eternity, they will clearly realize that it cannot be but more than an instant. . . .

Tell them that I shall ever feel the loss of not being able to be near them as heretofore to console them, but since first things must come first and before all else, the first thing to do is to fulfill the will of God. It was for the love of God that I left them and if I, for the love of God and with the aid of His grace, had the strength of will to do so, it will be to the point that they too, for the love of God, be content to be deprived of my company. . . .

Now is not the time to muse or fret over the happenings of life but rather to be conformed entirely to the will of God, striving to prepare themselves for a happy death which of all the things of life is our principal concern. For if we attain that, it matters little if we lose all the rest. But if we do not attain that, nothing else will be of any value.

Let them rejoice that they have a son who is a priest, though an unworthy one and a sinner, who daily in the holy sacrifice of the Mass prays for them with all the fervor of his soul and on many days applies the Mass for them alone, so that the Lord may aid them; that they may not lack their daily bread, that He may give them patience in their trials, resignation to His holy will, peace and union with everyone, courage to fight the temptations of the evil one, and last of all, when it is God's will, a tranquil death in His holy grace. If I, by the grace of God, succeed in becoming a good religious, my prayers will become more efficacious, and they in consequence will be the gainers. . . . I recall the occasion when my father was so ill that extreme unction was administered to him. I, being a religious, was at home at the time, and thinking that he was going to die, we two being alone, he said to me: "My son, let me charge you to be a good religious of your Father, Saint Francis."

Now, dear father, be assured that those words are as fresh in my memory as when they proceeded from your lips. Realize, too, that in order to become a good religious, I have set out on this course. So do not be disconsolate when I am carrying out your will, which is one with the will of God. I know, too, that my mother has never ceased to commend me to God in order that I may be a good religious. Now, dear mother mine, if perhaps God has set me in this course as a result of your prayers, be content with what God disposes and ever say in life's tribulations: "Blessed be God. May His holy will be done."

Good-by, my dear father! Farewell, dear mother of mine! Good-by, dear sister, Juana! Good-by, my beloved brother-in-law. Take good care of little Mike [who was then eight years and seven months old] and see to it that he becomes a good Christian and a studious pupil and that the two girls grow up as good Christians. Trust to God that your uncle may yet be of some service to you. Good-by and farewell!

From this house of the Holy Mission in this city of Cádiz, August 20, 1749.

> Your cordial friend in Christ
> Fray Junípero Serra
> Most unworthy priest

The original of this letter was discovered in Palma during December of 1912, the only complete letter from the first thirty-five years of Serra's life to have been discovered. Today, it is in the Capuchin Convent in Barcelona.

On August 30, 1749, nine days after the letter was dispatched, Serra and Palóu sailed from Cádiz on a journey that would take them across the Atlantic to the island of Puerto Rico. The voyage on the *Villasota* proved to be a slow, monotonous one of unvarying scenes of sea and sky, trying the patience of the eager missionaries.

Junípero made himself available as confessor to passengers and crew alike. He wore his missionary crucifix at night, suspended from a cord worn around his shoulders with Christ against his breast.

Early in October, fearing that the drinking water would not last, the ship's officers had little recourse but to ration it to one small glass at each meal. In the tropical heat, the lack of water and consequent thirst were the greatest tribulations Serra and Palóu had yet experienced. To those who grumbled or complained, Junípero advised, combining humor and asceticism with science, "It is nothing to worry about. I have found means to avoid thirst, and it is this: to eat little and talk less in order not to waste saliva." But Serra had some material assistance for his thirst, too. Among the crew was a Majorcan sailor who deprived himself of some of his own rationed water in order to provide Serra and Palóu with a little more. "He denied himself to make us more comfortable," Junípero later acknowledged in gratitude.

On the feast day of Saint Luke, the *Villasota* arrived in the port of San Juan, Puerto Rico, one of the oldest cities in the New World. Here, on the fringe of Spanish might in western waters, Spain had withstood her enemies for two centuries. With its massive stone walls rising from the sea, the fort is reminiscent of Cádiz in Spain from which the friars had sailed. In Serra's time the town was about one mile square, scarcely larger than his native Petra, and had about four thousand inhabitants.

According to arrangements made before sailing, the shipmaster was to provide food and shelter for the friars during their stay on the island. But once the small craft anchored, the captain reneged on his bargain. Junípero records the fact without bitterness, however. Fortunately, the contingent of missionaries found lodging near the walls of the city at Immaculate Conception, a hospice, that is, a friary admitting guest friars en route to the missionary field.

Here, Serra and his companions found their first outlet for apostolic zeal in America. Sensing that the parishioners were ripe for a series of sermons and services to renew their faith, as well as hoping to convert the city's unbelievers, Junípero announced at the conclusion of the rosary during the evening services:

> Tomorrow, for the comfort of the inhabitants, we shall begin a mission which will last as long as our ship remains in port. I invite all to come tomorrow night to the cathedral, where it will commence.

The people of the city were surprised, but the other missionaries were thunderstruck. The season was still hot, and the friars were worn and tired from their long voyage. Serra commented to Palóu, "What greater words of comfort can I give these poor islanders than to announce to them that a mission will be held during our stay?"

There was no doubt the islanders were ready; no mission had been held since the last band of Franciscan missionaries, also destined for the College of San Fernando in Mexico City, had passed through San Juan nine years before. On the third day after their arrival, the friars walked out to the public square and to street intersections, where as town-criers they heralded the beginning of the mission. Inviting all to attend, the friars launched a "spiritual attack upon the people's hearts in order to bring the captives from the world into the renewed service of Christ." For the missionaries, the citadel of the New World had been captured in the first assault. The assault on the hearts of the people to bring forth penitence and spiritual renewal would follow. These first street-corner "assaults" were made by means of spiritual pep-talks, singing of popular hymns, and calls for repentance.

The following night a procession was formed. Serra and the missionaries led the aroused city residents to the cathedral. "The commotion was simply great," Junípero later recalled. Fathers Cardona and Serra preached the rousing mission sermons on alternate nights, and Father Morán delivered the instructional sermons. Writing later about his participation in the mission, Junípero praised the other missionaries:

> Doubtless those good Fathers delighted in honoring me but here I found my own confusion and humiliation because at once I sorrowfully recognized in my heart the vast difference that existed between my sermons and the sermons of those good Fathers. Mine were chaff; theirs, gold and grain; mine cold as snow; theirs, warm and ardent as fire; mine were dark as night; theirs, clear and cheerful as the day. When the Father President preached, there was such commotion in the audience, such an abundance

of tears and cries and striking of breasts, that even long after the sermon was over, the lingering clamor could be heard. Thus moved and tearful, the people returned to their homes.

Similarly, Serra praised Father Morán, who preached the less fiery sermons and continued to lecture at the hospice even after the mission was over:

> When I preached, nothing could be heard, no tears, no moaning, even when I treated on those subjects naturally apt to move the audience and that in spite of my strenuous efforts in delivering my sermons. So it was made clear enough to everyone that I am the only one lacking that interior fire which inflames the words of the preacher and moves and fires the audience.

The most laborious part of the mission was the hearing of individual confessions—sometimes from three or four in the mornig until midnight. Yet, even now, during his first hours in the Western Hemisphere, Serra was demonstrating his selfless industry.

After eighteen days in Puerto Rico, the *Villasota* was ready to continue the voyage to Mexico. On October 31, Serra, Palóu, and the other Franciscans re-embarked after many fond farewells to their newfound friends.

A month-long voyage lay ahead through the islands and reefs of the Caribbean. Apparently, the voyage was as calm and monotonous as before until they were almost within sight of Vera Cruz, on the east coast of Mexico. On December 2, strong winds arose that drove the small ship away from shore in a southerly direction. The vessel began to leak, and the pumps were not able to draw out all the water. Soon, as the main mast threatened to break, the sailors begged the captain to run the ship aground so that at least some lives could be saved. So terrible was the storm that during the second night all gave themselves up for lost.

According to Palóu, during these hours of terror and danger, Serra maintained a serene composure. When asked if he was afraid, Junípero admitted that he was, but added that when he recalled why he had come to the Indies, his fears were allayed. The next morning the wind ceased and, on December 6, the *Villasota* cast anchor in the harbor of Vera Cruz. As he stepped ashore, Serra could note that during the ninety-nine-day voyage he had not been seasick once.

On shore, the Franciscans found brethren awaiting them, and after resting a few days, Junípero, Francisco, and their companions arranged for a thanksgiving celebration, the honors of the altar and pulpit to be shared. In Serra's own words, the sermon "was entrusted to my insufficient self." But as his biographer, Palóu, tells us, this "insufficient" preacher delivered a sermon that eloquently spiritualized the entire voyage, emphasizing the protecting mantle of God's providence.

II

MEXICO

. . . for I trust that God will give me the strength to reach San Diego, as He has given me the strength to come so far. In case He does not, I will conform myself to His most holy will. Even though I should die on the way, I shall not turn back. *They can bury me wherever they wish and I shall gladly be left among the pagans, if it be the will of God.*
—Fray Junipero Serra

CHAPTER SIX

COLLEGE
OF SAN FERNANDO

From Vera Cruz, men of war and men of peace, soldiers of the king and soldiers of the cross, started out on their missions of force or persuasion on the Camino Real. From east to west this "King's Highway" extended two hundred fifty miles from the Gulf of Mexico at Vera Cruz to Mexico City, then all the way to the Pacific at Acapulco, nearly another two hundred miles south-southwest. From north to south, it ran over a thousand miles from Santa Fe (in what is now New Mexico) into Central America, with the crossroads at Mexico City, Serra's destination.

The name King's Highway should not mislead anyone; this was not a wide, comfortable road over which travelers reached Mexico City with speed and ease. By all accounts, it was a very bad dirt road climbing from sea level to an altitude of 7,382 feet through tropical forests, over arid plains and high plateaus, and across formidable mountains, with volcanos and lakes and perennial snow.

After pausing briefly to recover their land legs, Serra and his companions were ready to be transported inland by the king's horses and men. In keeping with the royal agreement that the crown was to provide transportation and housing, the Dominican friars were dispatched to Guadalajara and the Franciscans to the College of San Fernando in Mexico City. Normally, a Franciscan was to abstain from using horseback as a method of travel; the Franciscan rule expressly stated that a friar "must not ride on horseback unless compelled by manifest necessity or infirmity." Yet the rule itself provided for two exceptions, one dealing with the length of the journey, conditions of the road, and the pressure of time, and the other with the illness of the friar himself. The missionaries in Vera Cruz fell under these exceptions to the rule and were therefore entitled to ride to Mexico City, since some were ill and others were on the verge of illness.

Along El Camino Real between Vera Cruz and Mexico City. The Camino Real route, no more than a well-trodden path when Serra traveled to Mexico City, wound through countryside such as this in the Jalapa region.

Now, in Vera Cruz, Serra and a friar from Andalusia chose to walk to Mexico City. Junípero was in good health and sincerely felt he had the necessary strength to maintain the Franciscan tradition the hard way. And this was just the first time in Junípero's thirty-four-year American career that he would demonstrate his dedication in this way. Bent upon a higher asceticism, he wanted from the beginning to identify himself with the *friales andariegos,* "walking friars," who had become so famous in the New World.

Serra and his companion started out without money or guide, their sole possessions their breviaries, books containing the prayers, hymns, psalms, and readings for the canonical hours. They "went with trust in Divine Providence, the best of all passports." They could rely upon Indian and Spanish hospitality, since the sons of Saint Francis were highly respected in Mexico.

Between December 15, 1749, and January 1, 1750, the two missionaries walked a little more than fifteen miles a day. Each morning after mass they set out, taking a little siesta around noon when the sun was warm and the travel most wearing. Their food and lodging were asked *por amor de Dios,* "for the love of God."

On one particular late afternoon, the friars reached the bank of a river swollen with rain waters. They could not cross to the small village where they expected to remain overnight, and they did not know where the river was fordable. In their predicament, they recited a prayer to the Blessed Virgin for guidance. Soon thereafter they noticed a figure moving about on the opposite bank. Serra called out in a loud voice, "Hail, Holy Mary! Is that a Christian on the other side of the river?" A voice replied, "Yes! What do you want?" Serra asked to be shown the ford. The villager responded that the two priests should walk along the bank until he pointed to the spot where they should cross. With the guide paralleling them across the river, the two friars walked for a considerable distance to the ford, where they crossed without mishap. The person who had aided them was a Spaniard, well dressed and courteous, but a man of few words. Inviting the two missionaries to his house, which was far from the river, he provided them with food and shelter. When Serra and his companion left the house the following morning to offer mass in a nearby town, they walked over a road covered with ice from the cold rain that had fallen that night. Years later, Serra confided to Palóu that he and his companion considered the man's hospitality an answer to their prayer, since the two surely would have died from the freezing rigors of the night.

There were further incidents on succeeding days that strengthened their belief that divine Providence was looking after them. One day, fatigued from the long march, the two men encountered a man on horseback approaching from the opposite direction. Asking where they were going, the horseman handed each a pomegranate with which to quench their thirst, giving them the strength to finish the day's journey.

One morning as they took their departure from a small farmhouse where they had stayed overnight, the host provided each man with a loaf of bread. But the two missionaries came across a starving old man on the road who begged for food or alms. Serra and his companion gave him the loaves they carried. Late that afternoon, as they rested alongside the road, a man on horseback passed. Asking where they intended to sleep that night, he opened his saddle packet and pulled out a loaf of bread, which he cut in half, handing each priest a piece. Later, in the pulpit, Serra described the incidents at the river and on the trail to illustrate the Providence of God.

But a serious problem developed. As Junípero trudged along day after day, his left foot became swollen, and he was bothered by a burning itch, which he blamed on a mosquito bite. One evening, upon arriving at a small farm, he could barely walk or stand. His condition was so bad that he was forced to remain at the farm for an additional day. Half asleep in the night, he unconsciously rubbed the swollen foot, and in the morning, it was raw and bleeding.

Palóu later identified the mosquito that stung Serra as the *zancudo,* a variety of Mexican mosquito whose sting can be fierce. Without proper rest and medication, there can be serious complications. In Serra's case, the result was an affliction that tormented him for the rest of his life.

Interior of San Fernando Church, Mexico City. This engraving from Serra's time shows the elaborately carved altar, which was covered with gold leaf.

With a festering foot, Serra hobbled painfully into the outskirts of Mexico City. On December 31, he and his companion remained overnight at the shrine of Our Lady of Guadalupe, where they inaugurated the new year by offering mass.

Serra managed to walk the last four-and-a-half miles to the College of San Fernando on the opposite side of the city. It was almost noon on New Year's Day, and now, more than six thousand miles from home and loved ones, the road of his missionary life was just beginning.

For the rest of his life, Serra would be under the jurisdiction of the College of San Fernando in Mexico City. The capital of New Spain, Mexico City at that time had almost one hundred thousand inhabitants and was the largest and most important metropolis in Spanish North America. The vast church and monastery of San Fernando on the western edge of the city were simple and severe in style. From the college's cloisters of prayer and penance, friars were to emerge, men of exalted spiritual ideals and austere living habits, capable of facing the challenges of the frontier.

Upon their arrival at their new home, Junípero and his companion first went into the church to pay their respects to *Jesús Sacramentado*, Jesus in the Blessed Sacrament. His first impression of San Fernando was not of the symmetry of its architecture but of the rythmic chanting of the office. "Father," he said to his companion, "we can indeed consider as well employed our journey here from so far away, together with the difficulties we encountered, if only to gain the happiness of being members of a community which so slowly and devoutly fulfills the obligations of the Divine Office."

A few steps away was the enclosure to Fray Joseph Ortés de Velasco, the college's guardian, and Junípero knelt to receive his blessing. Word spread of their arrival, and soon Serra was reunited with the other Franciscans from Spain. Embraces in the Spanish custom were exchanged all around. Fray Diego de Alcántara, one of the founders of the College of San Fernando, greeted Serra with the ancient reference his name provoked, "Would that we had a whole forest of junipers," for indeed the college was in need of new recruits.

Serra was promptly assigned a cell, and he became a regular member of the community. Junípero gave himself only a day to get his bearings; he had come to San Fernando to prepare spiritually for his missionary vocation, something he regarded as the greatest blessing of his life.

San Fernando was different in many ways from his convent back in Majorca. One hundred fourteen friars were housed here. Some of the cells and cloisters looked out upon orchards and fields, some on the two volcanoes that Serra would later come to know so well.

The daily routine was designed to enable those who professed themselves apostolic men to lead penitential lives. The entire community arose at midnight and until two in the morning chanted matins and lauds, said the litany, and spent an hour in meditation. A brief rest was then taken until around five when the new day began with prime and the other canonical hours, private masses, and the mass for the whole community. Only at the conclusion of these masses was a light breakfast of a roll and chocolate eaten. All in all about four hours a day were spent in these prayerful pursuits.

After this, classes followed in the languages of Mexico's Indian tribes, methods of organizing and maintaining missions, or theology. A noonday meal and a visit to the Blessed Sacrament preceded the siesta. The remainder of the day was occupied with vespers, more studies, compline, a litany, and another hour of meditation, until supper was served at seven, then more chanting followed by bed at eight.

Seclusion of the friars was strictly observed. Friends, relatives, or people who called upon the college for spiritual consolation were received in a small room near the entrance and not allowed inside the main structures. When their business was over, the friars immediately returned to their duties, since great stress was placed upon the avoidance of idle conversation. No friar was allowed to leave the monastery without permission of the superior and then only in the company of another. Recreation was taken in common in the patios or, when feasible, in walks outside the city. All wore habits of gray wool, woven from unbleached white and black fleeces since no dye of any kind was allowed.

Here, then, were formed the missionary minds whose influence one day would be felt from Mexico to northern California. The goal of training for apostolic missionaries was to become conditioned to privation, fatigue, and penance for the love of God and the sanctification of themselves and their neighbors. But even the best of them would not find it easy on the frontier. In later years, Serra would write from distant California that to the mission should come only those who were ready for extreme suffering and misery; on that score, he could offer them abundance.

As the weeks passed, and the infection in his foot healed, Serra was asked to hear confessions. Soon, he was familiar with Mexico City. Its sensuous life, slow-moving and carefree, was something Junípero had never encountered before. All around him were riches, flaunted shamelessly. Men and women dressed in the finest clothing and wore the most expensive jewelry. Sounds of dancing and singing could be heard at all hours throughout the city. Luxury was especially lavished upon the city's many ornate churches. The cathedral, built upon the site of Montezuma's palace, contained a solid gold statue of the Assumption surrounded by golden angels sparkling with jewels.

As Serra looked around him, he saw the poverty of the Indians whose ancestors had once owned virtually all this wealth. Although a submissive people now, the Indians lived on. Catholicism had taken a certain hold on them. Everyone at San Fernando knew they had to continue fostering it, and Serra began devising means for them to improve their lot.

Several months after Serra's arrival at San Fernando, his three other Majorcan friends, Juan Crespí, Rafael Verger, and Guillermo Vicens, arrived at the college. They were part of the second contingent of friars gathered in Spain by Pedro Pérez de Mezquía. One can imagine the rejoicing in the solemn halls of the college.

One day shortly after their arrival, while all were gathered in the cloister garden for recreation, Velasco expressed his sincere pleasure at their arrival and explained a difficulty that he now faced. In 1744, the College of San Fernando had assumed the responsibility of caring for the missions in the Sierra Gorda, a rugged mountain area about one hundred fifty miles northeast of Mexico City. Four priests had died within a short time, and a sister college had supplied replacements for six-month periods. Although the rules of the college required all newcomers to dwell there a year before being sent into the fields, Father Velasco felt that in these circumstances replacements had to be supplied immediately. "Now, who of you will volunteer for the Sierra Gorda?" he asked. Without a moment's hesitation, Serra

Market day in old Mexico City. On market day in Serra's time, just as in this 1864 drawing, several thousand boats laden with produce entered the center of the city over a network of canals to sell their produce in the shadow of the Mexico City cathedral.

spoke up, using the words of Isaiah, the prophet: "Here I am; send me!" Among the several dozen who volunteered, Junípero and eight others were chosen, including Francisco Palóu.

During the weeks of preparation that followed, Serra was designated by Velasco as the preacher for the feast of San Fernando on May 30. This was one of the few days in the year when the college was open to the public for a religious festivity. Palóu was once again in the audience, as he had been in Palma and Vera Cruz, and again reports the details.

For the annual eulogy on the life of the Spanish king and saint, San Fernando, Serra chose as his text the verse of Psalm 45: "My heart hath uttered a good word; I will speak my works to the king." Adapting his text to the subject, he used it to give unity to the discourse that unfolded the events of the royal life and its virtuous deeds. This sermon had such an impact upon Serra's listeners that many of the friars present asked Velasco why he was allowing Serra to leave the cloister for the distant Indian missions. Why waste such splendid talents among ignorant, illiterate people? Here, in Mexico City, his sonorous voice and great preaching ability could be employed to heighten moral standards among the people of the city. Serra should be retained at San Fernando.

But the guardian was not swayed by their arguments. As far as he was concerned, a university professor with the spirit of a child might be just the leader needed by the new missionaries and the Indians of the Sierra Gorda. Furthermore, he knew well why Junípero had come to Mexico in the first place—and to the missions he would go. Velasco even went so far as to appoint Serra president of the Sierra Gorda. But Junípero, pointing out his inexperience, politely declined the honor and asked to be relieved of it. Velasco yielded and the resignation was accepted. Serra was to begin his work as a simple missionary—the role he most prized.

CHAPTER SEVEN

THE SIERRA GORDA

The remote, untamed Sierra Gorda country that Serra and his associates were to enter in 1750 is located in the heart of the jagged mountain range called the Sierra Madre, which extends from north to south between the Atlantic seaboard and Mexico's central plateau.

In this vast region lived a few Spanish colonists and the Pames, whom Spain was unable to subdue until the nineteenth century, even though its soldiers and missionaries went far beyond this area in the meantime. Protected by natural barriers, the Indians roamed freely, eluding the Spaniards, and pillaged the scattered settlements in the valleys. The valleys are few and small and the arable land is rocky. The heat is extreme until October, though mitigated somewhat by the rains beginning in May.

The date for Serra's departure for this remote and difficult post was set for June 1, six months after his arrival in the New World. Soldiers and Christian Indians, accompanied by saddle and pack animals, came down the sierra to escort the padres to their new homes. Again Serra chose to walk, and this time Palóu accompanied him. For sixteen days the group marched over barely visible paths in the burning heat, plagued by mosquitos and fleas. Their way was through land inhabited mostly by coyotes, deer, poisonous snakes, parrots, tropical birds, and chiggers. For Serra, the journey was especially difficult since his right foot began to swell again and his sores became more painful.

Finally arriving in the straggling, barren village of Jalpan, Serra sized up the situation immediately. The church and mission were primitive structures of adobe and cane with thatched roofs, symbolizing the region's economic backwardness. There were less than a thousand parishioners, and not a single one going to confession or receiving Holy Communion even once a year—the minimum obligation of every Catholic. Serra's organizational abilities would be taxed to the fullest. Fortunately, he had in Palóu a loyal, hardworking assistant.

Immediately, the two men began to learn the complex Pame language of the Indians, employing as their tutor a Mexican who had been brought up among the Pames. After sufficient instruction, Junípero began translating the Christian doctrine and prayers into Pame. Within a few months, he was able to preach to the Indians in their own language and this, along with his gentleness and generosity, won their trust.

Serra now demonstrated all his pent-up missionary zeal and ingenuity. In his attempts to persuade the Indians to attend mass and go to confession more frequently, he himself knelt before Father Palóu for confession in the sanctuary of the church in full view of the entire congregation. Such an example had a profound effect: "If the good padre needs to go to confession, who am I to abstain?"

The confessions, of course, were genuine, not just exemplary acts. But Junípero had a flare for the dramatic and was using it to good advantage. Gradually, by persuasion, example, and passionate preaching, he succeeded in bringing the Indians to the church. Palóu records that on some days as many as a hundred approached the sacraments.

Using his imagination, Serra endeavored to draw the Indians to the worship of God by accentuating the splendors of the liturgy. Christmas was celebrated in Franciscan fashion by mystery plays similar to those of his native Petra, enacted by the children whom he trained for the purpose. During the Lenten season, and its culminating period of Holy Week, he carried out the liturgy in full splendor. To this Serra added the rosary, the Way of the Cross, sermons on moral topics, and hymns. All of this reflected the way he had been brought up in devout Petra. He realized that visual dramatization of religion was of prime importance with unsophisticated people. If such expression was still significant in his native Majorca after nearly a thousand years of Christianity, it was all the more important in the Sierra Gorda, where the faith was for the first time taking root.

At this time, the stations of the cross, today found in churches throughout the world, were a relatively recent innovation, originating with the Franciscans who had charge of the holy places in Palestine. The stations represent the stages of Christ's passion, and the worshiper meditates before each one, as a pilgrim in Palestine would visit the holy places there. Under Serra's leadership the stations of the cross became a procession in which both padre and people participated. A small cross, like the one on the hill at Bon Any in Petra, was erected on a slope outside Jalpan within sight of the church. Between these two spots Serra erected the fourteen stations. At each, appropriate prayers were offered in commemoration of Christ's sufferings, and after the stations of the cross were concluded, he would preach a sermon on the sufferings and death of Christ.

During the ceremonies, Serra himself carried the cross on his shoulders in imitation of Christ, a cross that Palóu states was so heavy that even he who was younger than his former teacher, could hardly lift it. Serra was not merely putting on a show. Although he believed in the visual and dramatic as a learning tool, he was at the same time practicing penance.

Ceremonies and processions such as these were frequent in the village. The days of Holy Week were given special importance. On Holy Thursday, Serra performed the ritual of the "washing of the feet" in imitation of Christ by bathing the feet of twelve old men from his congregation who represented the apostles. He then dined with them, afterwards delivering a sermon on the ceremony's significance. That evening there would always be a parade with the crucifix. On Good Friday, the observance commemorating the descent from the Cross was vividly performed. The loneliness and sorrow of Christ's mother were emphasized by the procession in honor of the risen Christ. Corpus Christi and the feasts of the Blessed Virgin and some of the other saints were occasions for other elaborate liturgical ceremonies. On Saturday nights there was always a procession in honor of Mary, during which the Pames sang the Rosary and carried lanterns. When word of the services spread, Spaniards from faraway settlements joined in the observances. There are extant no diaries or letters from Serra during this period of his life, so we have no firsthand accounts of his reactions to events like those we have when he reached the Pacific west coast. But, if at fifty-eight he was almost boyishly enthusiastic in Alta California, what must he have been like during his late thirties in the Sierra Gorda?

Serra began his missionary efforts in the rugged mountains as pastor of Jalpan, but it was not long before a new superior elevated him back to the position of president he had originally declined. On May 8, 1751, Fray Bernardo Pumeda was elected guardian of the apostolic college. Thoroughly familiar with Junípero's zeal and commitment, he sent Serra a patent placing him in authority. Serra now had no alternative. In obedience to his religious vows, he accepted. But after three years, when Father Gaspar Gómez replaced Pumeda, Junípero resigned as president, on the principle that "if it was an office of honor, it was right that all should enjoy it, and for the same reason, if it was one of labor, it should be allowed to pass from one to another." This viewpoint, hard to refute, was accepted by the guardian and his council.

During the eight years and three months Serra spent as a missionary in the sierra, he labored for improvement in conditions for the Indians. He realized that the more progress the missions made economically, the more stable and successful would be his religious ministrations. Through the college, he obtained oxen, cows, asses, sheep, goats, and farm implements. Palóu, equally competent and zealous, at first served as overseer of planting and harvesting until the Indians learned how to do it themselves. Blankets and clothing sent from Mexico City were provided as encouragement for their labors. Soon, the harvests were not only sufficient but sometimes abundant. The Indians were taught to sell their superfluous products (under the direction of the padres lest they be cheated), and with the money, Serra taught them to buy more animals, implements, and clothing. Women and children engaged in community labor, assigned tasks befitting their abilities.

As time went on, the Pames were presented with their own parcels of land on which to grow corn, beans, and pumpkins. Some were given oxen and seeds for planting. Women were taught spinning, knitting, and sewing. Serra encouraged the Indians to broaden their commercial activity by selling their wares in Zimapán, a mining center less than fifty miles away. Sisal ropes and mats of fine palm were sold for cotton, which was, in turn, used for weaving garments.

Documents recently discovered in the Biblioteca Nacional in Mexico City reveal that Serra ventured out of the Sierra Gorda on two occasions during all the years he was there. The first was in the late summer of 1752, while he was president; the other was early in March of 1758. Both were to the College of San Fernando in Mexico City.

On his first visit, he took the guardian a "trophy" that had given him the deepest joy, in short, the first tangible evidence of his religious success in Hispanic America. It was a statue carved by the Pames and representing the face of a woman, Cachum, "mother of the sun." It had been placed in a shrine high on a hill reached by a stone stairway, where some of the Pame chiefs were buried. The Indians prayed to the statue for rain, good crops, health, success in war, and suitable wives. As the Pames became more thoroughly Christian, they presented the statue to Serra, who presented it to the college for its archives.

Before being summoned back to the College of San Fernando in September of 1758, Serra finished supervising the construction of a large church in Jalpan, still in use by the descendants of the eighteenth-century Pames. Some years earlier, the prosperity of the missions permitting the taking on of such a project, Junípero had proposed the building of a large stone church, ample to hold the area's entire congregation. The project called for the skilled work of masons, carpenters, blacksmiths, and painters. Many of the Indians would learn these trades from the artisans, while the remainder served as laborers. Of course, the skilled workmen from Mexico City would have to be paid. Such monies would come from the alms given to the padres and from

Church of Santiago de Jalpan. The Church of Santiago de Jalpan, which Serra helped build, was the missionary headquarters for the Serra Gorda region, where Serra spent eight years. The exquisite facades pictured on this page and the next constitute the final phase in a church's construction, and were built with the help of artisans from Mexico City.

Church of San Miguel, Concá

53

Church of Santa Maria del Aqua de Landa (Purísima Concepcíon)

Church of San Francisco de Tilaco

the profits the Indians made from the sale of livestock and crops. Work on the church would be seasonal; it could only proceed during the October-to-May dry season. But even this schedule had to be contingent upon the need for labor in fields and farms.

Serra served as a laborer during the entire construction. Palóu writes that no one would have recognized the doctor of theology from the Lullian University in his torn habit girded with a piece of old cloth. Friars from San Fernando who visited Jalpan saw him carrying beams, filling in the cracks between the stones of the church walls, and making himself useful wherever needed. Years later, Palóu recalled one visit by Fray Bernardo Pumeda, the guardian. Apparently, Serra was in the midst of some twenty or more Pames who were carrying a heavy timber. Junípero, a little shorter than the others but wishing to help by equalizing the weight, placed the cloth that girded his torn habit between his shoulder and the beam. Pumeda commented to Palóu, "Look at your professor! See how he is making the way of the cross—and in what garments!"

Seven years were needed to complete the mission church. When it was finally finished, it was not only free from debt, but could boast of thousands of bushels of corn in its granaries, as well as money in the treasury. During Serra's tenure as president, other churches and missions were planned and built, and these still stand on the mountainsides and plateaus, monuments to his efforts in establishing the faith in the Sierra Gorda.

Jośe de Escandón was the military leader who finally defeated the Pames in battle in 1743. He promised to send them missionaries to teach them agriculture and Christianity if they would agree to settle. Missionaries had baptized some of them before that time, but it was difficult to instruct in the faith people whose lives were nomadic. Serra's missionary service there began in 1750, and during his eight years, much progress was made.

But Escandón also sent soldier families to secure the area and pursue fugitives. And with the arable land being as limited as it was, there were inevitable conflicts between the soldier-settlers, who wanted the land the king had promised, and the missionaries, who needed enough to support all the Indians living at the missions. The conflicts became so intense that the viceroy in Mexico City became involved.

Some of the soldier families wanted to found a town, and Escandón permitted it. But the Indians, backed by the Law of the Indies, which forbade Spanish settlements in mission territories, protested and threatened to defend their lands by force if necessary. Serra and the College of San Fernando sided with them.

The viceroy suspended the colony, but the townspeople protested and stubbornly remained; there were not enough soldiers to evict them. Meanwhile, commissions were appointed, alternative sites were considered, and other grievances were aired. The settlers were ordered to pay Indians for any work they did—and in the presence of padres to prevent cheating—and told to keep their cattle out of the Indians' fields. After a long, drawn-out long-distance legal battle, the settlers finally moved.

On January 29, 1755, the padres and Indians of Jalpan went out to the valley and formally took possesion of the land with the recognized legal formalities and by the usual signs of picking up rocks and plucking grass and throwing them into the air. This was Serra's first, but not last, experience of conflict between soldiers and missionaries, settlers and Indians.

During these same productive, yet often troublesome years, Serra was also appointed commissary of the Inquisition for the Sierra Gorda and served as a member of the Inquisition tribunal from 1752 on. Palóu states that in his capacity as commissary Serra was called upon from time to time to investigate reports of devil worship, witchcraft, and other superstitious practises in various parts of Mexico. Yet, in the Archivo General de la Nación in Mexico City, where there are over a thousand volumes of indexed material on the Inquisition, only one reference is made to Serra's direct involvement, although two other instances of his participation are now known. Throughout his tenure Serra averred that witchcraft was not practised by the Christian Indans, but by the *gente de razon,* or non-Indians, and in fact, as proof of this Serra had placed in the San Fernando archives the figure of the Indian goddess Cachum—which some of his converts had given him—"as a memorial of his spiritual triumph." It is also important to note that baptized Indians were not subject to the Inquisition.

CHAPTER EIGHT

TRAGEDY AT SAN SABA

Although Junípero Serra had renounced all personal wealth, the riches of a silver mine, and the hot, broad plains of northern Texas, almost kidnapped the founder of California.

The massacre of several Franciscan missionaries at San Sabá, Texas, prompted the guardian to reassign Serra there; in preparation he was to return to the College of San Fernando in Mexico City. Serra found the city clamorous and congested after the silence and primitive grandeur of the Sierra Gorda. He was stunned by the crowds, the traffic, the stores, the vast congregations in the churches, the almost nightly murders on the street, and the violence of the unemployed, who roamed the city in bands.

At the college, Junípero learned that the position of the Franciscan missions in Texas had suddenly become precarious. Father Miguel Molina, who had journeyed with him from Spain, was back to recuperate from a severe arm wound he had received during an Apache attack at San Sabá that had claimed the lives of Fathers Alonso Terreros and José Santiestevan.

As the sole survivor of the massacre, Molina described the events leading up to it. Two cousins had determined at any cost to further missionary work among the fierce Texas Indians. One, Fray Alonso Giraldo Terreros, a Franciscan of the Apostolic College of Santa Cruz in Querétaro, had already served as a missionary in Texas and hoped to extend his efforts into the San Sabá Apache lands. The other, Pedro Romero de Terreros, who had become wealthy from the Pachuca silver mines was to finance the effort. Fray Alonso established the mission of San Sabá de la Santa Cruz in April 1757. A *presidio*, or military garrison, San Luís de las Amarillas, was established two miles up river. There were no Indians living close by. The Apaches occasionally camped near the mission, but soon moved on. As it became more and more clear that they were hostile, the military commander recommended that the effort be abandoned, but the viceroy replied, "Stay." Even Fray Alonso was discouraged, but left the decision to his cousin and the viceroy. Again, it was, "Stay." Early one morning, over two thousand warriors on horseback, most of them Comanches, descended upon the defenseless mission, killing the friars and soldiers. Santiestevan was killed and beheaded as he prayed before the altar. While the other missionaries were being butchered and the mission burned, Molina managed to hide. With an arrow wound in his arm, he and a few others crawled away, eventually reaching the presidio under cover of darkness.

After listening in silence to the tragic account, Junípero remained undaunted; in a letter to his nephew, Fray Miquel de Petra Ribot, who had just become a Capuchin priest in Majorca, he said, "I realize my feebleness and nothingness for so glorious an enterprise."

This was why he had become a missionary, and the practical training he had received in his eight years in the wilds of the Sierra Gorda was surely the best preparation for coping with such a challenge. Along with being a saver of souls, a diplomat, a builder of churches and missions, and a tiller of the soil, he was a missionary whose religious fervor burned as ardently as ever.

Waiting for his superior to set a departure date, Serra joined again in the life of the college. Little did he realize that one man's offended pride would prevent him from going to Texas and lead to the abandonment of the entire San Sabá mission effort.

Pedro Romero de Terreros, the wealthy man who had financed the missionary project, had received word that Fray José García, the newly-elected guardian of the College of San Fernando, had chosen Serra and Palóu as replacements for the martyred friars. But Don Pedro objected on the ground that he had not participated in the selection of the missionaries as called for in the initial contract. If he were to pay the bills, he felt he had the right to determine who would take the place of Santiestevan and his slain cousin Fray Alonso. Letters of protest and explanation went back and forth for many months. Eventually, the viceroy died and the matter was dropped. Palóu returned to the Sierra Gorda and became prefect of the missions; Serra was appointed choirmaster at the college and put in charge of novices. Had it not been for the pride of Pedro Romero, Serra might have spent the remainder of his days in Texas.

Now, the cloistered walls of the college became a spiritual refuge after years of toil and prayer. But sought after by nuns and priests as a confessor and a leader of retreats, Serra's figure became well known. He concentrated on his spiritual development, and life in the city outside the walls of San Fernando held little interest for him. Palóu comments, "There was no person in the city whom he would ever visit. When those who were in need of him came for their own comfort to seek him at the college, it was only then that they learned he had departed on long missions in the alien districts of the seacoast, jungles, and sierras."

No explanations were offered by the guardian of the College of San Fernando for his failure to reactivate the mission at San Sabá. Whatever disappointment Serra felt for not being allowed to go was locked in his heart. During the next nine years, from 1758 to 1767, he dedicated himself to the internal life of the college and its preaching apostolate. He journeyed to the mining town of Zimapán and the desert villages of Mesquital within the archdiocese, and to the mountain dioceses of Guadalajara, Puebla, Oaxaca, and Valladolid, and to the Huasteca. It is estimated that between 1758 and 1767, Serra, despite his ulcerated leg, journeyed over 5,500 miles. And everywhere he went, he preached to Spaniards, Creoles, and Indians.

Everyone who met Serra was amazed at his self-discipline. Although at night he was terribly exhausted, he schooled himself to make do with little sleep. He would sleep from eight to midnight, then after the midnight office return to his prayers until dawn. Later, in California, the mission guards would ask when changing watch, "When does the father sleep?" And, Serra's eating habits were no less austere. Meat seemed repugnant and he ate it only rarely. He ate sparingly of fruit, vegetables, and fish, often finishing early, then waiting on the others or reading aloud.

To bring his body into subjection, he would use the discipline beyond what the college required, going to the choir loft at night to be unseen and unheard in his self-imposed blows and scourgings. He wore a sackcloth of bristles next to his skin or a coat with short, broken pieces of wire woven in.

In the churches and cathedrals where he preached, Junípero often chastised his body because of "my own imperfections and sins, as well as the sins of others." In imitation of Saint Francis Solano, he would drop his habit to the waist and begin lashing himself. On one occasion, Serra hid a large rock in the pulpit and, after delivering his sermon, called for the repentance of sin. Then with the crucifix in one hand, he grabbed the rock with the other and began beating his breast. In doing this, Junípero was imitating Saint Jerome in the desert when he, too, bruised his breast with stones. Saint John of Capistrano was his exemplar, when Serra, preaching on hell and damnation, burned his flesh with the flame of a taper.

With such acts, Serra was performing in the accepted manner of his times. The authorities in the college did not disapprove of such practices but suggested they be used with great discretion. It may look like fanaticism to us today, but it was fairly well at home in the religious and psychological matrix of Spanish New World culture in the eighteenth century—an outward manifestation of an inward spiritual discipline. And who is to say we are really very different? Serra and his contemporaries might well be astounded at the marathon runners and even the football players we so admire, who punish themselves and risk real and lasting injury for a purpose that would look to Serra like a kind of physical aggrandizement that leaves the soul untouched.

Because of impassioned dramatizations like these and otherwise, Serra was in great demand as a preacher. In 1767, responding to a request from Bishop Buenaventure Blanco of the diocese of Oaxaca, Junípero paddled up the dangerous Río Los Mijes where the heat, flies, and alligators made life hazardous. They were unable to disembark from the canoes for over a week because of the wild animals and poisonous snakes along the shore. After their exhausting trip, Serra and his companions had to walk over many miles of equally treacherous mountain terrain. Finally reaching Antequera, and exhausted as he was, Junípero preached a number of missions between February and May, performing hundreds of marriage ceremonies "for those living in sin."

While conducting a mission in the province of La Huasteca, Serra offered mass in a small town where only a few of the residents showed any interest in attending. Soon after Serra took his leave, an epidemic broke out, killing sixty people. When the parish priest noted that only those who had attended the padre's mission had not been affected, church attendance suddenly increased, not only among the townspeople, but also among the ranchers and farmers in the outlying districts. Palóu commented, "In all the province towns, a great deal of fruit was gathered for God who in His way abundantly rewarded the labors of his servant, Fray Junípero."

Another incident during this time further strengthened Serra's belief that divine Providence was watching over him. One evening when he and two companions were making their way back to the College of San Fernando after finishing their apostolic labors in La Huasteca, a journey that would take thirty-two days to complete, they found they would have to spend the night in the open. Selecting a spot by a small stream, they were greeted warmly by an aged couple and their grandson, who provided them with a little fruit and the shelter of their hut. The next morning, after thanking their benefactors, the friars continued their journey. A few hours later, they encountered several muleteers, who told them, to their astonishment, "In all the distance you traveled yesterday, there is not a single house or ranch. No one lives in this area because of the desert lands." Serra felt that "without a doubt, Jesus, Mary, and Joseph were in that hut by the stream that night," and cited "the poverty and the affection with which they lodged and fed us," as well as "the extraordinary inner consolation" the two had felt while within.

The following year, somewhere in the vast province of Zimapán, Serra almost lost his life. While Serra offered morning mass during a mission, someone apparently poisoned the wine. After drinking it, Junípero visibly changed color and lost his speech. Had not the altar boy been alert and aided him in time, he would have collapsed. The incapacitated Serra was carried to the sacristy, placed on a cot, and his vestments removed. A priest brought him a liquid antidote, which Junípero refused to take. Later, when offered some oil, he drank it, although it did not cause him to vomit. However, within a few hours, his speech returned, and he felt much better. Serra's first words quoted Saint Mark: "And, if they shall drink anything deadly, it shall not hurt them." Asked why he refused the first remedy, he replied:

Indeed my brother, it was not to offer you an affront, nor was it because I disbelieved in its effectiveness, nor because I had any horror of it, for in other circumstances I would have taken it. But I had just received the Bread of Angels, which by the power of Consecration ceased to be bread and was changed into the Body of my Lord, Jesus Christ. Sir, how could you ask me to take so nauseating a drink after tasting the divine Morsel which had been bread and then no longer was?

Serra was able to take his place in the confessional later that morning and to preach that evening. Although Junípero himself believed he may have had an upset stomach, Palóu always insisted that someone had tried to poison his friend.

Meanwhile, political and ecclesiastical events in Spain, France, England, Prussia, and Italy, as well as the American colonies, were destined to alter the course of Serra's life. The guardian of San Fernando had to keep abreast of the changes taking place in the Old World. Disquiet in Spain had been growing for some time because of the ever-growing threat from England and Russia to its overseas possessions. Out of such fears came the call for a graying Junípero Serra to missionize California.

CHAPTER NINE

THE CALL
TO BAJA CALIFORNIA

To the missionaries, Baja California meant a land wealthy in Indians to be evangelized; to the soldiers, assignment there meant banishment to *este último rincón del mundo,* "the last corner of the earth." To King Carlos III, the Pacific west coast from La Paz in southern Baja to Point Reyes above San Francisco Bay was an aegis against the invasion of foreign powers, especially the czar, whose explorers were already penetrating down the coast from Alaska, and the British, whose argosies were sweeping the world's seas and who believed that settlements were a more enduring claim to new territory than the planted standard and cross.

By the middle 1700s, England already had established a chain of colonies controlling an area extending from Baffin Island in the Arctic in northeast Canada all the way to Florida. Meanwhile, the once-powerful French nation had lost its domains in the Mississippi and Saint Lawrence valleys. New Spain's northern boundary extended in an undefined, defenseless arc from what is now Florida, Georgia, and Alabama, through Texas, New Mexico, and Arizona to Baja California.

Now, in 1768, with the announcement of the expulsion of the Jesuits from the Baja missions, a whole new story in the growth and development of California was about to unfold. In late June, Marqués de Croix, viceroy of New Spain, in consultation with José de Gálvez, the king's visitor general, recommended that the vacated missions of Baja California, each one a Jesuit oasis in the desert wilderness, be entrusted to the Franciscans of the College of San Fernando. At the time, the college was limited in manpower. Ten friars were in the Sierra Gorda, the others engaged at the college or providing missions nearby. Fray José García, the guardian, showed little enthusiasm for the undertaking. But since he had little choice in the matter, he called for fourteen volunteers, choosing Serra to serve as president of the missions of Baja California, with Palóu as his substitute.

At the time, Junípero was giving a mission in Mesquital province. Without revealing his reason, the guardian ordered that Serra return to the college at once. Arriving at San Fernando on July 13, Junípero received the guardian's blessing and was informed of his new position. Though shocked by the expulsion of the Jesuits, Serra expressed great joy over the new assignment. Characteristically, he was especially pleased that his opinion had not been asked and that he was going as an act of obedience.

Early on the morning of July 14, the missionaries bade farewell to their community and received the blessing of Father García. Everyone realized that for many of them this would be their last farewell. Near the college's entrance, García addressed the departing group:

> Beloved Fathers and Brothers, go forth with the blessing of God and Our Seraphic Father, Saint Francis, to evangelize that mystic field of labor in California entrusted to us by our Catholic Sovereign. Go! Go forth with the comforting thought that you have as your superior, Father Lector Junípero, whom by these letters patent I name president of all Your Reverences and of the missions. I have no more to say to you than that you obey him as you would me and that you commend me to God.

García then handed the patent of president to Serra, who tearfully received it without uttering a word. Then each missionary knelt, kissed the guardian's hand, and received his final blessing. When the members of the college accompanied the missionaries to the college gate, they found a large number of people in the plaza waiting to watch the departure. Many of them were losing their spiritual advisers. The gray friars mounted their steeds and trotted off upon a journey that would eventually take several of them as far as the Golden Gate and beyond, even as far as the northwest.

Traveling at the rate of almost twenty miles a day, the missionaries reached the city of Tepic near the west coast in thirty-nine days. There, Serra learned that a sloop was ready to transport the newly appointed governor of the peninsula, Don Gaspar de Portolá, and a few soldiers to Loreto on the east coast of Baja California. Junípero asked Portolá's permission for three of the Franciscans to accompany them. It was granted, and Serra, Palóu, and Gastón sailed with the group on August 24, 1767. However, the ship returned after encountering a bad storm in the Gulf of California.

Since the friars had time on their hands awaiting repairs to the damaged ship, Serra proposed that they give a mission in Tepic. But the townspeople were not in a receptive mood, and the presence of so many soldiers was causing confusion. Early in October, Colonel Domingo Elizondo, commander of the troops in the area, notified Serra that the padres should prepare themselves for departure later that week. Portolá decided to sail in a sloop and assigned the Franciscans a launch. Serra insisted upon seeing for himself whether the launch was large enough for his group, so he rode down to the harbor of San Blas to investigate, leaving Palóu in charge.

One day in mid-October a letter arrived from the viceroy in Mexico City. Palóu was astonished at its contents: The orders for the San Fernando missionaries had been changed. According to the new instructions, the Franciscans were not to sail to Baja California, but instead march northward to Pimería with a missionary group from the Apostolic College of Querétaro. Another group of friars, from the province of Jalisco, was assigned to Baja California. For Palóu, this change was surprising enough, but the motive for it was disconcerting. It was alleged that since the missionaries from San Fernando and Querétaro were members of sister colleges, they would get along better as neighbors. The Jaliscans would have the Baja fields all to themselves.

Of course, the Jaliscans were jubilant and the Fernandinos distressed. Palóu and his brethren had volunteered for a definite field, not just any mission area. Furthermore, they considered the Pimería as civilized enough to become a regular diocese and the warlike Apaches to the north of the Pimería as incapable of being converted to Christianity.

By special courier, Palóu notified Serra of developments. Serra hurriedly returned to Tepic, finding his Fernandinos hurt and frustrated, the Querétarans embittered, and the military complaining. In spite of his own disappointment, Serra calmly wrote to the viceroy pointing out the disadvantages of the new proposal and recommending a return to the original arrangement. Junípero then asked Palóu and another missionary to hand-deliver the letter to de Croix in Mexico City. The two messengers arrived at the Convent of the Discalced Friars of the Province of San Diego in Guanajuato on November 1, the Feast of All Saints, and that same afternoon obtained an interview with José de Gálvez, the visitor general. Gálvez explained to Palóu that he was not in accord with the viceroy's ridiculous idea, suggesting that he himself add a formal letter of protest to Serra's. The next morning, Palóu and his companion set out for Mexico City. Arriving on November 11, they received a swift response from de Croix, who, after consulting with his advisers, countermanded his previous instructions. Palóu immediately relayed the good news to Serra in Tepic by special courier.

At eight o'clock on the evening of March 14, 1768, the missionaries from the College of San Fernando embarked on the *Concepción*. The

Loreto Mission, Baja California, Mexico. The mission, Nuestra Señora de Loreto, was founded in 1697 by the Jesuits more than half a century before they were replaced by Serra and the Franciscans. Over the portal is the inscription: "Head and Mother of all the Missions of Lower and Upper California."

small ship reached Loreto two hundred miles up the east coast of Baja California on Good Friday, April 1. At the nearby mission, Serra met Father Manuel Zuzuárregui, the president of the Jaliscans. He had governed the Loreto mission for only eighteen days and had already recalled the friars who had been dispatched into the interior to take over the Jesuit missions. Now the Jaliscans were to return to San Blas and Sonora, where they had been ordered in the first place. Serra and his Franciscans were now ready for their work in Baja California.

In Loreto, the capital of Baja California (though the name "capital" was pretentious for this poor outpost on the frontier), Don Gaspar de Portolá and his officers extended a hearty welcome to the friars. The governor handed the church over to Serra but retained the living quarters under his supervision. He reserved two rooms for Serra and his assistant and provided each friar with table, chair, leather bed, candleholder, and bookstand. "Everything else remained in the hands of and served that gentleman and his household," wrote Palóu. The missionaries were the "guests" of the governor. Although Portolá supplied them with food, he charged the meals against the mission. Palóu remarks with disappointment that not a single bar of chocolate was offered to them.

Fifteen friars offered their masses early on Easter morning. Serra later celebrated High Mass and preached a fervent sermon. Portolá then read the letter from the viceroy that formally handed the Baja missions over to the Franciscans. But Serra and Palóu were surprised to learn that they were in charge of spiritual matters only. The everyday management of the missions was to remain in the hands of the military. Portolá explained that when the Jesuits were expelled, he had placed a soldier commissioner in charge of each mission so that the properties would be protected. The viceroy had agreed that this should continue until Gálvez decided upon new arrangements. Though it relieved the new missionaries of many burdens, it also impeded their work. For the time being, however, there was nothing to do but accept the situation.

Learning the location, distance, and needs of each mission, Serra began assigning his friars to them. Although all were pleased, none knew exactly what his responsibilities would be like in this rough country among half-starving Indians. Serra gave his Franciscans a paternal talk on their new work, urging all to labor zealously. Should any missionary die, he added, twenty masses would be offered for the repose of his soul by each of the other friars.

Serra remained for over a year at the mission in Loreto while his men conducted their conversion efforts in the nearby mountains and deserts. Agriculture was difficult due to lack of water; Baja California has the greatest variety of cactus in the world. Where small streams could be dammed, however, wheat, corn, beans, figs, olives, citrus fruits, and cotton could be grown. The harvest always depended on how much water could be found. The southern tip of the peninsula had the most fertile soil.

Upon entering the former Jesuit missions, missionaries counted an Indian population that had dwindled to only 7,149, "including infants at the breast." When the Fernandinos handed the missions over to the Dominicans three years later, the number had further declined to around 5,000, Palóu noting that "if it goes on at this rate, in a short time Baja California will come to an end." The depletion of the native population was due mainly to the constant epidemics and the prevalence of syphilis, introduced by Portolá's troops.

Meanwhile, Gálvez, displaying characteristic concern and imagination in attempting to safeguard Spanish possessions along the Pacific coast against Russian encroachment, ordered the immediate establishment of a naval base at San Blas on the west coast of Mexico, about four hundred miles northwest of Mexico City. Strategically located, the port would serve as a supply base for all Alta California exploration activities. Arriving there on May 13, 1768, Gálvez ordered the new brigantines, the *San Carlos* and the *San Antonio,* placed in readiness for a sea expedition to locate Monterey Bay. Three days later at a meeting with military personnel, he discussed the possibility of a land expedition. After a lengthy discussion, a plan of action was adopted and signed by the participants. Palóu noted:

> In consequence of all this, the illustrious Señor Don José de Gálvez, with the approval of all, agreed and resolved that there be made ready at once all the necessary supplies of provision, rigging, sails, and whatever else is thought useful and indispensable to be put aboard the two aforementioned new ships which are to undertake the voyage to the harbor of Monterey by leaving the coast and the chain of islands behind and undertaking the voyage on the high seas, thus to reach the proper latitude as far as the winds of the season will permit so as not to experience the delays, misfortunes, and sicknesses which were suffered by the expeditions of Don Sebastián Vizcaíno, and others made during the last two centuries.

With the conference completed, Gálvez wrote to Serra of his intention to settle Monterey in Alta (Upper) California. He then departed for Santa Ana, a small mining town near La Paz, where he set up permanent headquarters.

Upon receiving the news that a mission would be established in Monterey, Junípero ordered the ringing of bells and celebrated a special High Mass in thanksgiving. He immediately dispatched an encyclical letter to all the missionaries requesting that they, too, offer masses at their missions. Then by return mail, he congratulated Gálvez upon his arrival in Baja California and offered himself as the first volunteer "to erect the bold standard of the cross in Monterey." For Serra, the opportunity he had been waiting for at last materialized: that of planting the faith on "unworked soil." A number of enthusiastic letters were exchanged between Serra and Gálvez. On July 26, in a reply to Junípero's first letter of welcome, Gálvez acknowledged his appreciation of Serra's eagerness about the proposed northern expedition; from the very beginning he had had faith in his "beloved brethren of the College of San Fernando."

Serra then began a tour of the missions north of Loreto, probably to talk over with his missionaries prospects for the Monterey expedition. First, he went to San Xavier to see Palóu, and then north to the missions of San José de Cumundú, La Purísima de Cadegomó, and Guadalupe, where Fathers Martínez, Crespí, and Sancho were working. A trip of over two hundred miles through the scorching desert in August, it probably took Serra the entire month.

During that time, Gálvez was visiting the southern Baja missions.

What he discovered there angered him. Expecting to find the establishments more developed, he scolded the soldier commissioners for their poor administration. On August 12, he signed a decree turning the missions over completely to the Fernandinos. Throughout the remainder of 1768, as well as the following year, Gálvez was busy managing the affairs of Baja California.

It pleased Serra that in various ways Gálvez sought to promote the welfare of the Indians on the peninsula. Both in the north and in the south, certain missions had insufficient land and water to adequately maintain the number of converts, while missions with an abundance of both were without enough workers to cultivate the fields. Gálvez ordered Indians moved from one mission to another. He also authorized certain young Indians who had been orphaned to be sent to Loreto for training in handling coast vessels.

He had many other ideas for the betterment of the inhabitants of Baja, to whom he referred as "the poor Israelites." He wrote Serra that he wanted to lead them to the Promised Land, although he admitted he was not worthy of being compared to Moses. He hoped Serra and his missionaries would be so many more Aarons praying for him in the temple.

While ordering such civil, economic, social reforms from his headquarters in Santa Ana, Gálvez kept in close touch with Serra, whose swollen foot had been bothering him ever since he had arrived on the peninsula. On August 13, Gálvez wrote:

> I would feel bad if your Reverence would not be well and strong enough when the day comes to begin the overland march and you resolved to make the journey to Monterey, for it will be one fraught with hardship owing to the distance. However, I shall see to it that some provisions shall be anticipated which will facilitate the journey in so far as it is possible. But I repeat that I will never consent to Your Reverence going by sea.

Gálvez petitioned the viceroy for more missionaries for the expedition to Monterey. In his letters he took the opportunity to praise the work of the Franciscans:

> In the charity and zeal of the apostolic ministers who are in charge of the missions of this peninsula, I have found all the cooperation necessary to satisfy my desires. . . . They love the Indians with great charity and tenderness, nor do they lose sight of the public interest of the crown and its vassals.

On September 24, Gálvez notified Serra that the expedition's packet boats would enter the harbor of La Paz within a few weeks and therefore Serra should now appoint the missionary who would accompany the first ship, so that he would arrive there in time and not delay the departure. Gálvez added that he was in total agreement with Serra's concept of the missions in Alta California being a day's journey apart, with one friar assigned to each mission. In the event that only the missions of San Diego, Monterey, and San Buenaventura along the Santa Barbara Channel were established, two missionaries would be assigned to each. To strengthen such a slender chain, Gálvez planned to station soldier guards between the established missions until new missions could be formed. The visitor general added that he wanted the church's most opulent possessions to be taken on the expedition "for the service of God and the eyes of the Indians."

When Serra responded, he questioned the naming of the missions. "Is there to be no mission in honor of Our Holy Father, Saint Francis?" Gálvez replied, "Let him find the port bearing his name and he will have his mission there." San Francisco was to be the first mission established after Monterey "and Our Holy Father so beloved of God will facilitate its establishment by means of his powerful intercession." All succeeding missions were to be named after Franciscan saints; it was traditional that the missions founded by a particular order were dedicated to that order's saints. Names were selected by civil authorities in Mexico City after consultation with officials in the appropriate apostolic colleges.

Now Gálvez wanted to confer with Serra personally. He was to come south by launch, but the request was canceled due to heavy storms in the gulf. Gálvez then offered to send mules, muleteers, and servants to bring Junípero south. He also sent along a confidential letter containing the instructions he had drawn up for the new missions and asked Serra what he thought of them, "since I am very far removed from self-love and my labors are sufficiently bad to prevent their author from falling in love with them."

A month later, Gálvez again wrote Serra, suggesting that he and his missionaries persuade their Baja converts to settle in towns in the south. If they agreed, he promised to provide food and clothing for the journey, as well as certificates of identification. Gálvez also said he was ready to confer with Serra on the matter of stipends and salaries for the missionaries. Placing Palóu in charge of the Loreto mission, Serra began his journey on October 28. Three days later, to the joy of Gálvez, he arrived in Santa Ana. Equally honest and creative, Gálvez and Serra must have appreciated each other as they went about the serious business of doing what they believed to be God's work.

Among the questions resolved at their first meeting were the annual stipends for the friars of Baja, as well as those for the missionaries volunteering for the work in Alta California. From the Pious Fund amassed by the Jesuits in Mexico City from the donations of the affluent interested in sponsoring missionary activities, seven hundred pesos would be allocated to each of the missionaries assigned to the new missions, and a thousand pesos would be set aside for the founding of each settlement. The authorities at the College of San Fernando thought the allocations totally inadequate, though they were later proved wrong. Next, Gálvez and Serra discussed the sea and land expeditions to Monterey. Again, Junípero offered to go, suggesting that the secular priest not only administer Loreto but also serve as chaplain for the garrison, thus freeing two missionaries. In addition, Serra advised Gálvez to send a plea to the College of San Fernando for three more missionaries. Gálvez readily agreed, although he realized that at the time San Fernando had less than half a dozen friars to spare. But a large contingent of new missionaries was expected during the year from Spain under the leadership of Fray Rafael Verger, Serra's old friend and colleague from Palma. Upon receiving the request, the guardian of San Fernando, after careful deliberation with his advisers, complied, immediately dispatching Fathers Escudero, Vizcaíno, and de la Sierra to Loreto.

It was at this meeting that Serra selected Fray Fernando Parrón to accompany the sea expedition to Monterey. Parrón was ordered to proceed with haste to La Paz. To furnish the three new Alta California missions, Gálvez ordered the missions on the Baja peninsula to contribute whatever they could from their sacristies. Serra was authorized to requisition whatever he thought necessary. Because there was little time to send across the gulf for cattle, mules, and horses, Gálvez decided that these, too, should be supplied by the missions.

Final preparations were now in motion for the expeditions. January 9, 1769, was the date selected for the departure of the flagship *San Carlos* from La Paz. That morning, Serra, Gálvez, Parrón, and the town's inhabitants assembled on the shore. After Serra sang High Mass, all the members of the departing group received the sacrament of penance and the Holy Eucharist. In his oration, Gálvez said that the group was being sent to Monterey in order to plant the standard of the holy cross among the Indians. In the name of the king and the viceroy, he charged the explorers to preserve peace among themselves and to respect and revere their chaplain. Father Parrón knelt and received Serra's blessing, and Serra then blessed the ship and the banners. Then, Parrón, along with Captain Vicente Vila, boarded the *San Carlos*. Next, Lieutenant Pedro Fages and the twenty-five soldiers under his command, Miguel Costansó, engineer and cosmographer, and the ship's surgeon, Pedro Prat, climbed on board. On schedule, the *San Carlos* weighed anchor a little before noon and slowly started south down the gulf and around Cabo San Lucas, then north along the Pacific coast.

A month later, Gálvez dispatched the *San Antonio*, the second ship of the sea expedition, from Cabo San Lucas. He and Serra were both pleased with the leaders of the expedition, who had considerable experience on both land and sea. Vila of the *San Carlos* was a native of Andalusia and a pilot of the first class. Captain Don Juan Pérez of the *San Antonio,* a Majorcan from Palma, and all the others had experience on previous expeditions in Mexico.

Serra returned to Loreto with genuine contentment in his heart, knowing that this great enterprise—bringing Christianity and a settled way of life to the inhabitants of Alta California—had well begun.

CHAPTER TEN

OPERATION
ALTA CALIFORNIA

Although the official explanation for annexing Alta California was to extend the Catholic faith, there is ample documentation to show that Carlos III had been informed by the Spanish ambassador in Saint Petersburg that Russia intended to establish settlements along the Pacific coast. Thus, it was imperative that Monterey be secured. Once it was, Spain could employ its traditional means of expansion by establishing Spanish Christian culture among the Indians through the mission system. Had Russia not threatened Spain's northern flank, there is no evidence that Spain would have bothered to occupy Alta California during this period.

Don Gaspar de Portolá, that pleasant, genial man who had been assigned the dreadful task of carrying out the royal orders expelling the Jesuits from Baja, was to lead the overland expedition to Monterey. Gálvez's instructions to Portolá consisted of twelve points, the most important being to plant the flag of Spain on the hills overlooking the ports of San Diego and Monterey. Portolá, with Serra and a small guard, was to march as soon as possible to the northern Baja frontier mission of Santa María, where he would meet Fernando de Rivera and proceed to San Diego. Only the minimum of supplies was to be carted with them to Velicatá; a launch with the main provisions would rendezvous with them at San Luis at the northern end of the Gulf of California. The *San Carlos* and the *San Antonio* would sail on to meet the land expeditions in San Diego. Rivera was then to proceed to Monterey while Portolá remained in San Diego to help Serra establish a mission. In case Portolá decided to proceed to Monterey, Rivera was to scout and explore the country ahead of him. Gálvez then issued strict orders to Portola:

In order that our most commendable objectives may be attained, and to prevent difficulties and disaster in the outcome, the most prudent supervision must be exercised. Therefore I charge you with zeal and vigilance to maintain the most exact discipline over the soldiers of the expedition as well as over the muleteers, especially from the frontier on, so that the Indians will be well treated. The soldiers are to be punished as in the case of an irremissible crime if they offer any affront or violence to the women because besides being offenses against God, such excesses committed by them could also bring disaster to the entire expedition.

The visitor general then cautioned Portolá to travel slowly, since Indian opposition might be encountered. The native inhabitants were to be attracted with "affability, sagacity, and prudence." They were to be shown the great good that would come to them if they lived in brotherhood with the Spaniards under the sovereign protection of the king.

Near Monterey, the river and valley of Carmel were to be explored. Once the harbors of Monterey and San Diego were secure, an official document of possession was to be drawn up and dispatched to the viceroy with a diary of the journey. In Monterey, a mission and a presidio were to be erected, and once the Spaniards were settled, Portolá and Rivera were to return to San Diego, leaving Lieutenant Fages in charge.

Although the *San Carlos* and the *San Antonio* had already put to sea in January and February of 1769, the initial overland party still had not marched. Don Fernando de Rivera y Moncada, captain of the Baja soldiers, had already collected the horses and mules for the expedition and was waiting at Velicatá, two days' journey north of Santa Maria, and three hundred fifty miles south of San Diego. His orders from Gálvez had been to requisition horses and mules from the missions without endangering the survival of those establishments, giving receipts to the missionaries for the exact number of animals received. The missions would later be reimbursed with animals brought from Mexico across the gulf. Rivera was now at the frontier, impatient to move on to San Diego.

The chaplain and diarist for the Rivera party was Fray Juan Crespí of Mission Purísima. Serra's former philosophy student and Palóu's classmate was destined to become one of the greatest explorers of the Pacific coast. Now, with orders from Serra to join Rivera on the frontier, Crespí left his mission on February 26 and arrived at Velicatá on March 22. Two days later, Rivera, Crespí, twenty-five leather-jacketed soldiers, three muleteers, and forty-two Baja Christian Indians began their 350-mile journey. They arrived in San Diego on May 14, where the *San Carlos* and the *San Antonio* were waiting for them.

Meanwhile, the starting point for the expedition's second party was

Loreto, some nine hundred miles south of San Diego. With Portolá as commander-in-chief, and Serra as chaplain and diarist, the group was to follow on the heels of Rivera to San Diego. In the first words of his diary, Serra writes that it was a journey "I undertook from my mission and the royal presidio of Loreto in California bound for the ports of San Diego and Monterey for the greater glory of God and the conversion of the pagans to our holy Catholic faith."

Believing that Serra's infected foot had now become cancerous, Governor Portolá tried to dissuade the padre presidente from accompanying the expedition. He pointed out that Junípero's condition might delay the group and suggested that Father Palóu, younger and in better health, go in his place. Serra, recognizing that he was dealing with a practical soldier responsible for the safety and success of the expedition, nonetheless responded, "I trust in God that He will give me strength to arrive at San Diego and Monterey." He suggested Portolá start the journey without him; he would follow and meet him on the frontier. Serra then assigned Father Miguel de la Campa of Mission San Ignacio to accompany the expedition as the governor's chaplain.

On March 9, Portolá and his troops set off from Loreto and reached Mission San Xavier late that afternoon. There, he conferred with Palóu about Serra's physical condition, lamenting his inability to persuade Serra to change his mind. "I consider the attempt almost impossible, so I am writing to Gálvez about the matter." Portolá urged Palóu to request that Gálvez intervene. The next morning the expedition continued on its journey to Mission Santa María in the distant north.

Serra remained in Loreto during Holy Week, allowing him to sing High Mass on Easter Sunday and preach a farewell sermon. He had been at the mission for exactly a year. On Tuesday, March 28, Junípero commenced his trek to San Diego. He was provided with two servants, one of whom was José María Vergerano, a twenty-year-old from Guadalajara, but little else. Riding a sick and aging mule, Serra departed with no extra clothing and little in the way of food provisions.

> From my mission of Loreto, I took along no more provisions for so long a journey than a loaf of bread and a piece of cheese, for I was there a whole year, in economic matters, as a mere guest to receive the crumbs of the royal soldier commissioner, whose liberality at my departure did not extend beyond the aforementioned articles.

As he had in Puerto Rico when the captain of the ship had failed to provide for the friars, Serra merely recorded the fact, showing no bitterness. That evening, however, the mule bore a tired and hungry missionary into the San Xavier compound, where Palóu eagerly awaited him. Later, in his diary, Francisco noted:

For three days the Venerable Father stayed with me at the mission both because of the happiness I derived from his amiable companionship and the mutual love we bore each other since the year 1740 when obedience placed me under him as one of his students of philosophy, and to treat of matters concerning the presidency to which I had been named.

Palóu had been named by the guardian of San Fernando as Serra's successor in case of Serra's death, and this was their last opportunity to discuss the administration of the missions in Baja. Undoubtedly, their personal friendship prompted Serra to tarry a few extra days. Junípero wrote in his diary, "Reason enough for my delay here was the very special and long-standing mutual affection between this mission's minister, Father Lector Francisco Palóu, and myself."

In accordance with Gálvez's special instructions, Serra selected for the new Alta California missions from San Xavier's altar and sacristy a silver-plated chalice, a small bronze bell, a new chasuble (the sleeveless outer vestment worn by a priest offering mass) of cloth of gold and a used red one, and several other items.

Meanwhile, Palóu was concerned about the swelling of Serra's foot, which was now beginning to affect his entire left leg. Although he understood Junípero's resolve and ardent faith, he delicately mentioned the possibility that Serra's poor health might bring disaster upon the whole expdition, adding that since he was younger and stronger, he could go to San Diego in Serra's place. Junípero's reaction to the proposal was anger. "Let us not speak of that. I have placed all my confidence in God, of whose goodness I hope that He will grant me to reach not only San Diego to raise the standard of the Holy Cross in that port, but also Monterey." Palóu could only smile and note in his diary, "I desisted when I saw that the fervent superior greatly exceeded me in faith and confidence in God for love of Whom he was sacrificing his life on the altar of his apostolic labors."

Parting between the two came on the morning of April 1. Palóu wrote:

He said farewell, causing me equal pain for the love I felt for him and for the tenderness that I had owed him since the year 1740, when he began to be my teacher of philosopy. Since then we had almost always lived together, except when duty parted us, which was seldom and only for a short time. From this it may be inferred what reciprocal love there would be between teacher and pupil, and what sorrow that farewell would consequently cause us both, for we feared that we would not see each other again except in heaven.

Serra, so crippled that it required two men to lift him onto the mule and adjust him in the saddle, said, "Goodby, Francisco, until we meet in Monterey, where I hope we shall see each other and labor in that vineyard of the Lord." Believing instead that they would never see each other again, Palóu responded softly, "Goodby, Junípero, until eternity." Smiling, Serra affectionately chided Palóu for his lack of faith.

It was a long, slow trip from Loreto to San Diego, and Serra's diary, the only one he ever kept, records it fully. Making his way north, he arrived at Mission San José de Cumundú where Father Antonio Martínez, his old friend and co-worker from the Sierra Gorda, was stationed. Although away from the mission, the padre had left provisions for Serra's arrival. For a change, Junípero was comfortable. Since April 2 was a Sunday, Serra heard confessions, sang a High Mass, and preached.

The next mission, Nuesta Señora de Guadalupe, was more than a day's journey through rugged country. After traveling all day, Serra was prepared to spend the night in the open. On the road he met a dozen or so Indian families from Mission Guadalupe. Because of lack of provisions in the mission, Father Juan Sancho had had to send them out into the desert to forage for themselves. They had not been successful in their hunt, and the hungry children were crying. Serra's pack animals, abundantly laden by Martínez, were still half a day behind and would not arrive that night. From his own meager bag of supplies, Serra handed them cornmeal mush, first to the women and children, then to the men, explaining they could now return to their mission, since a launch was bringing corn by way of the port of San Luís. Then, after praying with them, Serra led them in singing "a very tender song on the love of God." (According to Palóu, the people of the region were known for the sweetness of their voices.)

The next morning, Serra resumed his trip over what he termed "very painful ridges." At noon, he rested for several hours at a small mission station, then continued his journey until he reached Mission Guadalupe after dark. Junípero had now come to the end of the mission trail that he had traveled before. From this point onward, he would be entering unknown lands, encountering unknown people.

In Guadalupe, Serra rested, allowing the pack animals to catch up. There were also letters to write and answer, and the friar in charge of Guadalupe was Fray Juan Sancho, a fellow Majorcan he had known as a young lay student in Palma before he entered the Franciscan order. During his stay, Fray Juan Gastón came over from Santa Rosalía de Mulegé on the gulf to pay his respects. He had been one of Serra's companions on the voyage in 1749 and had also worked with him in the Sierra Gorda.

Father Sancho had seen both the Rivera and Portolá expeditions pass through, and he told Serra that "of all the poor beasts that have passed through to Monterey, none were so broken down as the ones assigned to him." The padre therefore provided Junípero with the only fresh mules he had. Sancho also presented Serra with an assistant, Juan Evangelista Benno, a bright fifteen-year-old Indian altar boy who could read. Sancho outfitted the boy with clothing, a leather jacket and boots, and a saddle mule, much to his pleasure and that of his parents. Serra considered his young companion a favor esteemed beyond all others.

Two Christian Indians and the pack animals left Guadalupe on April 13; Serra, the young boy, a soldier guard, and the servants started out the following morning. Since Mission San Ignacio lay over a day's march away, Serra and his group had to spend the night in the open. Father Medina Veitía, the missionary at San Ignacio, thought-fully sent a prepared supper to Serra's camp from the mission. Early the next morning, he himself rode out on a mule to meet Junípero. The two padres rode together for a short distance, then Veitía went ahead in order to greet his superior properly. A few hours later, clad in a surplice, stole, and cope, Veitía formally greeted Serra at the church door.

The next day was Sunday, April 16, the day of the year Serra renewed his vows as a Franciscan. In the Convent of San Francisco in Palma and the College of San Fernando in Mexico City, the annual ceremony was conducted with becoming solemnity. Here, there were only Father Veitía and himself, but Serra carried out the renewal of his commitment to God by quietly uniting himself in spirit with his brethren throughout the world.

On the morning of his departure a few days later, Serra overslept and missed getting an early start. This was unfortunate, since the weather was extremely hot and the delay meant that he would spend two days and nights in uninhabited country before reaching Mission Santa Gertrudis. Arriving there on the morning of April 20, Serra was pleased to find Indians dancing before the church in welcome. He was formally received by Fray Dionisio Basterra. Junípero reverenced the cross extended by Basterra and blessed the people with holy water. Then, the two missionaries entered the small church in order to pray together.

Basterra embraced Serra and for some time the eyes of both welled with tears. Basterra had become more and more depressed over the last few months, since he was all alone in the mission without inter-preter, servant, or guard. When Rivera had passed through on his way north, he had requisitioned them. Basterra had appealed to Serra to intervene, and Junípero had immediately written to Rivera and Gálvez, to no avail. All Serra could do was send comforting letters to the melancholy missionary. Now, Basterra, a sad and lonely man, wept openly as Serra sympathized.

Serra remained with Basterra for five days, partly for Basterra's consolation. But he also had to attend to official business. Gálvez had ordered some of the Indians from Mission Santa Gertrudis to be transferred to Mission Purísima where there was a shortage of laborers to work the available land. Serra and Basterra gathered the natives from the various *rancherías* (villages) near the mission, explaining that it would be better for them to live at Purísima. There, at least, there was assurance of three meals a day, as well as an adequate supply of clothing. At Santa Gertrudis, they had often had to be turned away to forage for themselves. Serra's reasoning won over the Indians and they readily agreed. However, their decision was short-lived. They remained in the territory they knew so well, preferring less food and clothing to the new locale. Gálvez's orders and Serra's coaxing came to naught. In fact, three years later, Palóu reported that the Indians were still at Santa Gertrudis, some having fallen away from Christianity.

On April 28, after two days of strenuous travel, Serra arrived at Mission San Borja, where he was warmly greeted by Fray Fermín Francisco de Lasuén. Junípero wrote, "My special affection for this excellent missionary detained me here for the next two days which for me were very delightful by reason of his amiable conversation and manners." Lasuén's mission was very poor. Founded only seven years before, Mission San Borja was located in a region of Baja California notorious for its scarcity of water. In spite of the drawbacks, Lasuén had made considerable progress in feeding and converting the several hundred Indian families living near the mission grounds.

On May 1, Serra continued his journey toward the frontier mission of Santa María near Velicatá. After traveling four days, he stopped to say mass on the feast of the Ascension in the deserted church at Calamofué, little more than a ruined *jacal* (simple hut). The next morning, he arrived at Santa María. There, on the rim of Christendom, he met Portolá, Father de la Campa, and several members of the Portolá expedition. Most of the others had gone ahead to Velicatá.

Here were located the "poorest of all" the Indians Serra had yet encountered in the New World. There was little water and virtually no arable land or pasture. In fact, in time of drought, water was almost nonexistent; the land, alkaline, was useless. On Sunday, May 7, Serra sang High Mass and preached a sermon. Four days later, he and Portolá set out for Velicatá, saying farewell to "those poor people" whom he regarded as orphaned without a missionary.

CHAPTER ELEVEN

WITH A CROSS
AMONG THE INDIANS

After leaving Mission Santa María, Serra approached Portolá, asking, "If we move along at the slow pace of the pack train, we shall reach Velicatá only at the end of two days and tomorrow is Pentecost. May I ask the favor of pressing on in order that we can make the two days' journey in one?" Portolá agreed, and the small group traveled all day on May 13 to reach Velicatá in the late evening. They were warmly greeted by the advance guard of the party.

On Pentecost, 1769, Serra founded his first mission in a mud hut that had served as a temporary church when Father Lasuén traveled up on Easter to administer the sacraments to the Rivera expedition. The small *jacal* was cleaned and modestly adorned with a cross and a few bells. In stole, alb (a full-length white linen vestment), and chasuble, Serra blessed the holy water and then, with it, the church and the cross. He offered mass and preached on the descent of the Holy Spirit and the founding of the mission, which he designated San Fernando in honor of the patron of the apostolic college in Mexico City. After mass, possession of the surrounding territory was claimed in the name of the king of Spain.

The celebration took place "with all the neatness of holy poverty," according to Serra. Since the pack train was still on the trail, there were no candles on hand. The short stump of one and the wax taper of another was used, but neither lasted long enough for Father de la Campa to say mass. Smoke from the soldiers' guns, firing repeated volleys, substituted for incense. Though wood was lacking in the area, Serra noted that "the place in every other regard appears to be excellent and thus I hope that in time it will be a good mission."

But so far the most important thing was missing: a congregation of Indians to convert and for whom to provide. During morning prayers a few days later, Serra was informed by Father de la Campa, who had been assigned the mission, that a few people had arrived. "I praised the Lord," Junípero wrote, "and kissed the earth, giving thanks to the Divine Majesty that after desiring this for so many years, He granted me the favor of being among the pagans in their own land." Then, he hurried out to welcome twelve Indian men and boys. The sight of them convinced Serra that he really was now beyond the last lines of Christendom.

> Then I saw what I could hardly begin to believe when I read about it or was told about it, namely that they go about entirely naked like Adam in paradise before the fall. Thus they went about and thus they presented themselves to us. We treated with them for a long time; and although they saw all of us clothed, they nevertheless showed not the least trace of shame in their manner of nudity.

Serra placed both his hands upon their heads in token of affection and then filled their hands with figs, which they ate immediately. In turn, the leader of the Indians presented Junípero with roasted mescal and four beautiful fish, although the expedition's cook considered them spoiled and beyond eating. Portolá and his soldiers then offered leaf tobacco and various items of food.

Through an interpreter, Serra explained to the Indians that Padre de la Campa was going to remain at the mission in order to serve them. They had nothing to fear and should try to persuade their friends and families to come to the mission. Junípero asked them not to molest or kill the cattle, since whatever they needed would be supplied by the missionary. Portolá announced that their chief was now constituted the legal chief in the name of the king of Spain.

Leaving Father de la Campa and his primitive church, the expedition moved on to San Juan de Dios, arriving there on May 16. But Serra's foot had begun to bother him again.

> On the seventeenth I said Mass there although with great difficulty could I remain on my feet because my left foot had become very inflamed, a painful condition which I have suffered for a year or more. Now this inflammation has reached halfway up the leg. It is swollen and the sores are inflamed. For this reason the days during which I was detained there I spent the greater part in bed and was afraid that shortly I would have to follow the expedition on a stretcher.

Seeing Serra's pathetic condition, Portolá again tried to persuade him from making the journey. "Your Reverence is aware of the fact that you are unable to follow the expedition. We are only six leagues away from our starting place. If Your Reverence so desires, I will have you carried back to the first mission where you can recuperate, and we will continue our journey."

Serra's unbending determination was clearly evident by his reply:

> Your Honor, please do not speak of that, for I trust that God will give me the strength to reach San Diego, as He has given me the strength to come so far. In case He does not, I will conform myself to His most holy will. Even though I should die on the way, *I shall not turn back.* They can bury me wherever they wish and I shall gladly be left among the pagans, if it be the will of God.

Frustrated in this second attempt to deter Serra, Portolá had a stretcher prepared so that Junípero could be carried along the trail by the Christian Indians from Baja California accompanying the expedition.

Saddened that he would be a burden to those responsible for carrying him, Serra now departed from his practice of not using medicines for himself. Calling Juan Antonio Coronel, one of the muleteers, to him, he asked, "Son, do you know how to prepare a remedy for the wound in my foot and leg?" Surprised, the muleteer answered, "Why, Father, what remedy could I know of? Do you think I am a surgeon? I'm a muleteer; I've healed only the sores of animals." Serra replied, "Well then, son, just imagine that I am an animal and that this wound is the sore of an animal from which developed this swelling of the leg and the great pains I experience, which permit me neither to rest nor to sleep. Make me the same remedy which you would apply to an animal." Probably more to humor Serra than because he expected any results, Coronel took some tallow, crushed it between stones, and mixed it with some green desert herbs. After heating the concoction, he spread the mass over Serra's foot and leg.

That night Serra slept peacefully for the first time in months. The next morning, "I found myself much improved and I celebrated Mass." Later, in San Diego, Junípero wrote Palóu.

> I left the frontier in a very bad condition with regard to my foot and leg; but God brought it about that [through the muleteer] ... I was enabled to make the daily trek just as if I did not have any ailment. At present my sore foot is as clean as the well one, but from the ankles halfway up the knee it is in the same condition as my foot was. It is all one sore. However, there is no swelling but only the itching which I feel at times. In short, there is nothing to cause concern.

Portolá's expedition was still some three hundred miles south of San Diego with over forty days of uncertain travel ahead. In his sermon on Trinity Sunday, May 21, Serra exhorted everyone to good behavior

> on a journey whose principal end was the honor and glory of God. I blessed them in the name of the Father and of the Son and of the Holy Ghost, whose trinity of persons and unity of divine nature we celebrated

that day, and in the name of God, triune and one, marching orders were given and the trip was begun.

Later that day, the party made its way across a number of deep arroyos (stream-carved gullies) and encountered Indians skilled at making fine arrowheads. In one of the arroyos, they came upon a solitary, aged Indian, to whom they offered food. The man declared that he never ran away from strangers, though the rest of his fellow villagers did, and recalled that years previously a Jesuit had visited the area. Asked if he would become a Christian, he said yes. Asked when he would become one, he said, "Now." In his diary, Serra described how unconcerned the old man was about anyone or anything. "While he was standing there in the midst of our circle conversing with us, he squatted and, since he was untrammeled by clothes, he straightaway relieved nature while he continued to speak to us." Then, added Junípero, with not a little humor, "he remained as serene as relieved."

On the following day, while the pack train continued its journey, Serra remained behind writing letters. Sergeant José Francisco Ortega and a few soldiers remained with him. Now that he was beyond the missions, Junípero dispatched an encyclical letter to all the padres announcing that Palóu was now president of the missions of the Baja peninsula. To all his brethren, he added a "last farewell," since he was in an unknown land with unknown dangers.

As the group moved along, the expedition noted signs of where Rivera's expedition had passed or had come in contact with the Indians. They celebrated the feast of Corpus Christi on a large plain surrounded by hills. During the preceding nights, a mountain lion was heard in the underbrush near camp. "May God protect us from him," wrote Serra calmly. Over high mountains and across dry arroyos the cavalcade wound its tortuous way.

On May 26, two Indians were seen following the expedition at a safe distance. Some of the party's Christian Indians seized one of them, tied him up, and brought the bruised and frightened man into camp. Serra placed his hands upon the fellow's head and recited from the Gospel of Saint John. Then, he made the sign of the cross over him and had him untied. The young Indian was robust and about twenty years of age. Although badly shaken from his experience, he was taken to Portolá's tent, where he was given figs, meat, and tortillas. To everyone's surprise, he asked for a little atole, a thin porridge of corn and wheat, and was given some. He told them his name was Axajui, and he apologized for spying on the expedition. Serra tells us that "in exonerating himself of this venial sin, he fell into a pretty mortal one" when he said that his chief had sent him to spy on the Spaniards while the others went to lie in ambush among the cliffs in order to kill the padres and the rest of their party. Serra added dryly, "We generously forgave him of such like intentions." Axajui was sent back to inform his people of the good treatment he had received.

After several days of making their way over bare, rocky hills, they began to see small flowers of varying colors, a delight to the eyes after the monotonous desert landscape that had become so familiar. They passed Cieneguilla, the northernmost point reached by the Jesuit, Joseph Link, in 1766 during his search for the Colorado River. Serra had Link's diary with him. Unfortunately, it is no longer extant.

At this point, a group of more menacing Indians appeared, and for the first time Spanish soldiers were forced to shoot their rifles into the air in order to scare them away. But along the hilltops, Indians with bows and arrows continued to follow the expedition, which was now trying to cross the ravines. A more friendly group put on a mock battle for the Spaniards, a demonstration Serra and the soldiers seemed to enjoy. Among this group, Serra noticed the first women he had encountered in Alta California.

> Until now we had not seen any women among them; and I desired for the present not to see them [fearing that they went naked like the men], when amid these fiestas two women appeared, talking as rapidly and effectively as this sex knows how and is accustomed to; and when I saw them so decently clothed . . . I was not sorry at their arrival.

The youngest was the wife of the chieftain and carried food, a doughy form of pancake, upon her head, which she offered to the strangers. Serra, in thanking her, smeared his hands in placing them over her head and making the sign of the cross. She and the chieftain then explained how the food was to be eaten; the second, more elderly woman, joined in, talking animatedly.

On May 30, the feast of San Fernando, the expedition rested in an attractive valley that Portolá insisted should be named after the royal saint, not only because they were there on his feast day, but also because "it was the king among the places of [Baja] California." None of the other missions thus far established had such an excellent site—groves of cottonwoods and other trees, level land, running water, and good pasturage. There was even a small hill in the middle of the valley, where Serra envisioned a future mission. A name was suggested for the mission: San Pedro Regalado. Serra wrote, "May God, Our Lord, will that we may soon see it populated." As he explored the nearby rolling hills, he met other Indians, "humble and simple, who to all appearances are ready to receive the light of the Gospel."

As the expedition moved on through the month of June, the terrain became gradually lovelier. The group often spent the night under large oak trees. Near Santa Petronilla, the land was "so loaded with grapes that it is a thing to marvel at. I believe that with a little labor of pruning them, the vines would produce much excellent fruit." Rolling hills and plains alternated until finally,

> we found ourselves in the new Piedmont, or the foot of the sierra. . . . It seems the thorns and rocks of California are now behind us, for these very high mountains are of pure earth. Also there are many flowers, and beautiful ones, as I have already noted. And lest anything be lacking along this line, today [June 21] on arriving at our resting place, we encountered the queen of them all, the rose of Castile. As I am writing this, I have before me a branch of rose bush, with three petals opened, others in bud, and more than six unpetaled. Blessed be He who created them.

The flower Serra discovered was the small, five-petaled, pink wild rose known as *Rosa californica,* which was growing all along the Pacific coast from Baja to north of San Francisco Bay.

From atop a high hill on June 20, the scouts of the expedition saw the blue Pacific in the distance. Reaching its shores that evening, they called the spot Ensenada de Todos Santos (today, Ensenada); they were now less than eighty miles south of San Diego. The next morning, the party followed the coast along a level ridge to the northern corner of the bay, where they set up tents within a gunshot from the beach. "Here," wrote Serra later, "if the water could be properly utilized, great plantings could be made and enough water was at hand to supply a city." It would also make a good port, inviting the location of a mission on this "gentle coast with such a beautiful bay."

The following day was devoted to hunting and fishing. But Serra was able to report only failure. The fishermen arrived back in camp with no catch; the soldiers were such poor shots that they too were empty-handed.

For the final trek to San Diego, the cavalcade remained close to the sea. On June 23, the expedition came upon a large Indian ranchería where the travelers remained "with the greatest pleasure. The people were healthy and well built, affable, and of happy disposition. They were a quick, bright people, who immediately repeated all the Spanish words they heard. They danced for the party, offered fish and mussels, and pressed them to remain. "We were all enamored of them. In fact, all the pagans have pleased me, but these in particular have stolen my heart," Serra wrote.

The men were naked and carried their quivers over their shoulders; the women wore clothes. Their hair was cut and plastered tidily with white clay. On their heads, they wore a crown of beaver skin or fine fur.

On the following morning, the soldiers traded handkerchiefs for fish. The Indians were sharp businessmen, and Serra watched the proceedings with great interest. One small fish bought a small handkerchief; a bigger fish bought a larger piece of cloth.

Later that afternoon, the party left the ranchería, spending the night in the open along the beach. After a two-day march, they arrived at a spot that Serra named San Francisco Solano. Here there were a greater number of people living in one place than they had so far encountered.

> I cannot find words to describe their affability. Besides an uncounted number of men, a large number of women and children sat in a circle around me, and I pleased one mother who desired that I should hold her suckling child a little while in my arms. This I did with a great desire of baptizing it, until I returned it to its mother.

> I made the sign of the cross over all of them and blessed them, making them repeat after me: "Jesús, María." I give them what I can and I caress them as best as I may.

The coast of California was home to perhaps more Indians per square mile than any other area in the United States. More than a quarter of a million men, women, and children living in tribes of more than twenty-five linguistic groups enjoyed the easy climate and abundant food supply. The Indians Serra now encountered apparently cared more about receiving cloth than food. He noted that, although tall, they looked quite well-fed. Portolá commented that he would like to have a few of them to serve as grenadiers. Junípero laughed, adding that if he had given them all the cloth they wanted, he would have been surrounded by a large community of pagan Franciscan friars.

> What I should like to be able to do is to affix to their hearts the words, "Put you on the Lord Jesus Christ." May the most provident Lord and heavenly Father who clothes the little birds with feathers and the fields with grass, grant that my wish be accomplished in their regard.

The next day's travel proved difficult. Although the land was level, it was broken by innumerable gullies. In addition, many Indians were following the Spaniards. At the place the party stopped overnight, the number around them was so large that Serra did not even attempt to count them. They became uncomfortably more than affable. If Serra placed his hands on their heads, they placed theirs on his. If he sat down, they also sat down—very close. They were absolutely covetous of dry goods, some even begging Serra for his habit. Others asked Portolá for his leather jacket, waistcoat, breeches, and boots. Serra's spectacles were passed around among curious women, who were enthralled. But when the glasses were passed to one fellow, he dashed from the group with them. "God knows what it cost me to recover

The second Mission San Diego de Alcalá. The first of the missions founded by Serra, in 1769, it was moved from its original hillside site into the more fertile valley below. Here also, hostile natives attacked the mission, killing Padre Luís Jayme. The mission is named after Saint Didacus. Photograph by Carleton Watkins, ca. 1880

them," Serra wrote. The loss of his only pair of spectacles would have been tragic, with the nearest oculist at Guadalajara, nearly fifteen hundred miles away.

On the morning of June 28 the sound of horses' hoofs was heard approaching from the north. Sergeant Ortega, who had gone on ahead, and ten soldiers of the Rivera expedition came riding from San Diego. With them were fresh animals for the group and letters for Serra from Crespí and Parrón. Portolá and Serra learned that the ships had arrived, but that scurvy, the perennial scourge of seamen, had taken a dreadful toll among their crews.

Early the next morning, Portolá, his attendant, and eight soldiers set out to reach San Diego that evening. The rest of the party was to be led there by the newly arrived guards. But this last leg of the journey was extremely difficult due to the hundreds of gullies they still had to cross. Since the erosion that created them began in the hills and extended to the ocean, there was no alternative but to cross them. Serra later told Palóu that he crossed each one with a prayer on his lips, feeling he was in real danger. "But as all things in this world come to an end, they also did," he wrote philosophically.

On the morning of July 1, Serra could see the harbor of San Diego in the distance. Because of the various lagoons that cut into the coastline, detours required an additional half day. From the *San Carlos* and the *San Antonio* riding at anchor near the mouth of the bay, sailors arrived in a launch to greet the members of the expedition as they straggled in. The military camp was located on a hill farther north (in what today is Old Town), and there Portolá and Serra were reunited with Rivera's party. Junípero wrote:

> It was a day of great rejoicing and merriment for all, because although each one in his respective journey had undergone the same hardships, their meeting through their mutual alleviation from hardship now became the material for mutual accounts of their experiences. And although this sort of consolation appears to be the solace of the miserable, for us it was the source of happiness.

> Thus was our arrival in health and happiness and contentment at the famous and desired Port of San Diego. Thanks be to God.

Serra gave these last words two separate lines in large letters. He was jubilant. He had traveled nine hundred miles from Loreto, two thousand miles from San Fernando, and eight thousand miles from Majorca in order to reach Alta California. Now he stood looking out at the beautiful harbor, ready to raise aloft the cross of Christ.

III

SETTLING
THE AMERICAN
WEST COAST

As it is a whole year since I received any letter from a Christian country, Your Reverence may suppose in what want we are for news, but, for all that, I only ask when you can get an opportunity to inform me what the most Holy Father, the reigning Pope, is called, that I may put his name in the Canon of the Mass; also to say if the Canonization of the beatified Joseph Cupertino and Serafino Asculi has taken place; and if there is any other beatified one or saint, in order that I may put them in the Calendar and pray to them, we having, it would appear, taken our leave of all printed Calendars. Tell me, alas, if it is true that the Indians have killed Father Joseph Sala in Sonora, and how it happened, and if there are any other friends deceased, in order that I may commend them to God; with anything else that Your Reverence may think fit to communicate to a few poor hermits separated from human society.
Junipero Serra (from Monterey, 1770) to
Francisco Palou

CHAPTER TWELVE

WHERE CALIFORNIA BEGAN

From the first, Franciscan praise of the Harbor of the Sun was unstint-ed. Crespí called it a "pleasant port" and "fine harbor." For Serra, the bay was "truly beautiful" and "justly famous." Discovered by Cabrillo in 1542 and revisited and named San Diego by Vizcaíno in 1602, the harbor's renown had come through the descriptions of such early ex-plorers. When the padres arrived to occupy it, they were not disappoint-ed. Now, with orders from Gálvez to establish the first mission here, Serra and the others surveyed the area for a site.

Reconnoitering the grassy plains around Presidio Hill where the expedition was encamped, the padres noted that fresh water and ara-ble land were plentiful. Fields could be sown with grain, fruits, and vegetables. Willow, poplar, and sycamore trees dotted the river banks. Wild grapevines, asparagus, and acorns grew in abundance. Deer, an-telope, quail, and hares were abundant, as were the more ferocious wolves, bears, and coyotes. In addition to the abundance of food on land, the Indians, from rafts made of tules, fished for sole, tuna, and sardines and gathered mussels. "It is a good country," wrote Serra, "very much different from the land of Old California." There was no doubt it would make a good mission site.

Within a fifteen-mile radius of the camp, there were some twenty rancherías. All the Indian males walked about entirely naked. However, the women and girls, including the nursing babies, were clothed. They covered themselves with aprons made of leaves or reeds, gathered into a belt at one end and hanging loosely to the knees. Behind, they wore skins of deer or seals. Rabbit skins were used to cover their breasts and other parts of the body. Both men and women had their faces painted, and virtually all the men had their earlobes pierced. From their ears, and sometimes from their noses, hung seashells. For weapons, the Indians carried bows and arrows and war clubs.

They were friendly people and welcomed the Spaniards. However, their great interest in dry goods began to cause friction. Father Crespí noted that their avidity for stealing was unequaled. Costansó, the engineer, believed that only superior power and authority could restrain their tendency to rob. Ortega described them as intrepid, haughty, and very avaricious. But Junípero Serra, characteristically, looked ahead: "May God make a saint of him" and "May God give them and us His holy grace so that in a short time all will become Christians."

Although there had been great rejoicing when the four parties of the expedition reached San Diego, the immediate outlook for constructing a mission was bleak. By the time Serra arrived, twenty-one sailors from the *San Carlos* and the *San Antonio,* as well as a few soldiers, had perished from scurvy. During the Rivera expedition, food provisions had run out, forcing everyone to ration during the final days of the journey. Fathers Parrón and Crespí were weak. Serra was still in pain from his infected foot and leg. While the padres tried to minister to the souls, Doctor Prat did what he could with the bodies. Later, both Prat's charity and Junípero's kindness were officially reported to the king.

Meanwhile, Portolá and Captain Vila decided that the *San Antonio,* with the few sailors still in service, would return to San Blas for supplies and more seamen. Governor Portolá felt that he could continue the overland search for Monterey, leaving a skeleton guard with Serra in San Diego.

Before the ship's departure, Serra wrote letters to Palóu and the guardian at the College of San Fernando. In them, he made a few requests, one of which was personal. His two underhabits, or tunics, had to be replaced. Although one had been mended on the journey from Loreto, the other was quite ragged. He asked for a new one made of thick wool since, "It is very cold here"—surprising for San Diego in July.

Junípero then asked for prayers so that "the Divine Majesty may forgive me my many great sins and make me a worthy minister of His holy Gospel."

Above all, let those who are to come here as missionaries not imagine that they are coming for any other purpose but to endure hardships for the love of God and for the salvation of souls, for in far-off places such as these, where there is no way for the old missions to help the new ones because of the great distance between them, the presence of pagans, and the lack of communication by sea, it will be necessary in the beginning to suffer many real privations. However, *all things are sweet to a lover.* But these, my poor [Indians], have cost incomparably more to my Lord Jesus Christ.

Yet, even at this troubled beginning Serra possessed an optimistic vision of the future. To the guardian in Mexico City he wrote:

> We may not see it ourselves, but we can dispose matters so that some day our successors may see the holy Province of California, daughter of the College of San Fernando.

The *San Antonio,* with Crespí's and Serra's letters on board, sailed on July 9 and reached San Blas twenty-one days later. En route nine more sailors died.

On July 15, after a High Mass in honor of Saint Joseph was offered, the Portolá expedition began its overland search for Monterey. It was made up of seventy-four men: Fathers Crespí and Gómez as chaplains (Crespí the official diarist for the college), Ortega as scout, Costansó as engineer, Captain Rivera, Lieutenant Fages, soldiers, and Christian Indians from Baja California. Fathers Serra, Parrón, and Vizcaíno, along with Doctor Prat, soldiers, and Baja Indians—forty in all—remained behind at Presidio Hill. Which group, the Portolá expedition or the small colony left behind in San Diego, was in greater danger is debatable. One thing was clear, however: the lifeline of the Spanish Empire along the California coast was only a slender thread.

With the depature of the Portolá expedition, Serra turned all his energy to constructing the mission. Having selected Presidio Hill as the location, he and the others began erecting several simple shelters. One, a little larger than the dwellings, would serve as a temporary church. On the morning of July 16, 1769, Fray Junípero Serra founded Mission San Diego de Alcalá in honor of Saint Didacus. This Franciscan saint, a native of Spain who died at Alcalá on November 12, 1463, was born of lowly parents near Seville and was revered for the miracles he performed.

Two soldiers raised the cross as Serra blessed it. He then sang the High Mass and preached a sermon. It was the feast of Our Lady of Mount Carmel, a memorable day in Spanish history. On that date in 1212 Spanish troops had been victorious over the Moors at Las Navas de Tolosa. Later that afternoon, Serra inscribed the initial pages of the baptismal, marriage, and burial registers of the mission. He and Father Parrón became California's first missionaries. At Jalpan in June 1750, Serra had started almost from scratch. At Loreto in April 1768, he was continuing the work begun by the Jesuits. But now in San Diego, he would have to start from the very beginning in all matters—spiritual, economic, social, and linguistic.

Serra described his first months as unrewarding. When the local people visited the mission, he gave them trinkets and gifts in order to win their good will. Some of them, however, began to steal. They often teased or molested the sick soldiers. Unafraid, they mimicked the gunshots fired to warn them off. Problems grew daily. Although they refused Spanish food, they were still avidly interested in cloth. One night they were caught cutting the ropes and sails of the *San Carlos*. In order not to antagonize them, the soldiers remained patient and restrained. But the greatest barrier was lack of communication. The Indians, of course, did not know Spanish, and the soldiers and missionaries did not understand their language. The Baja Indians accompanying the party spoke an entirely different tongue, so were of no use as interpreters.

Within a month, the Indians had tired of the Spaniards' presence and decided upon a show of force. On August 15, the Feast of the Assumption, Father Parrón and two soldiers went out to *San Carlos* for mass. Meanwhile, Serra and Vizcaíno offered their masses in the mission chapel back on Presidio Hill, where several Spaniards went to confession and received Communion. Shortly after mass, four soldiers headed for the *San Carlos* in order to accompany Father Parrón on his return. Noticing that the mission had been left with little protection, a large group of Indians quickly assembled and attacked. As soon as the four soldiers left inside the mission heard the commotion, they ran for their muskets and pistols. The mission carpenter and blacksmith joined them. Chacón, the blacksmith, had just received Holy Communion. Unprotected by a leather jacket, he raced about the mission, crying, "Long live the faith of Jesus Christ and may these dogs, enemies of that faith, die!"

Meanwhile, Serra and Vizcaíno remained within one of the huts, praying to God that no casualties occur on either side. If any unbaptized Indians were to die, it might end all Serra's hopes. Although he was personally ready for martyrdom, he preferred to survive to preach the gospel. Now, on his knees, Junípero asked God to intervene. In one hand, he held a small statue of the Blessed Virgin. In the other, Serra later wrote, "her Divine Crucified Son, when the arrows were raining in upon us. . . . With such defensive armor I was in good hands. Either I would be spared from death or . . . I would die well."

José María Vergerano, Serra's servant, who had accompanied him faithfully from Baja California, came running into the hut, his neck pierced by an arrow. "Father, absolve me, for the Indians have killed me." Junípero was the only one present at his death.

He entered into my little hut with so much blood streaming from his temples and mouth that shortly after I gave him absolution . . . he passed away at my feet, bathed in his blood. And it was just a short time after he died before me that the little hut where I lived became a sea of blood. All during this time, the exchange of shots from the firearms and arrows continued. Only four men of our group fired while more than twenty of theirs shot

94

arrows. I continued to stay with the departed one, thinking over the imminent probability of following him myself, yet, I kept begging God to give victory to our Holy Catholic faith without the loss of a single soul.

On the Spanish side Father Vizcaíno, Chacón the blacksmith, and a Christian Indian were all wounded. Doctor Prat was soon on the scene, comforting them and extracting wooden splinters from their wounds. As the Indians carried away their dead, they realized for the first time the deadly power of Spanish arms. That evening, the warriors cremated their dead, and the wailing of women was heard from all the surrounding villages. But Serra was under the impression that none of the Indians died, suggesting that those who knew the truth kept it from him, realizing how painful the news would be.

The battle for San Diego, the first in the Spanish settlement of California, turned the tide in the Spanish-Indian relationship. Thereafter, the Indians became more peaceful. They began revisiting the camp, bringing along their wounded, no doubt hoping Spanish remedies would prove as powerful as Spanish arms. Prat, as usual, provided them with his kind, skillful attention. Any work at conversion, however, was halted while a stockade of poles was erected around the mission.

A week or so later, probably due to the promptings of a young Indian boy who had learned some Spanish and had been influenced by Serra, a crowd of Indians carrying a baby boy approached the mission. By hand signs, the child's parents indicated they wanted to have the infant baptized. Junípero was overjoyed. He covered the naked child with a bit of clothing and asked the corporal of the guard to serve as godfather. The other soldiers were also present in the crude chapel. For some fifteen minutes, Serra, clad in surplice and stole, read the initial prayers and performed the ceremonies before the actual baptism. None of the ritual, such as the anointing of the head and chest with oil and the application of spittle to the ears and nostrils, seemed to concern the Indians. But just as Serra lifted the baptismal shell filled with holy water in order to pour it over the infant's head, one Indian standing near by grabbed the child from the corporal's arms and fled with it in terror. Others followed, laughing and jeering. Serra stood there, confounded and frustrated in his first attempt at baptism in California.

Serra never forgot the incident, or the sense of frustration it engendered. Palóu says that even years later when Junípero described the event he had to dry the tears from his eyes, attributing the failure to his own sins.

As the months dragged on, Serra and his companions, completely isolated from the outside world, filled their lonely vigil on the hilltop with prayer.

Finally, on January 24, 1770, the seventy-four tired, hungry men of the Portolá expedition were spotted crossing the mouth of a canyon. Shots were exchanged in a festive atmosphere of jubilant triumph. As they entered camp, it was evident that every member of the expedition had survived. Amid comradely embraces, shouting, and pounding of backs, Serra and Juan Crespí knelt together in thankful prayer. However, it would be a long while before the men of the expedition would erase "the frightful smell of mules" that lingered about them. Along their hard road from Monterey, they had had to slaughter and eat most of their animals. During the six months of marching over nine hundred miles through territory hitherto "untrodden by Christian feet," the explorers had encountered innumerable Indians living along the coast. These people had been friendly and peaceful, and eager to have the Spaniards remain with them. Portolá, Costansó, and Crespí each returned to San Diego with detailed diaries of the discoveries made. Recorded were the places stayed, Indians met, possible mission sites, earthquakes experienced, and oil, animals, and wildflowers found. They had camped on the site of modern Los Angeles and predicted that a large city would one day rise there. They had discovered San Francisco Bay. But of all things, they failed to recognize Monterey and its bay. "How could you have missed it?" Serra asked Portolá, a situation as incongruous in Serra's mind as visiting Rome and missing the Pope. After all, Monterey was right where the early seafaring explorers had said it was.

Now it was time to dispatch letters to San Fernando with the important news. Writing to the guardian, Serra described his vision of fifty missions stretching along the California coast, concluding his letter by asking permission "to go about through these lands relying upon the Providence of the Most High if, through accident, human provisions fail."

With Portolá and his men returned to Presidio Hill from their expedition, there were more mouths to feed. But food supplies were meager. Unknown to everyone, the supply ship *San José* expected from Baja had been lost at sea. Now, as days stretched into weeks, Portolá decided that his troops had not come this far only to die of starvation, and therefore, San Diego might have to be abandoned. With reluctance, he explained to Serra that if a ship did not arrive by March 19, the feast of Saint Joseph, patron of the expedition, he and his men would march south to Baja. The idea of abandoning the toehold in Alta California was a severe blow to Junípero. His whole nature rebelled at the idea of turning back; after all, he had staked his life and health on the venture. His natural tenacity and his belief in divine Providence urged him to find a way to remain in San Diego.

Discussing with Crespí his determination to remain behind, no matter what, Serra found him of the same mind. Writing to Palóu, Junípero explained:

> Fathers Fray Juan Crespí, Fray Fernando Parrón, Fray Francisco Gómez, and I will remain to wait and see if the ships arrive and if as a result, we shall be able to establish a second mission. If we see that the foodstuffs are running low and hope is waning, I shall remain here with Father Fray Juan alone to hold out to the very last.

The two padres could not be left alone at the vacated mission on Presidio Hill; Serra therefore asked permission of Captain Vila of the *San Carlos,* still anchored in the harbor, for Crespí and himself to take refuge on the ship when Portolá headed south. If no ship arrived within three or four months, the two missionaries would return to La Paz by sea with Vila and his crew.

As March 19 approached, Serra, Portolá, and the members of the expedition joined in a novena of prayers to Saint Joseph. The following nine days were perhaps the most anxious of Junípero Serra's life. On the morning of the nineteenth, he celebrated High Mass and preached a sermon. After breakfast, the soldiers began packing for their departure the next morning.

Around three in the afternoon, a lookout spied a white sail on the horizon. The packet boat *San Antonio* had at last come into view. Immediately, the atmosphere in camp was transformed. Soldiers and missionaries followed the limping padre into the temporary chapel, where now their voices broke forth in thanks to God for the providential arrival of the supply ship.

For Junipero, the event was so significant that as long as he lived he celebrated a High Mass (at Carmel Mission) on the nineteenth of every month of the year.

CHAPTER THIRTEEN

ON TO MONTEREY!

Now that the provisions in San Diego had been resupplied, Portolá and Serra could look forward to further exploration in California. According to the orders of Gálvez, their primary task was still to locate Monterey.

Preparations got under way immediately. With new food stocks and materials, Portolá was able to plan and equip a second overland expedition, which was to rendezvous with the *San Antonio* at Monterey. On board ship, food and water were stored for the sea journey. After placing his personal effects in his cabin, Serra spent the afternoon in the mission chapel writing to Gálvez, Palóu, and the college. Later that evening, Captain Juan Pérez sent word that he should embark, since the ship would be sailing early in the morning. Placing the development of Mission San Diego de Alcalá in the hands of Fathers Parrón and Gómez, Serra climbed into a small craft and was rowed out to the *San Antonio*.

Crespí was to be chaplain of Portolá's second overland expedition to locate Monterey. There, Crespí and Serra would be reunited, and after helping to establish Mission San Carlos de Borromeo in Monterey, Crespí would march south to found Mission San Buenaventura somewhere along the Santa Barbara Channel. That would mean the two Franciscans would be separated by over two hundred miles, contrary to Serra's wishes but necessary if the mission system was to win over the Indians of the new land.

For both friars, it meant extreme loneliness. "Truly," Serra wrote Palóu, "this state of solitude shall be for me the greatest of my hardships."

Sailing out of San Diego harbor on the morning of Easter Sunday, the *San Antonio* was beyond the mouth of the bay when strong winds forced it back. For Serra, this "act of God" meant that everyone, sailors and soldiers alike, could attend mass at the mission on this greatest feast day of the Christian calendar. By seven the next morning, Serra was seated on the floor of his cabin, finishing his letter to Palóu: "Farewell, my most beloved friend. May His Divine Majesty unite us in heaven." After the letter was sent ashore, the small ship again set sail, with Captain Pérez, Doctor Prat, and the engineer Costansó joining Serra at the railing. Thus, on Serra's anniversary for renewing his vows as a Franciscan, a Majorcan missionary and a Majorcan sea captain were off in search of a second port for the settlement of California.

The next morning, April 17, the land expedition began its march northward. It was less than half the number of Portolá's first expedition; the group included Lieutenant Pedro Fages, twelve Catalonian volunteers, seven leatherjackets, two muleteers, five Baja Indians, a servant for Governor Portolá, and Fray Juan Crespí. Sergeant Ortega was left in charge at Mission San Diego, with eight soldiers, twelve Baja Indians, and the two missionaries.

Retracing the route they had taken the year before, the members of the expedition arrived in Monterey on Ascension Day, May 24, 1770. The journey had been made without the loss of a single man, or even a serious illness.

Although the *San Antonio* was not yet in sight, the explorers this time recognized Monterey Bay. Portolá, Crespí, and a guard walked over the hills to Point Pinos, where they had planted a cross ten months before. To their surprise, they found it surrounded by feathers and broken arrows stuck in the ground, signifying friendliness. Also placed before the cross were fresh meat and sardines, some only a few hours old. No Indians were in sight. In the nearby waters of the blue bay, hundreds of seals and otters were splashing and basking in the sun. With enthusiasm, Crespí wrote "This point forms a good roadstead of a beautiful beach of pure sand. . . . This is the port of Monterey without the slightest doubt."

The three-man scouting party then walked along the rocky coast south to Carmel Bay, where they encountered further overtures of Indian friendship. Soon, a small group of people approached them on the sand dunes, and gifts were exchanged. The Indians promised to return in a few days with seeds and venison. Portolá then established a camp on a small hill near Carmel Bay and sent for the rest of the party.

Seven days after the expedition's arrival, a lookout on a Monterey hilltop saw a sail and lit three large bonfires. Spotting the prearranged signal that Portolá had already arrived, Captain Pérez on board the *San Antonio* responded with cannon fire as the packet ship continued sailing the last few miles into Monterey Bay.

The next morning, Crespí, Portolá, and the men walked back over the hills from Carmel to Monterey Bay, where a rowboat took them out

The founding of Carmel Mission June 3, 1770. Serra's first mass in Monterey, the site of the original mission, is commemorated in this 1876 painting by Troisset. It was at this ceremony the Alta California territory was formally claimed for the Spanish crown. Serra is depicted beneath the historic Vizcaíno-Serra oak, the trunk of which is still preserved at the Cathedral Chapel of San Carlos, Monterey.

to the ship for a joyous reunion. The *San Antonio*'s passage had been slow and difficult. Captain Pérez battled winds that blew the small ship hundreds of miles in either direction, and as far south as the border of Baja, and as far north as the Farallone Islands west of San Francisco Bay. Several of the sailors were sick with scurvy. Serra described the voyage as simply "uncomfortable." Now on June 1, Serra, Portolá, Crespí, and the others discussed the founding of Mission San Carlos de Borromeo. All were in agreement that June 3, Pentecost Sunday, would be the appropriate day.

This second Franciscan mission in California was named by both the king of Spain, Carlos III, and the incumbent viceroy, Carlos de Croix in honor of Saint Charles Borromeo (1538–1584) who was born in Arona, Italy. His mother was a Medici, his uncle Pope Pius IV; Charles received the clerical tonsure at twelve. By the age of twenty-two, he was a cardinal and Archbishop of Milan. He took a leading role at the Council of Trent, and rigorously enforced the reform decrees of that Council throughout his influential diocese.

On Sunday morning, Portolá and his men greeted the ship's crew under a large oak tree near a ravine emptying into Monterey Bay. The oak was believed to be the very same one under which the Carmelites of the Vizcaíno sea expedition had offered the first mass in Alta Califor-

nia back in 1602. Serra's description of the auspicious occasion continues to breathe freshness:

> The day arrived. A chapel and altar were constructed next to the same
> ravine and oak tree, adjoining the beach, where it is said that Mass was
> celebrated in the beginning of the past century. The men of the land and
> sea expeditions coming from different directions met here at the same
> time, we singing the divine praises in our launch, while the gentlemen on
> land sang in their hearts.
>
> We arrived and were received by the clangor of the bells suspended from
> the oak. Everything in readiness, I vested in alb and stole, and when all
> were kneeling before the altar I intoned the "Veni Creator Spiritus." After
> the assistance of the Holy Spirit had been invoked in this manner to aid us
> in our plans, I blessed salt and water. Then all of us went over to a large
> cross prepared beforehand, which was stretched out on the ground. We all
> assisted in raising it and I blessed it, chanting the prayers of benediction.
> Then we planted it in the ground and all of us venerated it with all the
> tenderness of our hearts. With holy water I blessed those fields. Thus with
> the standard of the King of Heaven raised, the standards of our Catholic
> monarch were also set up, the one ceremony being accompanied by shouts
> of "Long live the Faith!" and the other by "Long live the King!" Added to
> this was the clangor of the bells, the volleys of the muskets, and the can-
> nonading from the bark.
>
> After this I began the High Mass to which I added the sermon on the
> Gospel of the day. All the while there was cannonading. When Mass was
> over, and after I had taken off my chasuble, we sang together the "Salve
> Regina" in Spanish before a very beautiful statute of Our Lady which stood
> on the altar. His illustrious Lordship, the Visitor General, had loaned it to
> me for this occasion, obligating us to return it later. . . .
>
> At the end, standing, I intoned the "Te Deum Laudamus" which we
> chanted to the very end with solemnity, observing the pauses, we added
> thereto in thanksgiving the versicles and orations in honor of the Most
> Holy Trinity, Our Lady, Most Holy Saint Joseph, patron of the expedition,
> and Saint Charles, who is the patron of this port, presidio, and mission.
> Thanks be to God for everything. While I was making my thanksgiving
> (having taken off the sacred vestments) after the Mass of that day, the
> officers conducted the ceremony of taking possession of that land in the
> name of His Catholic Majesty, setting up again and waving the royal stan-
> dard, pulling up grass, removing stones, and conducting the ceremonies
> prescribed by law, accompanied by the shouts of "Viva!" the clangor of
> bells, and musket shots. After this we all ate together along the beach and
> walked along it during the afternoon. Then the members of the land expe-
> dition returned to their Carmel and we to the bark. With this, the day's
> function came to an end.

On the following morning, the site for the presidio and mission was selected, a relatively flat area near the beach, some distance inland from the ravine and oak tree. Serra described the spot as "a pleasing stretch of land." After the soldiers moved their camp from the mouth of Carmel River to the new site, they aided the sailors in unloading food supplies, equipment, and material from the *San Antonio*. Two structures were quickly erected, one for the presidio and the other for the mission. Serra and Crespí would live on board the ship until more suitable dwellings and a chapel were ready for them.

From the very beginning, Serra believed that the permanent site of Mission San Carlos should not be in Monterey. The first ingredient for a mission was lacking: the presence of a large Indian village. In fact, no one lived along the shores nearby. Although plentiful in timber, the surroundings offered little drinking water. Serra noted:

> There is no ranchería in the vicinity of this port . . . if the Indians are determined to embrace our Holy Faith, we foresee a special difficulty in having them settle here. It might be necessary to leave the presidio and together with a guard change the site of the mission toward the area of Carmel, a locality indeed most delightful and suitable because of the extent and excellent quality of the land and the water supply necessary to produce very abundant harvests.

On June 14, the feast of Corpus Christi was celebrated. Feeling exuberant, Serra wanted a festive celebration full of religious splendor, a relief from the makeshift life they had all been living. But the preparations for the occasion brought out certain difficulties, which Serra recorded in a letter to Gálvez. The festival was particularly important in Mexico and called for special decorations, especially an abundance of lights and candles. The few wax candles they had could not withstand the strong Monterey breezes. Serra thought of using the single lantern that lit the *San Antonio's* cabin. But the day before the feast, while the crew was searching for medicine in the ship's hold, they discovered two boxes filled with lanterns. No one seemed to know whence they came, or for whom they were intended.

For the celebration, the sailors constructed a temporary chapel in one of the newly built storehouses. To Junípero, it was so beautiful that if brought tears to his eyes. Banners of the various saints were set up, and the patio through which the procession was to pass was strewn with green branches. Six of the new lanterns were placed on the altar inbetween the silver missal stand and the six candlesticks that had been brought from Loreto. (Today, these silver altar pieces can be seen on display in the Carmel Mission Museum.) Captain Pérez supplied tallow candles for the lanterns and candelholders. "All burned throughout the Mass, sermon, and procession without a single breath of wind affecting them," wrote the jubilant Serra. The procession of the Blessed Sacrament was accompanied by the constant clanging of bells, cannonading from the ship, and hymns and canticles of praise from the padres and soldiers.

Three weeks later, another celebration took place at the request of Captain Pérez, in fulfillment of a promise he had made during the troubled voyage from San Diego. While the ship was fighting heavy winds, Pérez, Serra, and the crew had daily recited prayers, promising upon safe arrival in Monterey to make a novena and celebrate a High Mass. During the evening before the festivities, sailors on board the *San Antonio* found two more unmarked chests. Upon opening them in Serra's presence, they discovered among the contents three oil paintings of saints:

> The joy I experienced was inexpressible. Together we went on land with my saints and we were to remain there. They were placed on the altar, the Most Blessed Virgin being already there, and not displeasing to her, she was surrounded by cardinals (Saints Bonaventure and Charles Borromeo) and a lay-brother sacristan (Saint Didacus). The altar was a thing to marvel.

On July 3, Serra celebrated a farewell mass in honor of Our Lady of Bethlehem, since her statue was being returned to José Gálvez in Mexico City on the *San Antonio*. The devotion to Our Lady of Bethlehem was important; she was the patron saint of all Spanish mariners. The statue lent to Serra by Gálvez, the inspector general, had been received as a gift from Archbishop Lorenzana. In a letter to Gálvez, Serra described the statue's position as the central piece of the altar, where she reigned, while he, "a poor, limping friar, bore her eucharistic son across the untilled fields of Monterey." The captain promised Junípero that he would leave the statue at San Blas with all due religious solemnity and see to it that a High Mass was sung for its safe return. Serra praised this religious sentiment and, with perhaps a twinkle in his eye, made Pérez and his crew promise that the religious ceremonies would not be followed by a fandango.

Since it might be another year before he could send any personal messages to San Fernando, Serra wrote at length. He felt keenly the lack of any news from headquarters in more than a year. To his superior, Andrés, he acknowledged total submission:

> I assure Your Reverence that at your slightest insinuation, I shall go further on, gladly and readily, or come closer home, or stay here, as long as my life lasts.

For the second time he reminded Andrés of the kind of men he envisioned as missionaries for California:

> subjects who do not turn their backs on hardships, and who do not become restless and anxious to return to the college almost as soon as they arrive

here. Those who come here dedicated to so holy a work must undergo hardships, as everyone knows. I must not lament over the hardships I have undergone and suffer at the present moment. They are not easy to describe. In these distant parts, one must expect to undergo some hardships, but these will be even more burdensome to those who are seeking every convenience and comfort. However, I shall not believe that any of those who may come here will be of that disposition.

Serra wanted padres who were every inch apostolic and able, ready, and willing to make sacrifices, even if they were intensely personal:

If someday I shall have to face any personal hardship, it will be this one, namely the great hardship for a sinner like me to remain in such a solitude, realizing that the nearest priest will be more than eighty leagues away and between us there will be land inhabited only by pagans with the roads pretty rough.

Serra looked forward to the day when more missionaries would come and all would enjoy the "worthwhile benefits of mutual encouragement, security, and solidarity."

The *San Antonio* sailed from Monterey on July 9, 1770. Aboard were Portolá and Costansó, both of whom deserved a leisurely sea voyage, several letters from Serra, and the statue, Our Lady of Bethlehem.

Spain's latest settlement was now left in charge of forty men, including the friars and Baja Indians. Nearly five hundred miles south in San Diego, there were only twenty-three. It would be a year before either group would see each other or receive supplies.

Upon receiving the news that a mission and presidio had been established in Monterey, Gálvez ordered all the bells in Mexico City rung. The massed clanging sounded like Rome after a canonization. Those at the College of San Fernando were especially proud that two of their own brothers, Serra and Crespí, had planted the cross over two thousand miles away.

Viceroy de Croix paid tribute to Gálvez, "the principal agent in the spiritual conquest," but did not overlook Serra's role.

The Reverend Father President of those missions, who is destined to serve at Monterey, states in a very detailed way and with particular joy that the Indians are affable. They have already promised him to bring their children to be instructed in the mysteries of our holy Catholic religion. That exemplary and zealous missionary also gave us a detailed account of the solemn Masses which have been celebrated from the arrival of both expeditions until the departure of the packet boat, *San Antonio.*

Reinspired by the news, Gálvez lost no time in planning further expansion and development in California. In early June, shortly after Fray Rafael Verger arrived in Mexico City from Spain with forty-four missionaries, de Croix asked the guardian to assign all the newly arrived friars to Serra in California. The ambitious viceroy projected ten new missions between Velicatá and the Golden Gate. Andrés, the guardian at the college, protested, arguing that the request was unreasonable. After all, the missionaries had just completed a 99-day sea voyage, the same length as Serra's in 1749, followed by a 33-day stay in the tropical climate of Ocón, where many had become ill. Moreover, college regulations required a year's residence at San Fernando in order for the friars to renew their apostolic zeal and learn how to be missionaries. After listening to such arguments. Gálvez backed down. But, later, after further discussion and prompting, Andrés consented to dispatch thirty missionaries, twenty to Baja and ten to San Diego and Monterey.

Meanwhile, election time was approaching at San Fernando, and in late November 1770, Andrés was replaced as guardian by Fray Rafael Verger. An entirely new governing board was elected as well. For the first time in the history of the college, its far-flung mission fields were ruled by three Majorcan ex-professors: Verger in command, with Serra and Palóu in charge of the two Californias.

Upon the shoulders of Rafael Verger fell the full impact of supervising the establishment and maintenance of the missions from San Blas to Monterey. And although he deeply appreciated his two excellent commanders in the mission areas, Serra's zeal often became a problem for him. Junípero was endowed with the vision to discern opportunities when they presented themselves, the optimism to risk all, and the courage to fight things through until the good was attained. But at times such a man might be too pressing in his demands, especially when he was unaware of the other exigencies that confronted the college. Verger felt that he would have to restrain Serra on occasion.

Verger was an administrator, much more practical and realistic than idealistic and visionary. As guardian, he soon gained the reputation of weighing matters with diligence and precision, careful to count all costs, and making his decisions prudently. But when Serra's zeal was stymied by government bureaucrats or military commanders, Verger would back his chief padre without hesitation. He was a friar of true feeling who shared the indignation of the missionaries at military abuses. He was horrified, for example, when he learned that of the fifty-one Baja California Indians who had accompanied the Portolá expedition from Loreto, only thirteen had survived to reach San Diego. Five had perished along the road; the rest had deserted because they were starving. Although they served as the expedition's laborers, the Indians had to shift for themselves when it came to food, receiving from the Spaniards a little atole, which "in truth was more water than gruel." Crespí, who himself suffered hunger and arrived in San Diego half-starved, blamed their treatment on Rivera, since the captain had brought along only half the provisions available back in Velicatá. Because of these tragic deaths, Verger recommended to Viceroy de Croix a number of changes in the rules affecting the use of Indians as porters and servants.

All aspects of the Spanish settlements in the Americas were strictly regulated by a tight interlocking directorate of Church and State: from the king through the Council of the Indies and the Board of Trade in Madrid to the viceroy and the military governor, down to the local presidio comandante, and from the Franciscan commissary general of the Indies in Madrid through the commissary general in Mexico and the guardian and his council in the College of San Fernando, down to the padre presidente and his missionaries in the field.

Little deviation from set rules was allowed; the apostolic college and viceregal palace worked hand in hand, sometimes in harmony, sometimes at variance. On the frontier, any conflict was exaggerated by the difficulty in communicating over the long distances involved. If clarification or interpretation of law was needed, it could take a year to ask the question and get an answer. In the meantime, new issues would have arisen. Thus, a difference in viewpoint between the padre presidente and the military commander could assume critical proportions.

CHAPTER FOURTEEN

HOMESTEADING

On July 9, 1770, the *San Antonio* sailed from Monterey for San Blas. Pedro Fages was left in charge as comandante by Portolá, and he and Serra settled down to developing their respective fields of activity and working out solutions to their mutual problems. While construction continued from the blueprints left by Costansó, the engineer, Serra and Crespí lived at the presidio with Fages and his troops.

Gradually, Indians from Carmel Valley began to visit the presidio, where they were kindly received. One of the Indians from Baja California was particularly successful in establishing friendly relations. Some of the people began to learn Spanish, and Serra and Crespí worked daily to learn their language. But it was not until December 26, 1770, that Serra for the first time poured the waters of baptism in California. The parents of a five-year-old boy consented to have their son baptized by Serra, who gave the lad the name Bernardino de Jesús, echoing a name familiar from his own boyhood days in distant Petra. Junípero invited the comandante to serve as godfather. By the following May, twenty more Indians had been born again of water and the Spirit. (Crespí and Gómez had already performed the first two baptisms in Alta California in July of 1769, when they baptized two dying infant girls along the trail during the first Portolá expedition to Monterey.)

Since the guard at Monterey was too small to be split up, the permanent mission at Carmel had not been founded, and the padres were obliged to remain at the presidio. Futhermore, permission had not been received from Mexico City to transfer the mission site to the Carmel River. Meanwhile, Indians, soldiers, and padres did some planting, though little was produced.

During the evening hours, Crespí kept busy rewriting the diary of his march from Velicatá to Monterey. Comparing it to Serra's diary as far as San Diego, he included sections of Junípero's journey in his own, identifying where both had been on different days. As a true diarist, Crespí omitted no details, but Serra considered his writing too wordy, repetitious, and full of superfluous detail. On several occasions, he suggested that Juan strive for greater condensation. Of course, this annoyed Crespí, Serra's one-time student. He responded with the pained annoyance of an author who believes he knows best what he saw and experienced. "Am I not supposed to describe things the way they were and how they happened?" Serra yielded, noting, "I let him follow his own bent." This was fortunate for history, since Crespí did not miss a single sycamore or willow along the entire route. So exact and detailed is his diary that even today one can retrace the old trails, as did Herbert Bolton, the historian who edited and prepared for publication the diaries of several California missionaries.

On January 20, 1771, the *San Antonio*, under Captain Pérez, sailed from San Blas with ten missionaries from the college destined for California. Arriving in San Diego three weeks later, Fray Antonio Paterna, their leader, found a mission in name only and was disappointed at its lack of growth. After supplies were unloaded, the ship sailed on to Monterey, arriving there on May 21 to great rejoicing. On May 30, the feast of Corpus Christi was celebrated in a ceremony even more splendid than in the preceding year. Twelve priests wearing resplendent vestments marched in the procession, and Indian boys, the first converts of the new mission, served as acolytes.

The ship brought mail for Serra and Fages. For Junípero, it was the first time in two years that he had received letters from the "land of the Christians." So keenly did Serra feel the lengthy silence that he referred to it as his "second novitiate." There was a letter from Fray Andrés, who by now was no longer his superior, and two letters from Viceroy de Croix. From the new missionaries, Serra learned that Verger was now at the helm of San Fernando.

The viceroy's letter to Fages explained that the ten missionaries were being sent so that the founding of the new missions on the California coast would not be delayed. He ordered that Mission San Carlos be moved to the banks of Carmel River and that Fages supply the missionaries with their proper portion of clothing, field implements, carpenter's tools, medicines, mules, and cattle. Five missions were to be established on suitable sites between Monterey and San Diego. Furthermore, the San Francisco peninsula was to be explored and a mission founded there. Fages was to cooperate with the father president (Serra), "and I herewith charge you very particularly to proceed to establish said missions without the least delay as an object demanding your first attention."

By June, Serra had drawn up a list of missionary assignments for the five new missions. Insofar as possible, he assigned the missionaries in pairs according to the regions of Spain from which they had come, believing there would be greater harmony between them if they had the same provincial and regional outlook. Crespí, originally destined for San Buenaventura on the Santa Barbara Channel, would remain as Serra's assistant in Carmel.

Fages, Pérez, and Serra held a series of meetings about the immediate exploration of the San Francisco Bay Area. They agreed the time was not yet opportune, since there were not enough soldiers for the purpose. If a mission for Saint Francis were established, there would be no guard to protect it. Serra offered to go along on the reconnaissance, suggesting an exploration by sea instead of by land: "I certainly wish to see the mission of my most beloved Seraphic Father established as soon as possible and insofar as I am concerned, it shall not be delayed one moment, with the help of God."

The *San Antonio* left Monterey for San Diego and La Paz on July 7, 1771. On it sailed five missionaries for San Diego and the two missions planned for the south, San Gabriel and San Buenaventura. Letters that Serra wrote during the period to the viceroy and the guardian, and sent via the packet ship, are revealing of his fondest wishes. To Verger, he envisioned the day when a ladder of missions would be established between Velicatá and Monterey, relieving missionaries and visitors alike of the burden of ocean travel:

> Then they can travel by land and rest at night, every third night at a mission belonging to the college and it would be quite tolerable a journey even to San Francisco. There would remain only the short sea voyage from San Blas to Loreto.

Serra then asked that more friars be recruited from Spain and Majorca to fill California's need. "I do not say that everything must be done in one day, but I do think that the ship should sail when the wind is favorable." Delay was not in Serra's vocabulary; his zeal was insatiable.

To consolidate the mission chain and strengthen the bond between California's new missions and the College of San Fernando, Serra suggested two forward-looking measures. The first was the founding of a hospice at either Tepic or Guadalajara for the missionaries assigned to California. There, two or three friars from the college would reside permanently in order to supervise the arrival of food supplies. They could purchase additional supplies from the Guadalajara farmers, which would save transportations costs. The second proposal was that a residence, or convent, be established somewhere in California, where the king, or some generous benefactor, could maintain six or more missionaries, constituting a standing body of replacements for those who became ill or wished to return to Mexico or Spain. Unfortunately, Serra's proposals were filed in the college archives. Had they been acted upon, the missions would have been saved many hardships.

Junípero also wrote to Palóu. With an intimacy reserved for his closest friend, Serra described how troublesome comandante Fages had become, referring to him as "a ridiculous little fellow." Although Serra and his missionaries were guests at the presidio, Fages proved to be a crochety host. For example, he demanded that the door of the friary face the interior of the presidio, not outside. Furthermore, he insisted on retaining the key of their enclosure "so as to lock us in and out when he pleased." Fages criticized the church and the cemetery and its cross, as well as the burial of an Indian a little off the precise mathematical lines prescribed. The padres were not to discipline the Indians without Fages' authorization; if the friars ordered the soldiers to punish the Indians, they were not to comply. Fages allowed four soldiers and a muleteer to work for Serra on condition that he supply them with rations. Serra readily agreed. Yet when the soldiers were later told to return to the presidio, they continued asking for their rations from the mission. Serra refused, on the principle of no work, no pay. When the situation was called to the comandante's attention, Fages said that it was only temporary; later he would return all his men to work for the mission. Serra reports that months went by with him seeing no sign of the laborers. After a year, Fages agreed to give Serra two men each day, but they were required to report to him what Serra ordered them to do. Without informing Junípero, Palóu forwarded the complaints to Verger at the college who in turn passed them on to the viceroy.

Also in his letter to Palóu, Serra touched upon a matter that shows his sensitivity and his scrupulous adherence to the truth. Serra, Gómez, Parrón, and Crespí were somewhat habituated to the use of snuff, which at the time was something of a custom among friars. The four missionaries had opened a case in San Diego, consigned to Crespí, which they unanimously agreed was "pure dirt" *("pura tierra")* and unusable. When their original consignment was depleted, they decided to try this "low grade" supply, sent by a Mexico City merchant named Trillo. After removing the top layers, they found to their surprise that the snuff was more compressed and of higher quality. The boxes were weighed and found to be correct, and "in time we found the snuff to be so good that when new containers arrived of definitely good quality, we did not begin to use them as long as the old lasted, and I can say that I will be glad if the new is as good as the old." Serra explained that in mentioning such a small matter, he wanted to correct a false impression he may have given Palóu in a previous letter. If his remarks "caused the merchant any harm, see to it that the harm is undone and the error rectified . . . to ease my conscience and out of love for the truth."

On the day after the *San Antonio's* departure, Serra, and two other Franciscans accompanied by seven soldiers, three sailors, and a few Baja Indians, left Monterey with a pack train for the Sierra de Santa Lucía. Five days later, they arrived at the head of the beautiful Valley of the Oaks. Serra chose a temporary site for Mission San Antonio de Padua near a small river that had sufficient running water even in July.

Bells were hung from a large oak and an improvised altar erected. In this sun-drenched valley on July 14, 1771, the feast of Saint Bonaventure, Serra gave spontaneous vent to the zeal that seized his apostolic soul. Ringing the bells wildly, he began singing out in his clarion voice, "Come, you pagans; come, come to the Holy Church; come, come to receive the Faith of Jesus Christ!" Father Pieras, watching him, asked, "Why do you tire yourself here if this is not the spot where the church is to be built? Nor is there a single pagan anywhere hereabouts! It is a waste of time to ring the bells." From the depths of his soul, Serra replied, "Father, allow my overflowing heart to express itself. Would that these bells were heard throughout the world, . . . or at least that they were heard by every pagan who inhabits these mountains."

While singing High Mass, Junípero noticed a lone Indian standing nearby, attracted by the sounds of the bell and the presence of the strangers. After mass, Serra approached the man, showing affection and offering gifts. Later that day, the man returned to his village with words about the kindness received. During the days that followed, the Indians brought the Spaniards seeds and acorns. Serra reciprocated with strings of beads and food made from corn and beans, which the Indians seemed to enjoy.

The name for Mission San Antonio de Padua had been selected by Viceroy Marqués de Croix. San Antonio, who lived in the thirteenth century, was a favorite of Serra's, since the saint was referred to as the wonder-worker by the Franciscan friars. And there was little question that in the nearby rugged Santa Lucía Mountains, the strength of a worker of wonders would be needed to convert the Tatché, Telamé, and Sextapay Indians.

On their return journey to Monterey, Serra and his party spent a night near what is now Soledad in the Salinas Valley. A few Indians approached, offering them wild seeds. Junípero, in turn, gave them seashells. A while later, a few women appeared out of the darkness. Serra later wrote that never before or after had he seen anyone like them. When he asked their names (he knew at least that much of the language), one woman answered with what sounded like the Spanish word *soledad,* "solitude." Greatly surprised, Serra turned to his com-

Mission San Antonio de Padua. Set in Los Robles Valley of the Santa Lucía mountains, Mission San Antonio was an unusually prosperous and peaceful mission. Founded in 1771, it was named after Saint Anthony of Padua. This photograph from ca. 1890 shows the mission before its full restoration in 1950.

panions and laughed, "Here you have María de la Soledad." Junípero never forgot the place where he had been so kindly received, nor did the Indians of the Salinas Valley forget him. In future years, they would send greetings to "el viejo," the "aged one" of the Carmel Valley. He wanted to return among them, but two decades would pass before a mission was founded there.

Back in Monterey, Serra lost no time in transferring his mission from the presidio to the new site along the banks of the Carmel River, with its commanding view of Point Lobos and the azure waters of tiny Carmel Bay. On August 5, Serra, with four soldiers and three sailors, began cutting timber and building a small stockade. On the feast of Saint Bartholomew, August 24, 1771, Serra blessed the cross erected for Carmel's first chapel and sang a High Mass. During the next six months, Junípero led the life of a religious recluse, watching and assisting in the building of the mission structures. On Christmas Eve, Crespí took up residence at the new site as Serra's assistant.

During the months that followed, food supplies began running low. Despite limited provisions, none of the padres suffered from hunger and Serra continued in good health. The Indians of the area were

"El Carmelo" in 1792. This pen and ink sketch was drawn by an artist with Captain George Vancouver's British expedition, which anchored in Monterey Bay. The buildings, from left to right, include the mission church, a tile kiln, a cattle stockade at the top of the hill, a storehouse, the quarters of the workmen, and the sacristy and quarters of the padres. An Indian village is in the background.

kind and hospitable and offered what little food they had. Milk and vegetables from the mission, along with a little meat and a few other supplies from Mission San Antonio, helped all concerned. With the delay of the supply ship, Serra began to realize that, if future settlements were to be established, something would have to be done to maintain a reliable flow of provisions to California missions.

The problems that plagued Serra during this time were varied. One of them was Juan Crespí. Serra liked Crespí and wanted to retain him as his assistant. But his friend began complaining of physical exhaustion. Serra suspected that Crespí was discontented and wanted to leave the Monterey area for a number of reasons, "the most important being the ugly climate"—cold and foggy. Crespí was sensitive to weather, something that never seemed to bother Serra. But Junípero promised to do what he could for his friend.

When Serra, as padre presidente of the California missions, received a letter from Mission San Diego saying that provisions were running low there, too, and that Father Dumetz, who was ill, had gone to Baja California to recuperate and return with help, he saw an opportunity to grant Crespí's wish. "Do you still want to go to San Diego?" Crespí indicated that he did and joined a pack train headed south. It was his second round trip overland, and he had just returned from duty as the diarist on a reconnaissance of the San Francisco peninsula. Rations had been insufficient and the group of sixteen men had suffered great hunger.

But months later, after settling in San Diego, he wrote Serra asking to return to Carmel, indicating that he preferred the cold and fog, as well as the daily treks between Carmel and Monterey to offer mass at the presidio, to remaining in San Diego. This time he promised to remain permanently. Serra was probably irked by his friend's vacillation. Yet in his response to Crespí, he said that both he and Father Dumetz should come to Carmel.

Such personnel matters were another part of Serra's duties. As head of a mission he was responsible for the material and spiritual needs of the Indian converts. As padre presidente of all the California missions, he had the same responsibility for the clergy, assigning them their posts and counseling them at need.

Though he on one occasion referred to Crespí's "childish changeableness," he also fully appreciated his friend's contribution. In a letter to Palóu, Serra wrote that "one thing is certain. The poor man in the matter of journeyings has labored more than all of us put together."

CHAPTER FIFTEEN

OVERLAND TO SAN DIEGO

In July of 1772, Carmel Mission was nothing more than a series of crude structures within a stockade, characteristic of the early years of all the California missions. The stockade was about sixty by forty yards; the main building, forty-five by six. The walls of the main building consisted of thick poles daubed with mud, inside and out, except for the principal rooms, which were whitened with lime. The roof was flat and earthen. One of the six rooms, all opening to the outside, served as a temporary chapel, or mission church. Near the stockade was the guard house and the kitchens. These buildings were constructed of the same material as the padres' quarters. Nearby was a number of small grass-roofed houses for the Indians. The mission had a small garden, although without a regular, knowledgeable gardener, little was produced. After a year's effort, Carmel Mission consisted of nothing more than this.

But in spiritual matters there had been greater progress: the padre presidente could proudly point to his little congregation of thirty Christians and a few baptized children "who had already gone to enjoy God." During the second year, because they could not feed any more people at the mission, Serra and Crespí baptized only those Indians in danger of death. So little food was available that the padres asked the Indians to forage for themselves. Later, when Junípero went out looking for them, or when the Indians returned from the surrounding hills of their own accord, they sometimes looked so emaciated they were hardly recognizable.

In August of 1772, Serra received disheartening news. Because of adverse winds, the overdue supply ship from San Blas had been unable to proceed beyond the Santa Barbara Channel, forcing it to return to San Diego. Serra was notified that food and materials for the two northern missions would have to be carted overland from San Diego by mule train. Hunger at Carmel and Monterey would continue.

There is "everything in San Diego and nothing here," Junipero wrote curtly to Palóu:

> All the missionaries grieve—we all grieve—over the vexations, labors, and reverses we have to put up with. No one, however, desires to leave his mission. The fact is, labors or no labors, there are several souls in heaven from Monterey, San Antonio, and San Diego.

Commander Fages and Serra conferred and decided that there was nothing to do but journey down to San Diego and bring back the supplies. On August 24, 1772, the first anniversary of the planting of the cross in Carmel Valley, the padre president, the comandante, a few soldiers, and a ten-year-old Indian servant, Juan Evangelista José, left Monterey for San Diego. Serra did not realize that he was not to see Carmel Mission again for a year and a half. His immediate goals were to transport and distribute the ship's food and materials, and to establish missions at San Luis Obispo and San Buenaventura. But circumstances decreed otherwise.

This was Junípero's first overland trip along El Camino Real. He had been only as far south as Mission San Antonio the year before. On this trek, he would come to know the coast of California, making mental notes that would later aid him in fashioning his chain of missions (or ladder, as he preferred to call it).

El Camino Real in California was the route taken by Portolá from San Diego to San Francisco in 1769, with a few adjustments made by Portolá and his scout and his engineer immediately after the expedition. Though the King's Highway was often no more than a difficult, serpentine trail through mountains and wilderness, it was nonetheless a regular road. The padres and soldiers always used the same route; at any given point, parties traveling in opposite directions would meet one another.

Now, during the height of the dry season, the tall green grasses of the canyons and hillsides had long since turned to yellow straw, scorched by the blazing sun all summer. In the distance, the coastal hills stood out fawn brown. Although the path was dusty, it was passable. With the rivers and arroyos reduced to mere trickles, the hoofs of the mules would not be caught in the mud. The heat was intense.

The first part of the trip was the familiar road to Monterey, five miles north over the hills through dense forests of pine. As they descended the northern slopes, Monterey Bay was spread out below them, curving away northwestward. Next, they turned east through a narrow canyon between the hills into the Salinas Valley. The road now ran straight and level between the broad Río de Monterey (now the Salinas River) and the western mountains. The valley is several miles wide and extends southeastward fifty miles between two mountain ranges. Nights, at least, were cooler here. Entering another canyon, the party climbed the Jolon grade and emerged near the San Antonio mission on August 27.

The mission was at the northern end of the San Antonio River valley, studded with oaks and a half a mile wide by twenty miles long. The party found there a small Christian community of twelve Indians. Few though they were, Serra was encouraged. Though the mission had not enough food to sustain more, many Indians had requested baptism, disclosing where their idols were hidden and telling the padres they could go and remove them. They also carried wood and water for the padres and gathered seeds for the mission. As soon as the mission could support more, a Christian settlement would surely grow here.

Climbing out of the San Antonio valley through low hills, the party crossed the Santa Lucía Mountains, where Fages had earlier conducted bear hunts to keep starving Monterey alive. The local inhabitants were friendly and still remembered with gratitude the soldiers who had rid the country of the ferocious bears.

On September 1, 1772, Serra raised the cross for California's fifth mission, San Luis Obispo de Tolosa. (Mission San Gabriel Arcángel was the fourth mission founded. Under written directions from Serra, Fathers Angel Somera and Benito Cambón had established Mission San Gabriel north of San Diego almost exactly one year before.)

San Luis Obispo was named after a young bishop of Toulouse, France, son of King Charles II of Naples and nephew of Louis IX of France. He had donned the habit of Saint Francis in 1294.

Leaving Father Cavaller, a four-man guard, and two Baja California Indians (and very limited supplies), Serra hurried on through the wide San Luis Valley, eager to reach San Diego. Arriving at the coast, the party began to pick up the pace through the great wind-swept sandbanks to the shores of the Santa Barbara Channel. Here hills and long mountains march down to the sea, sometimes jutting into the ocean as rocky points, but more often leaving narrow plains or rolling hills along the coast. There were over twenty large Chumash Indian rancherías between what are now Goleta and Ventura. In this "long stretch of paganism," Serra saw great possibilities for future missions, believing three would be necessary to take care of the multitude. He also learned, as others had before and after him, that travel could be dangerous at certain points along the narrow passage between mountains and the ocean. At one point, where the passage narrowed to a few hundred yards, hostile Indians confronted the party, seeking to impede their progress. Fages, with his few soldiers, made a show of force, and to Serra's distress, one Indian was killed.

The group continued along the coast to a large ranchería (on the site of present-day Ventura) that Crespí had named Asumpta and noted as a desirable spot for a mission. Junípero and Fages explored the territory and decided the broad alluvial plain twenty miles long by ten wide was suitable for San Buenaventura. There was an Indian town of five hundred and room for grazing cattle and growing grain, vegetables, and fruit. After winding through valleys and passess for seventy-five miles or more, on September 11 the party arrived at Mission San Gabriel. This was the only mission founded so far during Serra's presidency that he had not personally established—or even seen. Remaining there for two days, he was so delighted with the area and its inhabitants that he wrote the guardian at San Fernando that it was "without doubt the most excellent mission site so far discovered. Once it is sufficiently developed, it will be able, doubtless, to sustain not only itself but all the rest."

Serra saw that the padres were making headway in spiritual matters as well and had residing at the mission seven or eight orphaned youngsters, "precious creatures, one of whom spoke Spanish most beautifully."

The final stage of their journey took the party through the great plains of what is now Orange County down again to the shore. The road ran along the palisades at the edge of the coastal plateau, turning inland where the land slopes to the sea and skirts the wide rivers and lagoons north of San Diego.

By the time the party arrived in San Diego, Junípero had surveyed nearly five hundred miles of Alta California coast committed to his care. He now had a better perspective on and a fuller knowledge of his extensive mission field. But more pressing matters occupied him now. The padre presidente lost no time in trying to persuade Captain Pérez to make a relief run to Monterey. The distance by land was great and there were insufficient mules; any delay could only increase the suffering in the north. But the captain did not immediately agree. The *San Antonio* was not sturdy enough for the approaching rough weather, and he did not want to winter in Monterey. But Serra would not give up. He added a religious appeal:

> You must trust in God, our Lord, for whom you are performing this service since the main purpose of this enterprise is that of converting souls. Our Lord will not allow the weather to interfere since the services we are rendering are for His sake.

After Fages joined with Serra in pressing him to make the voyage, Pérez reluctantly agreed. Ironically, although Pérez reached Monterey

Mission San Gabriel Arcangel, ca. 1870

Mission San Gabriel painted by Ferdinand Dieppe, 1832. Founded in 1771 by Fathers Pedro Cambón and Angel Somera, Mission San Gabriel was named after the Archangel Gabriel. It was the most prosperous of the missions and was the gateway to Alta California from Sonora, Mexico. Dieppe's painting is now housed in the Santa Barbara Mission Archives.

and returned to San Blas without incident, the viceroy later rebuked the sea captain for sailing beyond San Diego and the comandante for urging him to undertake a voyage placing men and cargo in peril.

Fages and Serra had concurred on the need for sending supplies to Monterey by sea, but this was not typical of the mood between them.

During the next six months their differences crystallized into a open conflict over jurisdiction.

Pedro Fages was young, inflexible, and new to frontier life, as well as inexperienced at governing a mission territory. He was a disciplinarian whose methods, instead of improving his men, made them worse. And he claimed more power over the missions and the padres than his original orders warranted. In addition, he was ambitious and was being goaded on to establish more missions, both by Serra and by his superiors in Mexico. On this score, he faced the same frustrations Serra and the others did: insufficient supplies of food and not enough soldiers to face the unknown. His inability to keep his men from deserting not only created practical problems but was deeply humiliating to him, especially when he had to swallow his pride and ask the padres' help to persuade them to return. California was little more than three years old and already suffering from growing pains. The problem was at least partly the difference in temperament between the military commander and the padre presidente. The captain of infantry was proud, jealously protective of his authority, and concerned to impress his superiors favorably—and to these ends, on occasion, he was apt to infringe upon the rights of the padres.

Serra, whose apostolic zeal goaded Fages to look forward and, when necessary, cast caution to the winds, was keenly conscious of his responsibility toward his Indian charges. After all, the occupation was to colonize the country through the Christianization of the natives. This had been Spain's method in the New World through some three centuries of missionary activity. As far as Serra was concerned, the soldiers were a mere police force to guard and, when possible, assist the padres in the overall objective. Accordingly, when Fages refused the Indians grain, when he diverted them from mission labors to become servants for his soldiers, when he made decisions ostensibly on safety grounds that interfered with the padres' work, Serra found him an obstacle, not a support, in founding the missions. Matters certainly could not continue in their current state. If California's missions were to develop, and new missions be founded, conditions had to change.

Accordingly, on October 13, Serra held a meeting with his missionaries, suggesting that someone should go to Mexico City and place the problems of the missions' future before the viceroy; they agreed, deciding that Serra himself should be the one to go. Four days later, at five o'clock in the afternoon, the padre president and his twelve-year-old Indian servant, Juan Evangelista, embarked on the *San Carlos* for San Blas.

CHAPTER SIXTEEN

ON THE WAY TO COURT

As Serra sailed southward along the narrow peninsula of Baja California, he reflected upon the past thousand days. It had been difficult to face the uncertainties and disappointments on the frontier with the added burden of strained relations with Fages. Nonetheless, five missions had been founded, although at least three remained in a precarious state. Serra now felt that unless he could get the viceroy to transfer the comandante, the mission chain would not be established. On board the *San Carlos,* the padre presidente had time to marshal his arguments for proper presentation at the college and the viceroy's palace.

During the past year and a half, it had become evident to the civil and clerical authorities in Mexico City that the strained relations between the military and the religious in California were producing an embarrassing and dangerous deadlock. Something had to be done.

Pedro Fages, inexperienced, had been a surprising selection for Gálvez to have made. An insensitive man of impulse, Fages was everything antithetical to the innovative visitor-general. Although zealous in his service for the king, and always careful to maintain his dignity, Fages was nonetheless hated by his own troops. One noncommissioned officer reported to the viceroy:

In Monterey, starting from July, 1770, the comandante used to beat us with cudgels; he would force us to buy from him at three times their value, the figs and raisins in which he was trading; he would make sick men go and cut down trees in the rain and would deprive them of their supper, if they protested; he would put us all on half rations even though food might be rotting in the storehouse. We had to live on rats, coyotes, vipers, crows, and generally every creature that moved on the earth, except beetles, to keep from starvation. We almost all became herbivorous, eating raw grass like our horses. How many times we wished we were six feet under ground!

In a letter to his superior, Serra wrote, "In all fields, he strives to make trouble for us. But what does suffering matter if we finally succeed in accomplishing our spiritual ministry? After all, that is the only thing that counts!"

But Fages wrote his own letters of complaint to Mexico City. He explained that the soldiers under his command were of two basic types: Catalonian volunteers, who had come with him from Spain, and leatherjackets, who, though they were better equipped for the raw California conditions, were lonely, unschooled half-breeds who often raped or molested the Indian women. Desertion was a problem, and in addition, he had to deal with shortages of food, supplies, and mules to carry them.

The order Gálvez had originally issued and Serra had agreed to had left too much to individual caprice, which was dangerous when the personnel in high places changed so abruptly soon afterward and communication was so difficult. On his arrival, the new viceroy, Bucareli, faced quite a backlog of documents from California, as did Verger, new guardian at the College of San Fernando.

Junípero's decision to go to Mexico City was one of the most providential of his life. With charges, accusations, complaints, and criticisms piling up before the viceroy, this was the right psychological moment for a personal conference in order to clear the atmosphere.

Serra hoped to achieve with the viceroy a clear delineation of responsibility for developing the missions. He would explain that the padres wanted to get on with their work and not be hampered by the military. The new viceroy, Chevalier Antonio María Bucareli, who would serve until his death in April of 1779, had been recently appointed to replace de Croix and had hardly arrived from Spain when the Serra-Fages conflict was thrust upon him with all its confusing claims and disturbing charges. Bucareli, an intelligent, perceptive man, eagerly awaited Junípero's arrival, realizing that most of the problems in Alta California were due to the distance of communication, the lack of a fixed budget, and outdated organizational and decision-making processes.

On November 4, 1772, after thirteen uneventful days at sea, the *San Carlos* arrived in San Blas. Serra's first act was to dispatch several letters to Verger at San Fernando. One announced the padre presidente's presence on Mexican soil, described his reasons for being there, and detailed his difficulties with Fages. The second listed the points he intended to present to the viceroy, in case Serra should die on the road to Mexico City.

Meanwhile, because the missions of Baja California were to be transfered to the Dominicans, Verger consented to send north the additional ten missionaries Serra had requested, among them, Francisco Palóu.

On November 11, Junípero and his servant, Juan Evangelista, set out from San Blas for Guadalajara, over a hundred miles away, arriving there eight days later. Walking through the heart of the Sierra Madre, a region of high mountains and deserts, the two arrived at the convent of San Francisco so severely ill that the sacrament of extreme unction was administered. Later Serra wrote:

> Because the trip to Mexico has broken our health owing to the roughness of the road, we arrived in the city of Guadalajara burning with fever. The fathers ordered me to receive the sacraments since I was in danger of death for many days.

Although near death himself, Junípero was more concerned about Juan's health. He now brought himself to pray all the harder, asking God to spare the young Indian's life. Juan recovered and, while Serra was still suffering from intermittent fever, the two continued their journey toward Querétaro—over twice as far as from the coast to Guadalajara, but through less rugged country.

At the College of Santa Cruz in Querétaro, the fever struck Serra again. Consigned to the infirmary, Junípero believed that this time he was certainly going to die. The doctor at one point ordered the friars to give him the last anointing after vespers. But later that same afternoon, when another doctor made a casual visit, he found Serra completely well. "Is this Father going to receive the last sacraments?" inquired the doctor. "If he is, I am in a condition to receive them, too. Father, get up; you are all right; nothing is wrong with you." Turning to the attending priest, he ordered, "Inform the father guardian and do not administer the sacraments." When the superior came, the doctor laughed, "If it were not so late, I would have him get up because he is so well; but let him get up tomorrow and after taking food, he can continue his journey."

The next morning, with Mexico City over one hundred fifty miles away, Junípero and the boy continued their journey down a road familiar to Serra. For Juan, the experience was unparalleled: new sights, faces, and customs. Never before had he seen houses, monasteries, churches, and cities. The contrast between the splendidly adorned churches of Mexico and the crude adobe chapels of Carmel, San Antonio, San Gabriel, San Diego, and the brush hut of San Luis Obispo, was overwhelming. But most important, the lad saw a reassuring sight he could report back to his tribe: There were females among the new people. The institution of marriage existed here as it did among the Indians of the Monterey Peninsula.

Portrait of Viceroy Bucareli. After arriving in Alta California, Serra only returned to Mexico City once, partly to enlist the support of Viceroy Bucareli, who at Serra's behest drew up the first set of laws for California governing the rights of the Indians.

Silver monstrance presented Serra by Bucareli.

When the Spaniards first arrived in Carmel Valley, the Indians saw only men and mules, no women. In fact, no European females had arrived along the entire California coast by the time Serra and Juan left, leading to the conclusion that the Spaniards were the offspring of Portolá's mules. That deduction was part of what led Serra to argue for sending married colonists to California.

The two weary travelers reached the College of San Fernando in Mexico City on February 6, 1773. For several months after his arrival, Serra "was very weary and without appetite," though he joined the community round of spiritual exercises. Juan continued to serve Serra, and was introduced to Viceroy Bucareli and confirmed by the archbishop of Mexico, the Most Reverend Alfonso Nuñez de Haro y Peralta, in the grand chapel of the archiepiscopal palace.

After recuperating and talking matters over with the guardian, Verger, Serra sought a personal interview with the viceroy. The man from Majorca was now to meet directly with the alter ego of Carlos III. Bucareli received Serra cordially and listened with interest to what

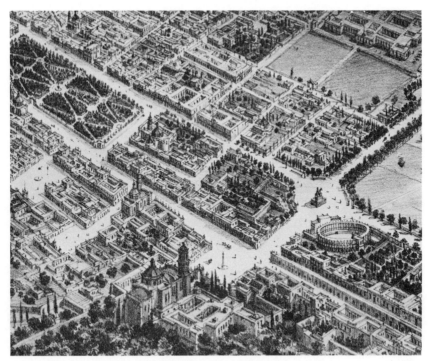

Aerial view of Mexico City, mid-nineteenth century

he had to say. Only a few months before, the viceroy had informed the king that the discord between the military and the missionaries manifests "a deplorable situation and the proximate ruin" of the new establishments in California. Now, impressed with Junípero's zeal and obvious knowledge of affairs, Bucareli asked him to put all his requests in writing and present them formally to the court, adding that he personally would like to contribute to the missionary effort.

Serra promised to draft the formal document as requested, but urged Bucareli to consider immediately a matter of pressing importance. California's food supply was very low. The supply ships that sailed from San Blas formed the lifeline of the missions and presidios; food and other goods needed to be shipped to San Diego and Monterey immediately. After listening to the impassioned plea, the viceroy ordered that a packet boat in San Blas be provisioned and dispatched with all haste.

Heartened by the meeting, and deeply touched by Bucareli's warm-hearted interest, Serra now felt he had a friend at court, a man at the highest level who was sympathetic. Once again Junípero Serra had gone forward.

CHAPTER SEVENTEEN

BEFORE
VICEROY BUCARELI

Upon returning to the College of San Fernando from his conference with Bucareli, Serra told Verger about the viceroy's request to put his petitions in writing for formal presentation to the court. Verger suggested Junípero list as briefly as possible the solutions he considered necessary, adding the reasons for each.

This legal brief, called the *Representación,* was completed and signed by Serra on March 13, 1773. It is written in beautiful calligraphy on durable paper; one copy, in California since Serra's time, is now in the archives of the Santa Barbara Mission. The *Representación* formed the basis of the first significant legislation for California, in effect a "Bill of Rights" for the Indians that would affect the military, post office officials, missionaries, colonists, the college, and even the Council of the Indies in Spain.

The thirty-two points covered every phase of activity in the mission enterprise, but one problem Junípero devoted a great deal of attention to was the personality of Pedro Fages. Serra asked that Fages be removed and that Sergeant José Francisco Ortega be appointed comandante. The padre presidente gave Ortega, who had accompanied the Rivera expedition to San Diego and the Portolá expedition to the Golden Gate, an outstanding character reference, describing him as a man respected by the Indians as well as by his fellow soldiers.

In the political atmosphere and practice of the day, and within the framework of Spain's bureaucratic empire with all its appointed officials, personal influence counted most. Junípero was now using the only means available to him: a direct, personal appeal to Bucareli. If California was to survive, either Fages or Serra would have to go.

According to Palóu, when Serra personally presented his *Representación* to Bucareli, he said:

Your Excellency, I place in your hands this petition in which you will see what I say is the undiluted truth, and what I explain is dictated by what my conscience obliges me to say. I consider my requests quite urgent and necessary, if the purpose of His Majesty, who has assumed such great expense, is to be carried out, which is the conversion of many souls who because they are unacquainted without Holy Catholic Faith, sigh under the tyrannical slavery of the enemy. Through the means and measures I suggest, I judge this purpose can be easily fulfilled. I hope Your Excellency will read [my recommendations] and decide what you judge to be just and fitting. This you may do with the knowledge that I must now return [to California] and that I desire to put [them] in operation as soon as possible. If this is done now, I shall return happy; if not, then I shall return somewhat saddened. However, I shall always conform myself to the will of God.

Within a few days, Bucareli informed Serra that his "alleviation" had been granted and Fages removed. Four years later, Bucareli wrote:

The little concord of Don Pedro Fages ... with the president of the missions ... compelled Father Fray Junípero Serra almost in a dying condition to come to this capital to present his requests and to inform me personally a thing which rarely can be presented with such persuasion in writing. On his arrival I listened to him with the greatest pleasure and I realized the apostolic zeal that animated him while I accepted from his ideas those measures which appeared proper to me to carry out.

During the months that followed, there were further consultations between the two men on these and other issues. One of the most important was the fate of San Blas.

In a report on April 22, Junípero responded to a plan to close San Blas as a port and send supplies overland to Guaymas, by sea to the northern end of the Gulf of California at San Luis, then overland to San Diego and the other missions. From his experience on the trail himself, he questioned the practicality of a plan that would require fifteen hundred mules to carry what two ships now brought from San Blas. In addition to the excessive time and expense, Serra saw social and moral dangers in sending so many soldiers and muleteers through Indian territory. "The pleasant prospect of so many women could be forgone only by a miracle; and many miracles would be required to forestall disorderly conduct."

Most of the requests that Serra made in his *Representación* were granted, a few were postponed, and in a few cases conditions were attached. Junípero felt that he had achieved everything he had hoped for. He was especially pleased with Bucareli's decree that "the government, control, and education of the baptized Indians should belong exclusively to the missionaries." The padres were to serve the Indians, as parents love and train their children. The new comandante, Fernando de Rivera y Moncada was to preserve harmony and cooperate with the missionaries. Ortega had not been acceptable to the viceroy because he was a sergeant, but he was shortly promoted to lieutenant and became the first commander of the formally recognized presidio at San Diego.

His six months of conferences in the palace now completed, Serra could reflect on a number of achievements: the promise of expeditions to explore and open up overland routes from Sonora and New Mexico; the separate marking of mission and military goods; the removal of immoral soldiers from the missions at the padres' request; the regulation of prices and standardization of weights; the recruiting of Mexicans on sailors' pay to the missions' fields; the protection of the padres' mail from tampering by military commanders; the provision of a doctor, blacksmiths, and carpenters, and of bells and vestments for the new missions; serious consideration of the shortage of mules; and pardons for all deserters.

Meanwhile, Gálvez, now a high official in Madrid, was still deeply interested in the venture he had so strongly sponsored. He could see that the man with the lame leg was still battling on. In Baja, Gálvez had not agreed with all of Serra's proposals; and even now, he disagreed with a few of Serra's ideas for California, especially those that allowed missionaries to interfere in military administration. Yet, he praised the work his friend was doing among the Indians to the king.

As Serra completed his preparations for the long, tiresome return journey to his headquarters at Mission San Carlos at Carmel, he took time to write a rare personal letter to his nephew, Fray Miquel de Petra Ribot. Miquel was known to Junípero as "Little Mike," although the man was now a Capuchin priest more than thirty years old. Explaining his infrequent correspondence, he wrote:

> It is not from a want of love that I have not answered some of the letters I have received from Your Reverence. When I left that beloved land of mine, I made up my mind to leave it not only in body. I could have kept up correspondence with various persons, for Your Reverence knows that I did not lack friends and acquaintances both within and without the Order. But if I was to retain forever in memory what I had left behind, what would have been the purpose in leaving it in the first place?

Turning to his work in the mission field, Junípero added:

> In California is my life and there, God willing, I hope to die. When that hour comes, some one of my fellow religious will not fail to write about my death so that others can commend me to God and thus you will be notified. What else does Your Reverence desire? You live among saints so that I do not believe you need my counsel. That would be the only reason my letters would be helpful to you.

In his letter Serra tried to inculcate Franciscan holiness in his Capuchin nephew, as well as epitomize Christian asceticism for all members of Christ's Mystical Body:

> Let us make good use of time. Our steps should be in conformity with the vocation to which God has called us; let us work out our spiritual salvation with fear and trembling, and with a burning love and zeal seek for the salvation of our brethren and neighbors. And may all the glory be to our great God.

In this, his last correspondence to Majorca, Junípero concluded:

> Whatever you can do in that apostolic ministry ... whether preaching by word and example, or hearing confessions with patience seems to me time spent in the best and most fruitful way. Although I am lukewarm, bad, and unprofitable, yet every day in the holy sacrifice of the Mass, I always make a memento for my only and most beloved sister Juana, your mother, and for her children, but in particular for my Capuchin. I hope all of you do the same for me so that the Lord may assist me amid the perils of a naked and barbarous people. Thus let our mutual correspondence be and let God do the rest.

In early September 1773, Serra and Juan Evangelista began their return journey to Carmel. Serra, nearly sixty, was in frail health, and the guardian of San Fernando authorized a coach for transporting Junípero, Juan Evangelista, and a companion, Fray Pablo de Mugártegui, as far as Guadalajara.

Before leaving the college, Serra asked permission to repeat what he had done twenty-four years before when he left Palma, namely perform an act of humility and esteem toward all his brothers assembled in the refectory. Permission was granted, and Junípero knelt and kissed the feet of each friar. He then begged forgiveness for all the sins he may have committed and, after receiving Verger's blessing, asked his brethren to commend him to God, for they would never see his face again. "In California is my life and there I hope to die."

CHAPTER EIGHTEEN

SERRA'S SECOND SPRING
IN CALIFORNIA

At three o'clock on the afternoon of January 24, 1774, Serra, Juan Evangelista, and his companion, Mugártegui, along with ninety-five other individuals, embarked at San Blas on the *Santiago* for the voyage to Monterey. Included among the passengers were two physicians, three blacksmiths, and two carpenters, some with wives and children—living testimony to the success of Serra's mission. After forty days at sea, the ship was within sight of San Diego. Despite viceregal orders to sail directly to Monterey, Captain Perez decided to anchor there, since there were no favorable winds to continue the voyage. When Father Vicente Fuster, Sergeant José Carrillo, and four leather-jacket soldiers came on board to welcome them, Serra learned that since the previous August everyone at the mission had been living on half rations.

At Presidio Hill, Serra greeted his fellow Majorcan, Luís Jayme, whom he had appointed to the mission in 1771. Serving under him were padres Vicente Fuster and Gregorio Amurrió, whom Palóu had placed there in 1773 (while he was acting as presidente during Serra's absence). The Franciscans were in good health and working hard. Since Serra had last seen it in October of 1772, nearly a year and a half before, the mission had made steady progress, even though California had almost succumbed to famine.

In their early years, all the missions had had to go through an experimental stage in agriculture. In San Diego, flood waters during the first year destroyed the crop. The second year seeds were planted farther away from the riverbanks, and water was so scarce that crops perished from lack of moisture. In 1773, Palóu reconnoitered the valley for better land. Jayme wrote Serra that inland would be a better location for the mission; Serra and Verger at the college approved, and the mission was moved. In 1772, Fages had complained that the Indians were too close to the presidio, and at the time, Serra considered it ridiculous to move them away from the mission. Now, both moved for agricultural reasons.

Confirmation that Bucareli had not forgotten California came on March 22, 1774, when a small band of Spaniards arrived at Mission San Gabriel. Captain Juan Bautista de Anza had been commissioned to explore the feasibility of transporting an entire colony overland from Sonora to California. To guide him across the hot, shifting sands of the Mojave Desert, Anza had enlisted Padre Francisco Hermenegildo Garcés, the missionary in charge of San Xavier del Bac in Arizona, from the sister college to San Fernando, Santa Cruz de Querétaro. In addition to his familiarity with the terrain, this padre-explorer was singularly attuned to the people who lived along the trail. Because of Garcés—and because of Serra's enthusiasm in Mexico City—the incredible had happened: California had been reached overland from Sonora.

On March 25, Anza sent four soldiers to nearby San Diego for food and supplies, as well as to inform everyone of the expedition's success. Serra was jubilant! A few days later, Garcés rode down to greet the padre presidente. The two had not seen each other since they had lived together in the hospice of Santa Cruz in Tepic back in 1768. Serra was primarily a mission builder, Garcés, an explorer preparing the ground for future missions. The two remained in San Diego during Holy Week, Junípero, with his friend's aid, baptizing ten Indian children during the time.

It appears reasonable to surmise that these two friars may have envisioned a second chain of missions to the northeast. In any case, some fifteen months after their rendezvous, Garcés became the first European to penetrate the great San Joaquin Valley, where he selected a suitable site for a mission near what is now the city of Bakersfield.

On April 6, Serra and Juan Evangelista left San Diego with Garcés for Mission San Gabriel, an exhausting journey of more than a hundred miles that took six days because of heavy rains and mud along the path. When the party finally arrived, they learned that Anza had left for Monterey the previous day, so Junípero rested at San Gabriel with his brethren, Fathers Cruzado, Lasuén, and Figuer for ten days.

During Serra's stay in Mexico City, he had commissioned oil paintings of the titular saints for the California missions that did not have pictures to adorn their altars. For the altar at San Gabriel, the padres had torn a picture of the Archangel Gabriel from a missal. Now Junípero produced an oil painting to replace it. The surprised fathers could not have been more pleased; the missal page was removed at once and the painting put in its place above the chalice.

On April 23, Serra and his party set out for San Luís Obispo, over one hundred fifty miles to the northwest. En route, they again passed

Mission San Luís Obispo. Still used as a church today, Mission San Luís Obispo is named after Saint Louis the Bishop. The photograph is ca. 1870, Carleton Watkins.

over the rolling plains of what is now Los Angeles and through the populous villages along the Santa Barbara Channel. A few days later, the group caught up with Anza near a village at Point Concepción. The explorer was reconnoitering the passes in the area for his expedition to found San Francisco. Since Serra and Anza had never met before, the padre begged him not to hurry off but to camp for the night nearby so that the two could talk over recent developments in California. Anza yielded, and the two men, soldier and friar, discussed their plans for California.

Next day, each went his separate way, and on April 30, Serra arrived at Mission San Luís Obispo, where he remained for three days. Six youngsters were baptized during his stay, bringing the total to fifty.

Having been told at San Gabriel that San Luís and San Antonio had received their paintings from Mexico during his absence, Junípero was tactful in mentioning that on his trip he had contracted a debt of eighteen pesos against the mission for a painting. The padres told him they already had one, but that San Antonio might like it better than the one they had, an attempt to pass the painting—and the debt—on to their brothers to the north. Serra dropped the matter and told them he would write and ask the college to transfer the debt to his own mission of San Carlos Borromeo in Carmel. But Junípero was not through.

Limping in to see their painting, he remarked, "Yours is pretty, but the one I have brought with me is still nicer," and suggested one of the two could be hung in the friary. But the padres still did not bite, not even curious enough to ask him to unwrap it.

When Serra arrived at Mission San Antonio on May 6, he found Fathers Pieras, Sitjar, and Murguía deeply appreciative of the painting of San Antonio and interested in the painting of Saint Louis, as well. They were more than willing to assume responsibility for the debt, if they could keep them both at San Antonio. But in the end Serra would not allow this, determined now to take the painting to Carmel.

On May 9, with Murguía and Juan Evangelista, Serra began the last stretch of his journey up the Salinas Valley, arriving in Monterey two days later. He was overjoyed at seeing the *Santiago* in the harbor and learned that it had arrived just two days ahead of him. No doubt Serra paid a courtesy call on Fages, who was still at the presidio. Late that afternoon, an hour's walk on the winding path over the pine-studded hill brought him home to Carmel and Mission San Carlos.

Palóu, now stationed at the mission, tells us Serra's arrival caused an outbreak of joy on the part of everyone. Junípero's prophecy to Palóu, "Goodby until we meet in Monterey," had finally come true. Crespí was also there, glad to be back, even in the cold and fog. Palóu, Crespí, and Dumetz had accomplished a great deal in Serra's absence. When he left, there had been twenty-two baptisms since the founding of the mission; on his return, the total was one hundred seventy four. Serra wrote to the guardian in San Fernando, "It seems all were glad seeing that after so many labors of mine, we obtained a remedy for all our ills both in provisions and measures. May God be blessed for all."

As Serra recounted his success with the benevolent Bucareli, Palóu described what had been the worst famine so far on the Monterey peninsula during the past eight months. For months, milk had been all that had saved them, comandante, padres, and Indians. The friars had been without a tortilla, or as much as a crumb of bread, for thirty-seven days. Meals consisted of gruel made of peas ground to flour mixed with the milk. For breakfast, a thin coffee took the place of their usual chocolate. While Anza was there, the padres could not even offer him that warm, satisfying morning drink. The Indians had had to forage for animals and fish.

But now, troops from the presidio were helping the *Santiago*'s sailors unload the ship's cargo of equipment and precious food supplies. By May 23, everything destined for the presidio and Carmel Mission, as well as what was to go to Missions San Antonio and San Luís Obispo, had been brought ashore. The heavy wooden boxes were placed in the royal warehouse, and the overflow was stacked high in the presidio patio. What belonged to the mission was carried over the hill by mules, and pack trains were sent lumbering on their way south to the other missions.

Serra wrote in thanks to Bucareli and expressed his joy in a letter to the guardian:

> Now all of a sudden we see ourselves supplied with such abundance that we do not know where to store all the victuals. The rations have been increased. The pay has been raised. And relieved from anxiety, all the people are in the greatest mood for rejoicing.

Chocolate, tortillas, ham, flour, oil, and wine were passed out to everyone. And to the great joy of his family, Juan Evangelista was safe at home with stories of what he had seen and the people he had encountered in the distant land.

In his letters to Bucareli, Serra wrote:

> After so many journeys by sea and land, I am home well and safe in the missions of Monterey, so greatly favored by Your Excellency. Now all the land, heretofore so melancholy and miserable, is rejoicing because of the abundant provisions and most fitting measures with which Your Excellency has consoled us. . . . All the inhabitants are so happy and so contented that there is seen no trace of sadness except in those who have to leave. [They are no less] indebted to the piety and zeal of Your Excellency than to those men who began the colonization and spiritual conquest . . . they do not even have a fear of the future.

CHAPTER NINETEEN

A FRESH START

Rivera's arrival in Monterey on board the *Santiago* to replace Fages brought sincere joy to Serra's heart. The two were old acquaintances, who had met in Baja in 1768 and seen each other at intervals since then. The new comandante of the area, however, was not a happy man; he had been recalled to duty after he had obtained permission to retire because of illness. In 1773, he had purchased a hacienda in his native region of Compostela (south of Tepic) upon which he still owed a great deal. Because Bucareli wanted to confer with him in person, Rivera had had to borrow money to make the trip to Mexico City. Now, in isolated Monterey, he feared he would face many strenuous years and never see his homeland or his hacienda again.

After showing his letter of appointment to Fages and being proclaimed military commander, Rivera and Fages together made an inventory of the presidio's assets. On May 26, he rode over to Carmel to call upon Serra and the missionaries. Three days later, Serra returned the visit at the presidio and invited Rivera to a celebration in Carmel the next day in honor of San Fernando. That afternoon, the new commander obligingly returned to the mission with the padres and slept there overnight. But the next morning Rivera returned to the presidio without having attended the festive services. Serra was both surprised and disappointed. A week later, on June 2, the feast of Corpus Christi, several sailors and soldiers arrived from Monterey to participate in the solemnities. Again, Rivera failed to appear—and at one of the most important religious events in the Spanish-speaking world. Serra found his behavior so extraordinary that he registered his surprise in a letter to the college.

On June 11, the *Santiago* sailed north to explore the coast of the Pacific northwest. On board was Juan Crespí, assigned as ship's chaplain and diarist.

Daily mission life. This pen sketch by Alexander Harmer of Santa Barbara vividly represents the day-to-day activity of constructing a mission. Lumber, adobes, and tiles were the primary materials used. The native workers' clothing was manufactured on mission looms, and weaving, along with sheepshearing and the building trades, were important mission industries.

Meanwhile, the demoted Fages remained in Monterey until July 19, when he began the overland trek to San Diego to embark on the *San Antonio* for Mexico. There is no record of the parting words between Serra and Fages, but Serra was sorry the commander was leaving, since during the past month he had sensed a change in Fages's attitude. It was too late for anything to be done about that, but unknown to the officer, Serra wrote to Bucareli about him. The viceroy was so touched by the Christian spirit of the letter that months later he informed Junípero that Fages, who had arrived in Mexico City terribly ill, would receive the viceroy's "studied attention."

Serra now settled into the daily routine of mission life. Juan Evangelista's stories of his journey were having their effect; Indians began arriving at Mission San Carlos from all over. On August 24, Serra wrote:

> Every day Indians are coming in from distant ranches in the Sierra.... They tell the padres they would like them to come to their territory. They see our church which stands before their eyes so neatly; they see the milpas with corn which are pretty to behold; they see so many children as well as people like themselves going about clothed who sing and eat well and who work. With all this, together with what God, our Lord, shall accomplish in their souls, is there any doubt then that they will be drawn to us?

Junípero's great hope for the future rested with the children. Describing how happy they were, he wrote the guardian:

> The spectacle of seeing about a hundred young children of about the same age praying and answering individually all the questions asked on Christian doctrine, hearing them sing, seeing them going about clothed in cotton and woolen garments, playing happily and who deal with the padres so intimately as if they had always known them, is, indeed, something moving, a thing for which God is to thanked.

Junípero became especially close to one of the families who had been helpful to him from the beginning. Tatlun, chief of a ranchería, had already brought several of his own children for baptism. Now, he and his wife were receiving instructions. When the chief presented his four-year-old son for baptism, Serra blessed the child in his own name and the name of the viceroy and asked José Cañizares, captain of the *Santiago,* to serve as godfather. Junípero Bucareli was duly baptized.

Harvest time for 1774 was rapidly approaching. The padre presidente wrote to the viceroy that the Indians of the Monterey peninsula were applying themselves in fields, orchards, and woodlands. The collected food was brought to the mission storehouse from which it was rationed daily to the converts. While the wheat harvest was in progress between July 18 and August 11, large schools of sardines appeared in Carmel Bay. This was too good to miss! The Indians continued harvesting in the morning but went fishing in the afternoons, working hard at their double occupation for twenty days. The fish were dried in the sun, in a method similar to that used by the Chumash Indians along the Santa Barbara Channel.

Juan Evangelista personally gathered thousands of the silvery fish to send as a gift to Bucareli in the name of his people. Ten months later, the young man received a letter of gratitude from the viceroy, who said the gift was appreciated by his court in Mexico City and that the salted sardines were delicious.

In a letter to Bucareli, Serra described the scene on one Sunday during the harvest season: The white sands and blue waters of Carmel Bay made a picture like "sitting in a beautiful theater." Since it was a day of rest, the Indians spent the afternoon searching the nearby rocks for mudhens, then roasting the fowl over their fires.

On August 27, the *Santiago* returned to Monterey from its exploration of northern waters. Serra was elated at the ship's safe return and amazed at Crespí's accounts of the trip. The ship had sailed as far north as what are now the Queen Charlotte Islands off the coast of British Columbia. From Crespí's and de la Peña's diaries, Serra wrote to Bucareli that "there are people, and many of them, who are industrious, skillful, sociable, and friendly." Although the coast was foggy, mountainous, and snow-clad, Serra envisioned missions as far north as Alaska, with California serving as a giant stepping stone, a parade of crosses rising from the western mountains with thousands of converts attracted to them. Why stop at San Francisco? As always, postponement was not Serra's way. Had it been left to him, he would have extended his ladder of missions to the glaciers of the frozen north.

Despite generally favorable conditions in Carmel, Serra had several problems to work out. He was interested in further developing the small non-Indian town that was growing up next to the mission. It included the houses of three soldiers, two sailors, a blacksmith, and a carpenter as well as a warehouse and the corporal's home. Junípero encouraged these individuals to build whatever they wanted, since they might serve as examplars to the recent converts to Christianity.

Three Spanish sailors who had married Indian women, and three others who were about to do so, hoped to remain in the valley as colonists in order to take advantage of new land grant regulations drawn up in Mexico City for military personnel. If they colonized the area, they would receive not only two years' pay, but also food rations for five years for themselves and their families. They wanted their own homes and their own fields to work. Serra supported them. As soldiers, they would often be transferred from one mission to another, forced to leave their already cultivated fields and transport their wives over long, rough roads without shelter at night. Unless such colonists began to live permanently near the mission, Serra felt the missions would never become formal settlements.

Junípero was also anxious about a number of missionaries who were "unemployed" since he could not found the new missions for which he had permission due to lack of soldiers and mules. At Carmel alone, he had four "extra" padres. Though Palóu, Murguía, Dumetz, and Tomás de la Peña were not idle, their morale was sinking; they did not have their own missions to manage as they had expected. Rivera seemed to oppose the founding of more missions, causing Serra to ask, "What are we doing here since it is plain that with this man in charge, no new missions will ever be established?"

In the meantime, Palóu was assigned to the fields with the Indians; Murguía supervised the women; Dumetz taught the children; and de la Peña worked in the gardens. They were also engaged in prayer three times a day and taught the basic doctrines of Christianity to the catechumens whenever possible. Meanwhile, Serra was always busy. Every detail of mission life demanded constant attention: the Indians, soldiers, colonists, crops, buildings, mules, ships from San Blas, his own missionaries, Rivera, the viceroy, and the College of San Fernando. All his responsibilities required a great deal of writing. Junípero confided to Verger that half his life was being consumed in writing letters to Mexico,

San Blas, Tepic, and the various California missions. He was becoming more of a scribe than a missionary. He did not even have time to visit the missions as often as he should. But as father president, "the solicitude of all the churches" tell upon his shoulders, and this meant frequent use of paper and quill.

CHAPTER TWENTY

CONCERTS
IN CACOPHONY

The period between March of 1773 and May of 1774 was generally one of hope and optimism, buoyed by gratitude, although friction was beginning to grow between the new comandante and the padre presidente. Junípero had lacked enthusiasm for Rivera from the very moment he learned of his appointment. In fact, the reformed Fages had proven more cooperative. In Madrid, Gálvez, too, had had misgivings when he learned of the appointment. Now, between Monterey and Mission San Carlos, disputes and misunderstandings were an almost daily affair.

The most important centered around the matter of founding new missions. Five were already established between the harbor of San Diego and the Bay of Carmel; Serra's aim was to establish as many more as possible in the intervals. In particular, he wanted to see Mission San Buenaventura, so long delayed, become a reality. The padre president had proposed its founding to both Fages and Rivera, but each had refused on the grounds there were insufficient soldiers for its protection. But Gálvez in Spain had ordered a mission along the Santa Barbara Channel to be the third founded, and in Spain it was considered to be already in existence.

Serra envisioned ten or eleven California missions being developed in his lifetime, "on a ladder with conveniently placed rungs." With missions founded at suitable intervals, weary wayfarers would spend only three days and two nights in the open between them. As matters now stood, the first mission south of San Carlos was San Antonio, nearly seventy miles away. Beyond was Mission San Luis Obispo, another seventy-five miles to the south. From San Luis Obispo to San Gabriel there was a gap of two hundred twelve miles, and between San Gabriel and San Diego, the distance was one hundred sixteen miles.

Obviously, more missions were needed if the gaps were to be filled in.

Serra, frustrated, continued to try to find ways to found new missions with the insufficient soldiers and supplies on hand. The hardware and altar pieces for San Buenaventura had remained in crates since 1769; the problem was to obtain the necessary soldier-guards. Junípero was willing to sacrifice some of Carmel's protection, but that would not be enough. However, if nine of the twenty-six soldiers at the presidio in San Diego were transferred north and added to three or four from his own mission, San Buenaventura could finally be founded. Rivera, however, refused to budge, insisting that such a slender guard was imprudent for that populous and dangerous locale. "Indeed," Serra commented dryly, "the Indians might revolt; who can deny that?" As for himself, he was unafraid, ready to move on despite the risk, and fearing that otherwise no new missions would be established at all. The comandante wanted to be safe and sure. Junípero called it "military prudence," and did not refer to it in a complimentary manner.

Clashes between Rivera's "military prudence" and Serra's "imprudence" increased, fueled, as always, by the fact that Mexico had not sent mules and soldiers as promised. On one occasion, Junípero learned that a number of unburdened mules were being dispatched to San Diego, and asked permission to send twenty sacks of flour to Mission San Luís Obispo. The comandante refused, saying that carrying such a load might delay the mules on the road.

Serra used this and other incidents to stress to the guardian at San Fernando the need for more mission mules. He was still waiting for the hundred or so the viceroy had promised him from Sonora. He suggested the viceroy be asked whether those mules were indeed on their way to California and added that the future growth and development of the mission depended solely on Rivera. "Every day it becomes more apparent to me that we shall gain little even on those points which have been resolved by the council and ordered to be observed by the viceroy."

Rivera seemed to resent suggestions coming from anyone else. He would delay for months replying to Serra's simplest requests. Although foodstuffs and dry goods were stacked high in the warehouse, he postponed their distribution—to the point that hunger became a problem once again. The mission Indians, workmen, and padres— even Rivera's own soldiers—were receiving only a small fraction of what had been received. People would gladly have paid for the food and materials, but Rivera denied them even that. Serra wrote:

> My Mexican blacksmiths are in rags. They have not even been able to get hold of a pair of breeches, nor pots, frying pans, ladles, or grinding stones.

He asked the guardian to confer with Bucareli as soon as possible— prodding the viceroy to help.

Another point in Serra's long letter to the guardian was a complaint that Rivera was obstructive when asked to remove immoral soldiers from the missions—something the viceroy had promised Serra in Mexico City would be done. Serra became more and more insistent that soldiers with families, especially Indian wives, should be replaced and allowed to remain as settlers. He wanted to purge the libertines and encourage settlers with Indian relatives to remain near their wives' families. A short note to Bucareli written the day after the long letter to the guardian began abruptly:

Evils that are not remedied in the beginning customarily are cured later only with difficulty. Now we are at the beginning of a new administration and having observed the need of proper remedies, it has not seemed good to me to defer asking for them.

Clothing remained a problem for the missions.

To clothe the nakedness of so many girls and boys, women and men, even moderately, not only to protect them from the cold, which is quite severe here during the greater part of the year, but also to foster decency and urbanity especially among the weaker sex, I am confronted with an almost insuperable difficulty.

In 1775 Serra explained in a letter to the viceroy that there was no longer any cloth at all left in the missions. With the salaries of the missionaries, and by using their old habits and one hundred shepherds' blankets, they had been able to clothe the naked. But now there was nothing left.

Before any reply had time to come from Mexico, some of the problems had been solved. The rations were adjusted, but not in time to prevent Rivera's receiving a second order on the matter. Once again the difficulties and delays in communication between Mexico City and Monterey did nothing to help the situation.

By November of 1774, the families Rivera had gathered in Sinaloa, and whom Lieutenant Ortega had brought overland from Baja California, arrived in Monterey. Now, Rivera was ready to undertake the reconnaissance of the San Francisco Bay area preparatory to founding the sixth mission. On November 30, sixteen soldiers and Palóu, along with supplies for forty days, headed north. On December 4, Palóu planted a cross on the highest peak overlooking the wide entrance to San Francisco Bay. When the party returned to Monterey on December 13, Palóu presented his diary to the padre presidente, who immediately forwarded it to the viceroy.

Not until six months later, on June 28, 1775, were Serra's hopes for establishing new missions revived. On board the *San Carlos,* which had just anchored, was a letter from Bucareli ordering the construction of two missions and a presidio in the San Francisco area. For their establishment, Captain Juan Bautista de Anza and his 177-member party of soldiers and settlers were due in Monterey with additional supplies. Junípero was "filled with joy" but again wrote asking for a mission along the Santa Barbara Channel. Indians there had recently attacked the Monterey pack train, threatening the missions' slender lifeline.

The year 1775 was especially difficult for Serra. Realizing that time was racing by, and that the Santa Barbara Channel missions were no nearer to being founded than when Fages was governor, Serra continued to plead with Rivera for cooperation, and relations continued to deteriorate.

Finally, Rivera and Serra received instructions from the viceroy to select the sites for the two new missions and the presidio. Bucareli's letter to the comandante was a duplicate of the one sent to Serra, but written out by the viceroy's secretary. Serra's letter was in Bucareli's own handwriting.

Unfortunately, the viceroy's penmanship was terrible, so illegible that Junípero, as well as the other padres, misread it. In the letter, Bucareli informed the comandante and the padre presidente that the first responsibility of the Anza expedition would be to provide escorts for the founding of new missions along the Santa Barbara Channel and the San Francisco peninsula. From that, Serra surmised that most of Anza's thirty soldiers were meant to serve as mission guards. In a postscript, Serra read "thirteen men" instead of "the six men as escort that I assign to each mission." To Junípero, *seis* looked like *trece*. He showed the letter to Palóu and de la Peña, both of whom also read "thirteen." Serra later commented that he was no more in doubt than if he had read the large lettering of a choir book. On the basis of reading "thirteen," an eager Junípero walked over to the presidio in Monterey to begin his negotiations with Rivera.

In late June, when Rivera paid a visit to Mission San Carlos, Serra told him about Bucareli's letter, something he had not done up to this point. The captain asked Junípero if the "thirteen" was written in alphabet or numbers. Serra responded, "In alphabet, and in Bucareli's own hand." Rivera knew the padre presidente was in error, but remained silent, perhaps thinking he had snared Serra in a lie. On several other occasions when Serra brought up the thirteen guards, Rivera only smiled, making no comment. Serra later commented, "He kept the news for the worst possible occasion he could think of."

On August 10, a second letter arrived for Serra from the viceroy authorizing the establishment of missions along the Santa Barbara Channel. He left it to Serra and Rivera to decide based on the number of soldiers available. Rivera began the discussion by asking Serra what guards he had for founding more missions. Junípero answered that he would provide two from his own mission, plus two from Mission San Diego. With these four, as well as others who could be spared from the presidios, he could establish at least one, it not two, missions. Rivera was adamant that he would not release any of his soldiers from the two presidios and refused to discuss the matter any further.

Late the following morning, Serra and Murguía went to the presidio. Rivera received them pleasantly enough in his office and began to joke about Mission San Buenaventura, which had been planned as far back as the 1769 Portolá expedition (of which both he and Serra had been members). Junípero laughed and asked Rivera if he remembered the time he came to him one night behind Portolá's back to ask for something to eat for himself and his men. Serra had given him a few corn cakes, the only food he had. Rivera smiled, responding that he did indeed remember the incident. Serra wrote:

> Thus we spoke about our adventures in olden times and all with such good humor that I forgot all my cares and I considered it a closed case that the foundation [of new missions] would take place.

Then, almost abruptly, Rivera became serious. He demanded to know "How many men did you ask for, to found just *one* mission?" He emphasized "one" in such a way as to suggest that there would be no discussion about founding more than that, although, of course, the viceroy had approved the establishment for two. Surprised, but undaunted, Junípero repeated what he told the officer earlier: four soldiers from San Carlos, or two each from Carmel and San Diego, to be added to those assigned from the presidios. The comandante sat back, remaining silent.

After a few moments of reflection, Rivera stood up and said, "We will consult the viceroy in Mexico." Serra was shocked; that would put the matter off for another whole year. Choosing his words carefully, Junípero answered:

> The viceroy has put the [exact number of guards] into our hands so that we can work out the problem. There is nothing further to do or consult about. He already knew when he wrote how many soldiers were at the presidios and how many soldiers the mission had.

Everyone in the room realized that Bucareli expected the comandante and the padre presidente to decide on the basis of the existing soldiers in Alta California and on the condition that the established missions not be jeopardized.

After a long and thoughtful pause, Rivera replied in a tone of finality that no more than six soldiers could be provided.

Our difficulites are minor. With what you offer, the men are assured. Let us put the number at twelve and then we can start San Buenaventura. When that mission was to be established earlier, fifteen soldiers were stipulated, but twelve will be sufficient, and let us give this glory to God that along the channel the name of Jesus will begin to be heard and His Excellency, no doubt, will greatly rejoice over it.

But Rivera answered, "Not more than six!" All the missions founded to that time had but six guards and that number would be allowed for future missions unless contrary orders arrived from the viceroy.

Stunned, Serra asked, "Then we have not agreed on ten?" "No, no," retorted Rivera, "only on six!"

Serra sat back, silent, but deeply disappointed. He reminded the commander that though the existing missions had only six soldiers for protection, no mission had actually been founded with so few.

Rivera now stated for the first time what he had known all along: that the viceroy had definitely written the ultimate number of regularly placed guards would be only six. Serra later wrote, "I, who was centered on my 'thirteen' mistakenly said, 'The viceroy does not say that.'" Rivera rejoined, 'Yes he does!' And I shouted, 'He does not!'"

Flushed, Rivera started pacing the room, a man whose pride and honor had been wounded. He spoke about his many years of service to the king, how he had honorably served in the army, and how he had never been reprimanded by the viceroys under whom he served. Now, this father president, a man of prayer and a doctor of sacred theology, had impugned his integrity. Serra listened quietly, "It seemed to me better to let his anger wear itself out."

Flushed, Rivera sat down, saying nothing. After a few moments, Serra began to speak:

Señor Don Fernando, even if other considerations do not suffice to convince you that it was neither my intention nor my desire to anger you and much less to obscure your honor, at least this much you may hold for the present; that I came here to ask you for favors and insults are not the means to obtain them. I did not come here with the intention of speaking about the missions of the San Francisco area for the means therefore are lacking. I came to speak about the missions on the Channel and this by order of the viceroy. By mere chance, and because you brought the matter up, we spoke of . . . the thirteen soldiers. The matter being so, all of a sudden it turned out to be six men instead, without your saying you had a letter.

At this point, Rivera pulled out Bucareli's letter in the clear, neat handwriting of the viceroy's secretary, plainly stating that six soldiers were to constitute the guard for each of the proposed missions. Serra wrote:

As if accused by his own conscience for not having undeceived us for so long a time, he showed us a folded sheet of paper, saying that he was going to write us that information and thus the matter would be clarified since he had not informed us about it before the conference started.

Of course, with the proof of the letter on the table, the comandante had cornered the padre presidente in a mistake. Writing of the embarrassing event to the guardian of San Fernando, Junípero observed: "And they call me lector (reader)," alluding to his official title as a professor in the Franciscan order.

The next morning, after mass, Rivera again met with Serra, Lasuén, and Murguía. Junípero's sermon had been based upon the text of love for one's neighbor; he pleaded with the audience to bear molestations with patience, to forgive injuries, and to live in peace. Now, Serra listened quietly as the comandante reiterated that on the basis of the viceroy's instructions, only six soldiers would be assigned as guard for the development of new missions. Everyone present realized that Mission San Buenaventura could not be founded; the nature and number of the area's Indians required at least ten or twelve soldiers for protection. Therefore, the only compromise possible, claimed Rivera, was to establish Mission San Juan Capistrano, midway between San Gabriel and San Diego. The padre president reluctantly nodded in agreement.

When Serra and Murguía left the presidio that Sunday morning, "after a few peaceful words with the officer," Junípero sincerely believed that Rivera had been pacified. But a few days later, both Father Lasuén and Father Dumetz informed him that the comandante was still very angry. Determined to resolve the matter once and for all, Junípero walked back to Monterey the following Sunday and, after mass, met with the officer alone in his room. When asked why he remained resentful, Rivera replied that he had many reasons. Serra insisted upon hearing them all. Citing Saint Bonaventure, who had written that a man's actions were often different from his motives, Junípero explained that from the beginning he had had no intention of insulting the comandante. Yet, if his words or actions had inadvertently done so, he was sorry. But only by hearing Rivera's complaints could he be in a position to apologize and make amends.

Rivera then related his resentments, some dating back several years. Most of these dealt with rations, supplies, mission servants, Serra's letters of complaint to the viceroy and the guardian, and most important of all, the issue of San Buenaventura. As far as the comandante was concerned, it would be difficult to iron things out. Therefore, all future discussions would be handled in writing. Sad and disappointed, Junípero returned to Carmel where he wrote the guardian:

We have gone back to writing, which is the greatest of all my labors, an occupation which has been the most repugnant occupation in all my life; and sad to say, it seems to me that I am more a scribe than a missionary; even so, I realize that I do not write as much as I should.

Even when they began putting things in writing, misunderstandings arose. In late September 1775, they decided to give up corresponding in order to exchange views verbally. But again the situation grew explosive. Once more, they returned to corresponding; again the situation grew even worse. Bucareli tried admonishing them both by letter but was quite ineffective. Serra apologized repeatedly to Rivera for his own faults and mistakes, and was willing to forgive and forget. But two men so different in temperament could never work together smoothly.

Their differences were personal, but they were also rooted in the conflict between the right of a religious order to set its own goals and conduct its own affairs and the military sense of responsibility for the security of Spain's new land. Rivera wrote to the guardian at San Fernando, where he had received hospitality:

It is not possible to give satisfaction or to please people in everything in this place. Your Reverence may well rest assured in this matter and if you still retain any doubt, then come here and take a walk about the place. Let me hand you my *bastón* [badge of military authority], and I am willing to wager that neither will Your Reverence succeed. Let this news suffice . . . a padre can think as a religious. I must think as a Christian. Moreover, I have the obligation of thinking as a captain and in all matters I have to render an account. The padre is free in this regard.

In another letter on the same day, he said, "There are times when I am all out and somewhat disconsolate in not being able to satisfy and condescend to all that the Father President wants."

CHAPTER TWENTY-ONE

FIRE AND BLOOD
IN SAN DIEGO

With the decision made to establish Mission San Juan Capistrano, Father Fermín Francisco de Lasuén left Monterey to join Father Gregorio Amurrió at San Luis Obispo. They traveled together as far south as Mission San Gabriel, and leaving Amurrió there to assemble the necessary furnishings for the future mission, Lasuén rode on to San Diego with Lieutenant Ortega to make the final arrangements.

Lasuén, Ortega, and a few soldiers reconnoitered the site between San Gabriel and San Diego. After dispatching his report to Serra, Lasuén returned to San Gabriel to assist in moving to the new mission.

Meanwhile, in October of 1775, a number of problems had arisen at Mission San Diego over the disciplining of a few Indians. During the previous year, the mission had been moved from the Presidio Hill site four miles into the valley, where abundant water rendered the land more suitable for agriculture. However the harvest was still very small. For that reason, although some four hundred Indians had been baptized since the founding of the mission, most of them could not live there. Instead, they lived in nearby rancherías, where they were led in prayer by the better instructed among them. From the beginning of Serra's spiritual conquest, the Diegueños had proven most difficult to bring under mission influence.

On October 2, Father Luís Jayme and Vicente Fuster allowed some of the mission Indians to leave the grounds for a day's excursion into the nearby hills. Among those leaving was Carlos, chief of the village nearest the mission, and his brother, Francisco. On the open road, the brothers robbed two elderly non-Christian Indian women of their bags of seeds and fish. A complaint was made to the padres, and when Carlos and Francisco heard about it, they fled during the night, fearful of punishment for their thievery. Five others of rank joined them. Not long afterward, word reached the mission that they all had been killed. Ortega dispatched soldiers to investigate and learned that they were still alive. Ortega did not press the search, since he had to send troops to Lasuén to help establish Mission San Juan Capistrano.

But Indians were not Ortega's only problem. His own soldiers objected to going out to establish the new mission. Realizing that supplies were meager, they feared they would have less to eat there than at San Diego. They adamantly refused to help in constructing the initial buildings—even though Ortega explained that he and the padres would assist in the work. After all, the king was not paying them to be common laborers. Realizing he might have a mutiny on his hands, Ortega unsheathed his sword and, with all his authority, demanded: "Am I commanding here loyal servants of the king or traitors? Are you servants of His Majesty?" At first no one responded. Then slowly they indicated they were ready to do as commanded. On October 19, Ortega, Lasuén, and twelve soldiers left San Diego for San Juan Capistrano. Nine soldiers and a sergeant would remain at the new mission; Ortega and three others would return to San Diego.

The party arrived at the chosen site on October 29. The following morning the cross was raised and blessed, and mass was celebrated in a hastily constructed *enramada*. The Indians appeared pleased. Soon, most were helping the Spaniards cut timbers for the chapel and dwellings. By the time Father Amurrió arrived with the furnishings and cattle eight days later, a corral had been built, the buildings laid out, and wood cut and tule gathered.

That same day, a messenger brought the news that Indians had attacked and burned Mission San Diego.

Throughout early October, Carlos and his confederates had gone from one village to another inciting revolt. Late in the month, a few Indians had been flogged at the mission for attending a pagan dance, and Father Fuster had threatened to set fire to their village unless they moved it away. A number of angry villagers joined the runaways.

In the days that followed, the padres were warned on several occasions that an attack on the mission was imminent. Father Jayme had sent Diego Paje, the mission's Indian interpreter, into the hills to plead with Carlos and his band to return, and Paje had succeeded in persuading two of them to come back. Told that there was a plot brewing to massacre all the missionaries and soldiers, Jayme refused to believe it. He simply loved the Indians too much to lend any credence to such a tale and admonished those who brought it for their lies. Jayme, in fact, tended to attribute any bad qualities among the Indians to the bad example set by the Spanish. Earlier he had written Palóu,

I feel very deeply about the fact that what the devil does not succeed in accomplishing among the pagans is accomplished by Christians.... The uprisings which have occurred in some of the rancherías closest to us were due to the fact that the soldiers had dishonored the wives of some of the Indians.

Fearing they would still receive severe punishment for the thefts, Carlos and his accomplices made their preparations to attack the mission and presidio on the night of the full moon. Between six hundred and a thousand Indians were to be involved from over forty rancherías. Half of them would surround the mission; the others would move down the valley and attack the presidio. The flames of the burning presidio would signal the attack on the mission. All the Spaniards were to be killed. A group of women would accompany the warriors and carry whatever loot they could into the hills.

On the evening of November 4, 1775, a small group of Christian Indians arrived at Mission San Diego to stay overnight in order to hear mass the next morning. The padres retired to their respective quarters: Fuster to the warehouse and Jayme to the padres' structure. The four soldiers, two blacksmiths, the carpenter, and the visiting son and nephew of the lieutenant retired to their quarters. It was a brilliantly moonlit night, the weather chill enough for an open fire outside the guardhouse. Undetected, six hundred or more Indians reached the mission between one and one-thirty in the morning. Of these, half continued down the valley road toward the presidio.

The story of what happened next has been told by Palóu and others, but that of Father Vicente Fuster is the sole eye witness account.

The Indians first surrounded the huts of the Christian Indians, threatening them with death if they tried to escape. This was accomplished without the guards noticing anything. Meanwhile, other Indians crept into the church, removing the statues of the Immaculate Conception and Saint Joseph and handing them to the waiting women. Although chests filled with vestments and church furnishings in the sacristy were broken into, even that noise failed to attract the guards. Father Fuster states, "The sentinels were sound alseep."

One of the attackers ignited his firebrand at the bonfire outside the guardhouse and ran about, touching it to nearby structures. Soon, the crackling flames awakened the missionaries, the soldiers, and the other Spaniards.

Fuster jumped from his bed and raced toward the soldiers' barracks, where he found the troops already firing their muskets. The others, except for Jayme, also gathered there for protection. One of the soldiers, without a leather jacket, was already slumped on the floor, gravely wounded. Soon, another soldier was put out of action. The carpenter, Urcelino, who had been ill, grabbed a musket but was pierced by an arrow. He cried out, "Ha, Indian, you have killed me.

God forgive you!" He was only wounded, but he died five days later.

When aroused by the flames, Father Jayme walked calmly toward the Indians with his customary greeting, "Love God, my children." They seized him and pushed him to a nearby gully. There, they stripped him to his underwear and shot more than a dozen arrows into him. They finished by pulverizing his face with clubs and stones.

With the guardhouse now in flames, Fuster and the others dashed toward the padres' quarters, unable to reach it, they took refuge in a one-room building completed just the day before. From here, the soldiers continued to fire. Worried that he had not seen Jayme since the attack began, Fuster sneaked away from the shelter and ran to the padre's sleeping quarters, which were already burning. He fought his way through the flames only to find the bed empty. Fuster later realized how fortunate he had been that the burning roof timbers did not fall and crush him as he came running out.

Returning to the barricaded structure from which the soldiers were firing, Fuster was met by one of the men asking where the mission powder was kept for shooting off the cannon on festive occasions. Fuster turned and ran to the already burning warehouse where it was stored and brought out the untouched box. The soldier took what powder he needed and they put the box in the open, away from the fire. Fuster shouted for everyone to retreat to the nearby kitchen, which was enclosed on three sides by adobe walls. They all scrambled over to it carrying the powder and guns and used trunks of clothing to barricade the open side.

Soon, however, the attacking Indians concentrated all their ferocity on the kitchen. So great was their deluge "of arrows, stones, chunks of adobe, and firebrands thrown at us that it seemed they intended to bury us." But from this new vantage point, the soldiers were able to wound a number of their attackers. During the battle, one of the soldiers received nine arrow wounds; another, three; and another, four. Fuster later wrote Serra,

> It is impossible to estimate for Your Reverence the number of arrows that were aimed at my head and which terminated their flight in the adobes, but thanks be to God not a single one hit me.

One arrow actually struck a cushion he was using to protect his face. The padre pulled it out himself.

> For the greater relief of their anxiety, the soldiers handed me the box of powder. Can Your Reverence imagine how great was the affliction of all of us in seeing so many flames above the soldiers because of the many firebrands thrown at us and the danger of the powder being ignited?

As the peril became great, Fuster spoke to the soldiers, who were still firing their weapons:

> Comrades, the situation is very bad, the enemy numerous, we but few. Let us have recourse to God and to Mary Most Holy. Let us truly ask this Holy Mother to favor us, to repress the fury of our enemies, and to allow us to be victorious over them. To obtain this favor, I on my part promise to fast nine Saturdays and to celebrate nine holy Masses in her honor.

The soldiers also promised to fast and to hear the masses.

> And it seems that the Holy Mother sensibly heard our supplications, for many times I took the burning firebrands right off the top of the powder bag. In this place where I was, I received a terrible blow from a stone which hit me on the shoulder and though I felt the pain of the blow, I tried not to show it outwardly in order not to afflict the others with me nor did I say anything about it until after two days when it became necessary to apply some ointment of oil.

Now, the defenders longed for the light of morning. "So long did the night seem," wrote Fuster, "that it appeared like enduring the pains of purgatory." During the hours before daybreak, the rain of arrows lessened, although a shower of stones, rocks, and firebrands continued. Fuster worried that the Indians would make one last attempt to kill them all before morning. Just as a faint glow began to lighten the eastern sky, a hail of arrows descended upon them.

> [I heard] those who had formerly been my faithful children giving orders that all of us should be done away with, . . . But a well-aimed shot from a musket unbraved them and made them flee in a hurry.

With this final attack, the battle ended. Those who were supposed to attack the presidio had not done so, since they saw the mission on fire and feared the presidio's soldiers had been alerted by the flames. After pausing to pillage the mission, the Indians quickly retreated into the hills.

Emerging from the adobe shelter, Fuster began shouting for Jayme. Upon recognizing two of the Christian Indians running toward him, he asked, "Where is Father Luís?" They responded, "We do not know." "Their answer," wrote Fuster, "was a penetrating sword piercing my heart." Then slowly, Christian Indian women began appearing, sad and distressed. Indians from adjacent villages came carrying weapons, assuring the padre they had pursued the attackers and they were far away.

> I came forth from that kitchen of sorrow and when I stood before them, they embraced me and acknowledge me as their father. I cannot adequately describe this action for I do not know if anxiety or joy filled me the most.

Fuster asked if they would help him find Jayme. Then he sent the other Indians out to search for the animals, to alert the presidio soldiers, and to bring water to put out the fires that were still burning. Those who went to the arroyo for water found the lifeless, mutilated body of Jayme and ran back to Fuster.

Great was my sorrow when I laid my eyes upon his person for I saw him totally disfigured. I realized his death had been a most cruel one which indeed was to the liking of the barbarians. I saw that he was entirely naked except for the drawers that he wore, his chest and body pitted like a sieve from the savage blows . . . of the clubs and stones. Finally, I recognized him as Father Luís only insofar as my eyes noted the whiteness of his skin and the tonsure of his head. It is fortunate that they did not scalp him as is customary among these barbarians when they kill their enemies.

Hardly had I looked at my departed Father and companion when I fainted nor did I return to my senses for some time. Who knows what would have happened to me if the Indian women, when they saw me fall on the body of the deceased Father, had not caught me in their arms. They took care of me in this manner until they could give me water to drink, and having washed my face with it, I returned to my senses. It is not possible for my quill to describe the anguish and sorrow I felt for there is a great difference between experiencing something and describing it. When I thought over the loss of my companion whom I loved and reverenced, my own lukewarmness confounded me when I recalled the excellence of his virtues. However, "The Lord gave; the Lord took away; blessed by the name of the Lord."

After Fuster revived, everyone at the mission retired to the presidio, carrying in a sorrowful procession the bodies of Father Jayme and the blacksmith José Romero. Also borne on stretchers were two of the more seriously injured soldiers—one of them José Arroyo, Ortega's nephew—and the wounded carpenter Urcelino, who died within a few days. Fuster walked the four miles alongside the stretcher bearing his friend's body. Jayme had been only thirty-five years old at his death.

The funerals were held on November 6, and afterward soldiers were sent to salvage what they could from the mission—door hinges, field instruments, and any wheat that had not been burned. Not many animals had been killed, but they had been scattered and had to be rounded up.

Fuster sent word to Ortega at San Juan Capistrano and to San Gabriel, asking one of the fathers to come down. Ortega and Lasuén decided their plans for San Juan Capistrano would have to be abandoned for the time being: The site was too exposed and the local Indians had withdrawn and appeared to be preparing hostile action.

Leaving nine soldiers to escort Lasuén and the cattle and supplies back to the presidio the next morning, Ortega hastily departed as the sun was setting on November 8. Riding hard through the night, he reached the presidio at San Diego by eleven o'clock the next morning. Padres, soldiers, cattle, and supplies were to follow more slowly, under orders to stay close together and exercise great vigilance along the way. The expedition arrived in San Diego at nightfall on the eleventh. The arrival of Lasuén and Amurrío brought some solace to Fuster.

All through November an attack on the presidio by over a thousand Indians was expected. Loyal Christian Indians reported that the first assault had been merely an attempt to find out if the soliders possessed true valor and that an attack on the presidio would be next. But nothing further materialized. Ortega investigated, and was eventually satisfied that Fuster was correct in believing that the Indians of the mission village and three, at least, of the forty rancherías had remained loyal.

Meanwhile, from the gutted mission, some forty small sacks of wheat had been salvaged. The burned censer, chalice, ciborium, cruets, oilstocks, and other items were brought to the presidio. Fuster decided to send the censer to Serra to demonstrate the intensity of the fire. The other articles would be dispatched to the College of San Fernando.

Not until the end of the month was the news of the tragic event relayed to Rivera and Serra. Ortega apparently felt he could not spare a single soldier for the overland trip to Monterey. Fuster urged both Serra and Rivera to come down to San Diego as soon as possible. Belatedly, the tale of California's first major disaster was now being carried by six soldiers up the four hundred fifty miles of El Camino Real.

The couriers arrived around eight o'clock on the night of December 13, and Ortega's letter was immediately handed to Captain Rivera, who was dining. The comandante read the account of the disaster and immediately rode over the hill to Carmel. Serra received the news just after nine. Rivera's announcement was shocking:

> Father President, I have just received an ominous report from San Diego which obliges me to set forth immediately on the road for that place; for the Indians have rebelled, burned the mission, and killed Father Fray Luís.

After a stunned silence, Serra, in a hoarse voice, whispered, "Thanks be to God. Now that the terrain has been watered by blood, the conversion of the San Diego Indians will take place." Then, the padre presidente fell to his knees and in prayer paraphrased Tertullian's "*Sanguis martyrum, semen Christianorum,*" "The blood of martyrs is the seed of the Church." Serra told the comandante that a solemn requiem High Mass for the soul of Jayme would be celebrated the next day and invited the captain and his soldiers to be present. Rivera declined, saying that he would be preparing to leave for San Diego. Junípero suggested that a padre accompany him. But Rivera rejected the idea, on the grounds that he intended to travel as fast and as light as possible and not even rest at the missions along the route.

"With this answer," wrote Serra, "my intention to go down there to aid in the re-establishment of the two missions, destroyed by one blow, was frustrated."

Since the padre presidente did not have time to write instructions to the fathers at the presidio and Mission San Gabriel, and since Rivera would undoubtedly hold an investigation and report its results to the viceroy, Serra immediately wrote to Bucareli himself:

I leave all to God for in human affairs I have no other refuge but the authority of Your Excellency. I tenderly supplicate you to give orders that the two missions be restored in all their completeness as soon as possible in their respective locales. Since we are living in a vale of tears, not all news or events can be happy ones.

Serra feared that the tragedy would interfere with mission development, as it had at San Sabá, where "the soldiers are still in their presidios and the Indians in their paganism." There, the viceroy had insisted on the Indians being punished before the mission could continue. Toward the end of his long statement, he appealed to the viceroy:

Your Excellency, one of the principal items I requested from the visitor-general at the beginning of these conquests was that in case the Indians, whether pagans or Christians, would kill me, they should be pardoned. And I have been most anxious to renew this request as quickly as possible. I want to see a formal decree from Your Excellency on the said matter for me and the other religious, present and future, and it will give me special consolation to have it in my hands during the years that God may deign to add to my life.

It is indeed just that the soldiers guard and accompany the missionary as long as he lives as the very apple of their eyes, nor am I one to look upon this favor with disdain; but if despite this the Indians should kill a missionary, what good are we going to obtain by waging a military campaign against them? The military will answer me by saying: "We will inflict an exemplary punishment on them so that they will not kill others." To this I reply: "To prevent the Indians from killing others let the soldier protect us in better fashion than they did the now deceased padre and allow the murderer to live so that he can be saved." This is the purpose of our coming here and the title which justifies our presence here. It should be conveyed to the murderer, after some moderate punishment, that he is forgiven and thus we shall fulfill our [Christian] law which commands us to forgive injuries and not to seek the [sinner's] death, but his eternal salvation.

Serra, in anticipation of his own possible martyrdom, had already forgiven his potential murderers. Bucareli was not only deeply touched by his plea but also receptive to his idea.

After seventeen days of hard riding, the last through heavy rains, Rivera and his ten soldiers reached Mission San Gabriel around midnight on January 3, 1776. Before the drenched commander could dismount and change his clothes, he received the news that Lieutenant Colonel Juan Bautista de Anza and his colonists were expected soon. Late the next morning, the Anza expedition, one hundred seventy-seven in number—including Father Pedro Font, soldiers, and colonists—arrived at San Gabriel. The intrepid guide once again was Padre Francisco Garcés from Mission San Xavier del Bac on the desert near present-day Tucson, Arizona. The padre had traced the route across the vast Mojave Desert two years previously, and a prudent Anza considered his assistance invaluable because of his close friendship with and understanding of the Indians along the trail. As sad as the situation was in San Diego, the mission bells rang in celebration of this second success of an expedition in reaching Alta California from Sonora overland.

Anza now learned of the tragedy. He not only granted the soldiers Rivera asked to borrow, but also offered to accompany the commander to San Diego. Rivera needed all the manpower he could gather, since he was determined to capture the rebels, restore peace and tranquillity, and ensure the presidio against future Indian attacks.

After a delay of a month and a half, the Anza expedition departed Mission San Gabriel for Monterey on Ash Wednesday, February 21, 1776. Slowly wending their way along the coast were Captain Anza; Lieutenant José Joaquín Moraga, second in command; Manuel Vidal, the commissary; Father Pedro Font, diarist and chaplain (cousin of Fray Pablo Font who knew and wrote about Serra at the College of San Fernando); ten soldiers as escorts; twenty new recruits for Monterey and their wives, children, and servants (one hundred six in number); twenty muleteers; four families of settlers (seventeen persons); one hundred forty mules loaded with baggage and provisions; and four hundred fifty saddle animals. What a spectacle the cavalcade must have made as it passed over the rolling plains of what is now Los Angeles County, along the Santa Barbara Channel, up the coast to Point Arguello, over the hills to San Luís Obispo, and then north through the Salinas River Valley. As word spread of the passage, Indians from all the nearest rancherías flocked down to greet them, slowing their progress. Three children were born along the way; one woman died in childbirth. Without other incident, the expedition arrived in Monterey at four-thirty on Sunday afternoon, March 10.

The small presidio had never seen such a crowd of people and animals. Tents were erected in the plaza and fortunately, its overflowing

Mission Carmel 1884. The present building at Carmel was begun in 1793 and dedicated in 1797. After falling into ruins in the 1840s it was restored in 1884, the year of this photograph.

larders were able to sustain the large number. That evening was devoted to great rejoicing. Early the following morning, Fathers Serra, Palóu, Murguía, Cambón, and de la Peña walked over the hills from Carmel to greet Anza and the colonists, while Crespí and Pieras remained behind at the mission. In the Monterey chapel, Father Font sang the High Mass in thanksgiving for their safe journey. The four fathers from Carmel composed the choir, and presidio soldiers fired salvos and volleys, "all this causing tears of joy to flow."

Serra invited Anza and Font to San Carlos, an invitation that was eagerly accepted. Font noted in his diary, "It was decided that we should go to the mission of Carmel to yield to the urging of the Reverend Father President, but principally because in the presidio there was no place for us to lodge."

At the mission later that afternoon, seven padres welcomed the visitors "with singular joy" and "the festive peals of the good bells." At the church door, Father Murguía officially received the party. Font sprinkled Anza with holy water; then, after venerating the cross, everyone entered the church in procession and sang the Te Deum. After offering thanks there, the visitors were shown to their guest quarters.

The next morning, Font toured the mission and grounds, noting in his journal that the site had been an excellent choice, although fog was common. Situated on a slight rise of land near the Carmel River and the Pacific Ocean, Mission San Carlos had "a rather spacious and well-made church" built of palisades and tule. A few simple oil paintings hung on the walls. The padres lived in three adobe rooms adjacent to the church. Font noted that about four hundred Indians lived at the mission. He praised the sardines and salmon caught in the bay.

It is a most beautiful site and pleasing to the view because it is so near the sea and in a country so charming and flower covered that it is a marvel . . . In short, although the rest of the missions are very good, this one seemed to me the best of all.

About his walk through the garden just a stone's throw away from the mission, Font observed:

> It is a delight to see it so clean and full of vegetables, cared for by Father Palóu with such diligence that he spent all the day working in it and had it very well laid out.

Bordered with gillyflowers in bloom, the gardens contained cauliflower, lettuce, and other vegetables and herbs.

> And the finest thing about that country is that without irrigation all such vegetables are raised than which there are no better in Mexico. Indeed, one squash grown here would ordinarily last two or three days.

In the nearby fields were crops of wheat, barley, beans, chickpeas, and lentils. "It was really a benediction of God to see such fine fields planted without irrigation." It would be another five years before Mission San Carlos would have an aqueduct leading from the river to the fields. Until then, all plants and crops had to be watered by hand.

Anza and Font remained at the mission as Serra's guests. "Everyone knows," wrote Junípero, "that I did my best to give [them] a welcome hospitality." The table was set with careful attention. When Anza arrived, it was Lenten season and a yearling sheep was killed. When offered jerked beef, Anza's cook informed the padre that his master did not eat that kind of meat. Chickens were therefore provided until the lieutenant colonel departed for San Francisco. After Easter, a cow was slaughtered so that Anza could have fresh meat, though Serra, the padres, and the mission Indians did not eat as well. For the journey north, Anza was provided cured and fresh salmon, vegetables, and spices. "We made a general offering of everything we had here," Serra wrote the guardian in San Fernando.

Meanwhile, Pedro Font and Junípero Serra had ample opportunity to talk over recent developments in California. Foremost in their minds was the recent tragedy at San Diego. It was now obvious that the veneer of Christianity there had proven to be a thin one. In a sense, the attack was a vindication of the fears expressed years earlier by Fages. It had to be acknowledged that in their failure to follow up the initial attack, the Indians had lost an opportunity to permanently destroy all the Spanish settlements in California, an enormous investment for Spain's weakened economy during the past six years. Only seventy soldiers were guarding the five missions and two presidios along the 500-mile coastal strip.

It appeared to Font, who had visited the tragic scene and spoken with Father Fuster, that Indians from over fifty rancherías had taken part in the attack. What was especially difficult for Serra to believe was the fact that some of the mission structures had been ransacked before the general attack, indicating possible treachery on the part of some of the Christianized Indians.

On an equally tragic note, the discussion turned to what had recently occurred at San Gabriel. The wife of an Indian chief from a nearby ranchería had been raped by one of the mission soldiers. The chief later attacked the guilty guard, firing an arrow that bounced off the man's leather shield. In the fight that followed, the chief was killed and his head cut off and impaled upon a pole to warn off other members of his tribe. Fortunately, the Indians were pacified by the padres, who were able to win back their confidence. Later, the son of the slain chief was among the first to come forth for baptism.

Font also informed Serra about the personal differences that existed between Anza and Rivera. Anza knew that the comandante was opposed to establishing new missions in Alta California, but he planned to reconnoiter the San Francisco peninsula anyway in order to place a presidio and mission there. Furthermore, Rivera had complained to Anza about Serra. "I have never seen a priest more zealous for founding missions than this Father President. He thinks of nothing but founding missions, no matter how or at what expense they are established." Serra also learned for the first time the reason for Rivera's two-year grudge against José Ortega. Both he and the lieutenant had served together in Baja and both had come north in the earlier Portolá expeditions. Rivera's anger at Ortega stemmed from Serra's having nominated the one-time sergeant for military commander of Alta California instead of Rivera.

The long discussion ended on a happier note, however. Serra was able to inform Father Font that he had presided over the marriage of Juan Evangelista, whom Font had met while the young boy was at the College of San Fernando three years before. The padre presidente was proud of the fact that he had not only baptized his one-time servant in March of 1771 but had also presided at his marriage just a few months before on December 2, 1775.

At three o'clock on the afternoon of March 22, Anza and Font bade goodby to the padres and returned to Monterey to leave on an initial expedition to reconnoiter the San Francisco area for a suitable mission site.

Meanwhile, in San Diego, Rivera was busy investigating the rebellion. Carlos was reported to be in the neighborhood, although thus far he had eluded capture. However, during the night of March 27, he sneaked onto the presidio grounds and hovered around the improvised church, remaining undetected. Early the next morning, when Father Fuster went into the chapel to offer mass, he discovered Carlos behind the altar. The Indian ringleader was shrewd enough to realize that it might be more prudent to make contact with a padre before giving himself up. Furthermore, as a Christian convert, he may have had some knowledge about the right of asylum.

The right of such sanctuary dates back to ancient times. It is the right of those guilty of crimes to take refuge in a church and not be forcibly extricated by civil authorities except under certain conditions. Authorities of the Catholic church had always insisted that its sacred places were immune from civil intrusion, and this was written into the law of Christian countries, including, of course, Spain. However, opposition was growing and in the two centuries preceding, four popes had issued legislation limiting the right of asylum.

After hiding Carlos in the chapel and offering mass, Fuster returned to his quarters and consulted with Fathers Amurrió and Lasuén. Then, he calmly walked to Rivera's headquarters and informed the comandante, "Señor, let us handle things in peace and quietude. I am notifying you that Carlos has taken refuge in the church." This was a startling announcement. After a few moments of reflection, Rivera replied, "Let Your Reverence keep him there. I am caught unawares. I will think the matter over and determine as to how I shall proceed." When Rivera indicated he might not recognize the right of asylum, Fuster ended the conversation by saying, "I am a minister without faculties in this regard; in case of doubt, the cause must go to the bishop who has the competent jurisdiction."

Late that afternoon, Rivera reached a decision. He sent a note asking that Fuster hand Carlos over to him before sundown. Anticipating the padre's objections on the basis of canon law, Rivera included his reasons for making the request.

After consulting Lasuén and Amurrió, Fuster prepared a written response.

> I ought to advise you, in case you do not know it, concerning the major excommunication promulgated by Popes Gregory XIV and Benedict XIII against those who command and execute an act against those who have sought asylum.

Fuster reiterated that as a simple priest he had no power to hand over Carlos and that the matter would have to be decided by the bishop in Guadalajara. Before sending his reply to Rivera, Fuster made a copy for the Franciscan archives in San Fernando and had Lasuén and Amurrió sign it.

Upon receiving Fuster's reply, Rivera summoned his soldiers and surrounded the church. Girded with a sword, and holding his baton of authority in one hand and a lighted candle in the other, Rivera entered the chapel, seized Carlos, and dragged him away to the guardhouse, where he was put in stocks.

The three padres watched the drama from the door of their dwelling. Fuster protested loudly against the action, exclaiming that the comandante and all those participating in the arrest were now excommunicated. "All right, padre," Rivera shouted back. "Your Reverence may protest, but there goes the protest," pointing to the prisoner being shoved toward the guardhouse.

In the days that followed, Fuster appealed to the commander in the name of the church, the king, and the viceroy to return the prisoner. Only in that way "can you partially repair the injury you have done to the Church by your violent extraction." The padre argued that Carlos was no longer a threat, since the chief had roamed the area for five months without inciting new attacks and finally came of his own accord to seek refuge in the church. "What misfortune do you now expect?" Fuster demanded.

With Carlos in the stockade, Rivera traveled to Monterey to see Serra about his excommunication. Fuster asked the comandante to deliver to the padre presidente a sealed envelope (containing copies of the missives he sent to the viceroy in Mexico City) and a personal letter to Serra. The evening before his departure, Rivera wrote to his military friends in Mexico City that he was in the midst of "the greatest tribulation and sorrow" he had ever experienced.

The comandante arrived in Monterey on the night of April 15 and the next morning sent word to Serra of his presence. Fathers Serra, Murguía, Cambón, and de la Peña immediately walked over from Mission San Carlos to greet him. Rivera handed Serra the two letters sent by Fuster. Noticing that the seals were broken, Serra asked why. Rivera smiled and apologized, saying they had been broken unintentionally along the road. However, he was prepared to take an oath that he had no knowledge of the letters' contents. Junípero took his word for it, saying he required no such oath. After all, the comandante could not afford to complicate matters by opening the personal mail of the padres. Serra and the other friars then listened to Rivera's story. The padre presidente told the commander that he would take the documents back to the mission, read them carefully, study the issue involved, and provide him with a response within a few days.

At the mission, Junípero and the other fathers carefully read over the documents and came to the unanimous conclusion that Fuster had been correct in excommunicating the comandante. Serra delivered his opinion to Rivera through Father de la Peña on April 17. Since Anza was no farther south than Mission San Antonio de Padua on his way back to Mexico City, Serra sent Father Cambón after him with all the letters from Fuster, asking that he deliver them to the guardian at San Fernando.

Since there was no higher ecclesiastical authority in California to appeal to, Rivera accepted Serra's verdict. The comandante returned to San Diego, restored Carlos to the church, and, on May 18, was absolved from the censure of excommunication by his one-time friend, Fermín Lasuén. The case had come to a conclusion, but the repercussions would be felt for some time.

In retrospect, it is difficult to accuse Fernando de Rivera y Moncada of a crime, since the commander believed he was acting in good faith on a precedent set in Baja California. Padre Vicente Fuster was under the clear impression that he was defending an ecclesiastical right asserted and upheld over centuries in multiple papal documents. In the interests of defending the right of asylum, and of protecting the fugitive Carlos, it appears the friar may have overreacted. In any event, at the end of that summer, Bucareli's pardon arrived. And responding to Serra's letter of months before asking forgiveness for the insurgents, the viceroy ordered that any Indians still incarcerated be released immediately so that true peace would return.

CHAPTER TWENTY-TWO

REBUILDING
AND EXPANSION

Twice Rivera had foiled Serra's attempts to get to San Diego. Not until seven months after Jayme's tragic death did the father president arrive to console his distressed missionaries, and not with an escort of soldiers but on board the *San Antonio*.

When the packet boat arrived in San Diego harbor on July 11, 1776, Comandante Rivera and Fathers Lasuén and Amurrió scaled the deck ladder and were greeted by the ship's officers. Captain Peréz noticed that when Rivera learned that Serra was an unexpected passenger, a "great fear" seized him.

Apparently, Rivera was reacting to a rumor that Serra was planning another trip to Mexico City. The comandante still recalled the results of his previous pilgrimage to the palace of the viceroy. Bucareli's esteem for Junípero and his general concurrence with Serra's proposals were already known. Rivera must have feared that the viceroy would take Serra's side against him on every issue.

A week or so later, Serra and a group of nearly thirty sailors and workmen, protected by six soldiers, marched out to the ruined mission in the valley. The workers carried molds for making adobe bricks and were armed with guns and pistols. For nearly three weeks, they worked with Indians, digging, excavating stones, and making over seven thousand adobe bricks. These, plus those salvaged from the burned-out buildings, would be used for the walls of the new structures. While Serra was toiling alongside the sailors and laborers, word arrived that Rivera had urgently ordered everyone to return to the presidio. A report had been received that Indians were going to attack the mission. Immediately, camp was broken and they all returned to the presidio.

According to those around him, Rivera was in a confused state of

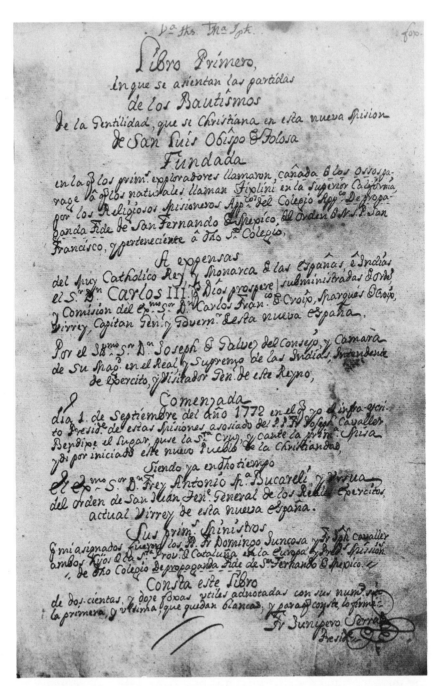

Title page of the Book of Baptisms for Mission San Luis Obispo, 1772. At the bottom is Serra's signature with his distinctive rubrica. The missions kept careful records of baptisms, marriages, and burials, as well as statistics on the mission economy.

mind. The embarrassment of the excommunication and the constant disagreement with Serra were taking their toll. The captain of the *San Antonio* overheard him say, "It seems to me these devils are trying to make me break with the fathers." At that point, Father Santa María responded jokingly, "Now, Señor, resist the temptation."

There is little question that Rivera's mind was turning tangled suspicions and hostilities into devils. The comandante felt his presence was necessary in San Diego, but thought he should be in San Francisco if a mission was to be founded there. He had no confidence in Ortega at San Diego and little in Moraga at San Francisco. And now, Serra's unexpected arrival and desire to reconstruct the destroyed mission further upset him.

Since Serra was forced to postpone rebuilding his gutted mission, he began gathering and examining the church goods ruined by the fire. A silver chalice with its paten and spoon were shipped to the College of San Fernando for repair. Some mission items were still in the hands of Indians in the nearby rancherías. Cautiously, the padres were attempting to retrieve them. On September 16, Junípero inscribed a new baptismal register to replace the burned one, adding to it a brief history of the mission and the names of those he and the other padres remembered having baptized. For the forgotten ones, he wrote: "May God, our Lord, have them inscribed in the book of life." In similar fashion, registers for burial and marriage were reconstructed. One cherished article salvaged from the ashes was a catechism in the Diegueño language that had been written by Father Jayme.

Toward the end of September, an Indian arrived at the presidio with information that Corporal Guillermo Carrillo was leaving Velicatá for San Diego with military reinforcements for service in Alta California. This was good news; it meant that Mission San Diego could be rebuilt and the abandoned plans for the mission at San Juan Capistrano reactivated.

A week or so later, when Carrillo and his troops were spotted on a hill overlooking the harbor a few miles south of San Diego, there was great rejoicing, and the bells rung in honor of their arrival. On September 29, the feast of Saint Michael, Junípero sang a High Mass "for the health and well-being of the viceroy."

To his surprise, there were three letters from Viceroy Bucareli in his mail. They indicated that the royal treasury, not the College of San Fernando, would pay all expenses for the delivery of supplies to the missions to be founded in the San Francisco area; that the twenty-five soldiers were being assigned to reinforce the mission guards; and that the Indians guilty of the November massacre were to be pardoned and Missions San Diego and San Juan Capistrano to be refounded.

Serra acknowledged the letters, saying:

Mission San Juan Capistrano. Founded in 1775 and named after Saint John Capistran, its church was architecturally the most ambitious of the Franciscans' undertakings, but it was virtually destroyed in the great earthquake of 1812. In this early photograph (ca. 1876), the ruins to the right are the remnants of the old stone church. The photograph also shows parts of the original mission structure such as the tiles on the cuartel roof (long, low building on left).

Words fail me to express my obligation to you and the pleasure, happiness, and consolation that are mine as a result of your measures and Your Excellency's gracious sentiments. I know that the only return that Your Excellency can expect from me is my cooperation and that of the other religious who are here furthering the advance of these spiritual conquests. For this purpose, our Catholic monarch (may God preserve him) contributes so liberally. May Your Excellency be assured that we shall pursue with all our strength the work we have begun.

Fired with new zeal and energy, Serra was once again ready to go forward. After Rivera and Lasuén departed for Monterey, Serra, Fuster, and a number of soldiers and Christian Indians again began to rebuild Mission San Diego. The seven thousand adobe bricks that had already been fashioned when Rivera interrupted construction were still waiting to be used. Since the foundations had already been laid, work could proceed, and before the winter rains set in, in fact, a great deal of planting could be accomplished. When Junípero was satisfied that matters were well in hand, he left for the narrow valley of San Juan Capistrano with Fray Amurrió, eleven soldiers, and eleven mules bearing packs and provisions.

Arriving there on October 27, 1776, Serra found still standing the cross Lasuén had erected the previous November. When Portolá passed this spot in 1769, he looked out over the vista and called it the "most inviting valley I have ever seen since the trees, water, pasturage, and so many wild grapevines remind me of a vineyard." Although Governor Portolá christened the area, Viceroy Bucareli chose the mission's patron saint, San Juan, surnamed Capistran, one of the few lawyers ever canonized.

The bells that Lasuén had hastily buried when the courier brought news of the revolt the year before were now unearthed. At the sound of them, the Indians came, and according to Palóu, rejoiced "to see that the fathers had returned to their territory." On November 1, the feast of All Saints, Serra sang a High Mass at an improvised altar in a rough shelter and declared California's seventh mission founded.

On the return trip from San Gabriel, where he had gone to bring supplies for the new mission, Serra had a narrow escape. Alone with a single soldier and a young Indian interpreter, he was walking over a low hill ahead of his small pack train when suddenly he came face to face with a large group of armed Indians in war paint, ready to strike. The Indian from San Gabriel shouted in their own tongue not to kill the padre. If they did, they would be pursued and killed by "the king's soldiers who are following close behind." The ruse worked, and the Indians hesitated, lowering their weapons. When they stepped back, Serra called to them, placed the sign of the cross over them all, and gave them glass beads. The party reached San Juan Capistrano without further incident. Later, Serra told Palóu that he thought his end had come.

Passage for Serra and Lasuén along the Santa Barbara Channel during early December was more of a problem than usual. Strong winds blew, and rain came down in torrents. The Pacific was especially rough, surf rolling in over the sand all the way to the base of the cliffs, making it impossible to ride along the flat beach. The party had to climb to the cliffs above. That forty-mile stretch was as trying as tiring. The assistance given by the channel Indians brought tears to Junípero's eyes. At one point, they transported him in their arms from the beach to the cliffs above. Later, large numbers accompanied the gray-robed padres as they rode and walked from ranchería to ranchería. Serra describes how they sang with him on the march. All this increased his feelings for the "Canaliños." Along the way, he tentatively selected the sites where new missions would be established: one at the southeastern end of the channel (San Buenaventura), another midway, at Santa Barbara, and the third near Point Concepción.

Serra and Lasuén probably spent Christmas at San Luís Obispo. There they caught up with Rivera and his guard; for some reason, the comandante was taking his time in returning to Monterey. While at San Luís Obispo, Junípero proposed that Lasuén take over Mission San Diego with any padre companion he desired. Even though Serra asked him to "sacrifice himself for the love of God," Lasuén said an assignment at San Diego was "against his inclination and he would go only if commanded under obedience." Lasuén remained at San Luís Obispo until, "bowing his neck to the yoke," he accepted transfer to San Diego, where subsequently he handled his stewardship exceedingly well.

Meanwhile, Serra left San Luís Obispo and without incident reached Mission San Carlos on January 12, 1777.

Awaiting Serra in his room was a small bundle of letters from Mexico City that Captain Anza had delivered a few months before. With the excitement of a voluntary exile eagerly awaiting news from home, the tired padre presidente quickly thumbed through the packet. When he spotted a patent, that official circular letter with its tell-tale yellow-brown markings, Junípero spontaneously accorded it precedence over all others. Since the epistle was from a major superior, his hands must have trembled a little out of apprehension.

As he carefully read and reread the lengthy statement, Serra was seized by conflicting emotions: distress, incredulity, frustration, and defeat. For nine years now he had been pushing himself to the limit, not only for the settlement of the land he had grown to cherish but, more importantly, for the people he was growing to love more each day. Now, the official gratitude of his religious superiors in Mexico City was equivalent to censure. It was a restriction of his responsibilities that left the title of padre presidente meaningless, without the authority to accomplish what was needed for the missions.

The lone and aging man slumped down in his chair, hurt and crushed. For the first time in his life he felt like retreating. Could he not resign in dignity and with distinction? Had he not volunteered for the foreign missions for a period of ten years and was he not about to complete two decades? Could he not plead old age? He was in his sixty-fifth year and could argue that he deserved retirement. And his health was not good. A bronchial problem he had suffered since childhood had become aggravated into an asthmatic condition. Furthermore, his sore and ulcerated foot and leg still caused him constant pain.

In anguish, the padre presidente knelt to pray. But, as he subsequently confessed to Fray Francisco Pangua, the guardian at San Fernando, his thoughts "turned to asking for retirement from so angelical an employment," especially since the patent had been signed by every member of the college's governing board. Certainly Serra was satisfied with the course his life had taken. It had been bountiful and, as hard as it had been, that life as a religious pioneer had given him a great deal. He was disappointed, but like so many others who have seen and experienced worth and worthlessness, Serra realized that the world into which he was born was one of cruelty and brutality, and at the same time one of divine beauty.

After protracted reflection kneeling before his Lord, a broken and dispirited Junípero Serra rose refreshed and rejuvenated in resolve:

I am not going to give up. While my first reaction is to resign, I am not doing so because I think it is better with the help of God to work toward amendment and let myself entirely to the dispositions of Divine Providence and to obedience.

During the week that followed, the padre presidente of Alta California's fragile mission system wrote a lengthy response to the college; ten months later the censure was revoked.

CHAPTER TWENTY-THREE

A NEW DRAMA:
DREAM OR NIGHTMARE?

During Serra's six month's absence, Fathers Dumetz, Murguía, de la Peña, and Crespí had baptized twenty-three more Indians, bringing the total number at San Carlos to four hundred and forty-one. Also, during this time, the presidio of San Francisco and Missions San Francisco de Asís and Santa Clara had been founded, bringing the number of missions now on Junípero's laborious ladder to eight.

Before his voyage to San Diego, the padre presidente had selected and crated some of the finest church items for the long-awaited dedication of a mission to Saint Francis. Now, upon his return, Serra was informed that while he had been away in the far south, the foundation beside the Laguna de los Dolores had been laid on October 9, 1776, by his dear friend and fellow Majorcan Francisco Palóu.

Anza, on an earlier expedition to the Golden Gate in the early spring of 1776, had surveyed the terrain and selected a site for the presidio near the mouth of the bay. The mission was to be next to a small stream and lake, where Palóu in the same year offered the first mass on June 29 (which is popularly regarded as the founding date of the city of San Francisco)—five days before the Declaration of Independence was signed in Philadelphia. Formal ceremonies establishing the presidio took place on September 17, the feast of the Stigmata of Saint Francis. Afterward, the officers took formal possession of the area for the king. October 4, the feast of St. Francis, was designated for the formal opening of the mission, though the actual ceremonies were postponed until October 9. Rivera had delayed the founding, so Anza had left Lieutenant Moraga in charge, and Moraga and Palóu had presided.

Now, with the other Alta California missions prospering, Serra was feeling content. But a letter arrived at Carmel that filled him with even greater joy. A radical change had been ordered by the king;

Loreto, which had been the capital of the two Californias, was to be supplanted by Monterey. Named as new governor was Don Felipe de Neve. He would become the supreme civil ruler over the two Californias, from Cabo San Lucas to San Francisco. At the same time, Rivera was transferred to Loreto in Baja California as lieutenant governor.

This news meant that Alta California was now considered more important by the king than Baja, the mother colony. There was public recognition in Madrid and Mexico City of all that the padres had achieved. Junípero wrote Bucareli of his happiness in "the fact that I have lived to see and am actually seeing our Monterey at whose birth I assisted become the headquarters of so large a province." The ebullience of his correspondence during this period manifested his tremendous new optimism at signs that the king was interested in California and that a new civil authority had been appointed with whom he could see eye to eye.

The viceroy made it very clear to the newly appointed governor how important it was to have harmony in the Californias.

California has suffered confusions that must be banished and is in need [one who can] . . . plant good order. This can never be attained unless harmony and cooperation are observed between the royal ministers and the reverend missionary Fathers.

Bucareli's instructions to Neve express in the strongest terms his approval of Serra's policy toward the Indians.

The good treatment of the Indians . . . [is the only way] to win them over. [That policy] belongs particularly to the missionary Fathers. . . . [You are] to protect and aid them. You are to instill respect for them. . . . I am so satisfied with the zeal and the religious comportment of the Reverend Father President and of the other missionaries that I promise myself felicitous results as long as this above-mentioned charge is carried out.

To Serra, Bucareli wrote that he had instructed Neve "to act in accordance with your reverence in all things. I hope . . . that you will do whatever seems feasible and inform me as to what you need so that I can give reality to your desires by supplying the proper measures."

In the long drama of Serra's life, a new act had now begun. On the cold morning of February 3, 1777, Serra first met Neve at Monterey. Shortly afterward the edict was read that made Monterey the capital of the two Californias. After a conference with Neve, Junípero returned to Carmel filled with optimism. A few days later, Serra wrote to Bucareli,

I am very much inclined to believe that this gentleman has quite justly merited the approval of Your Excellency; I have begun to experience . . .

much from his equity, prudence, and zeal. . . . I, with the help of God, will lend all my strength toward cooperating with him and toward helping him in whatever holy purposes [he lays before me]. . . . [Circumstances] augur well for that peace I have so long desired.

Plans went forward for the channel missions once more. On his way north to Monterey, Neve had paid particular attention to conditions in the area and was in agreement with Serra and Bucareli that three missions were needed—both to strengthen lines of communication and to serve the large population. All three—Serra, Neve, and Bucareli—agreed that founding of these missions should be postponed until the latest ones, at San Juan Capistrano, San Francisco, and Santa Clara, were better established.

On June 17, 1778, the *Santiago* put in to San Francisco with news and supplies, and mail was sent south to Monterey by the overland military courier service. From San Fernando, Serra received a patent giving him official permission to administer the sacrament of confirmation. He was also pleased to hear that Verger, his old friend and supporter, had once again been elected guardian.

But the news from Bucareli was not so good: A letter dated January 14, 1778, informed Serra that jurisdiction for the northern provinces of New Spain, including Baja and Alta California, had been transferred to a commandant general headquartered at Arizpe, Sonora (about seventy-five miles south of the present-day Mexico-Arizona border). This was a bitter disappointment to Serra. It meant that from now on he would have to send his requests and appeals to Teodoro de Croix (nephew of the former Viceroy Carlos de Croix). Junípero, and the California missions, would be deprived of Bucareli's sympathy and generosity. Furthermore, this new division of government complicated the structure of church-state relationships. The College of San Fernando remained in Bucareli's jurisdiction, as well as the supply ships that sailed from San Blas. But Governor Neve would serve directly under de Croix, who was new to the area and would be slow at first to make decisions.

Meanwhile, de Croix wrote to the padre presidente from Mexico City on August 15, 1777, indicating that he had heard a great deal about Serra's zeal and prudence in governing the missions, and assured him, "Your Paternity will find in me all you could desire for the propagation of the faith and the glory of religion."

Acknowledging de Croix's letter, Serra congratulated him on his appointment and reiterated the hope that missions would be founded along the Santa Barbara Channel. Since 1769 both the military and the missionaries had realized that this passage was the most hazardous section on the Camino Real. Had the Indians realized their strength, and known of the Spaniards' fears, they easily could have cut California in two.

About the people who lived there, Serra wrote, "I have always found them endearing. . . . Señor, they are our sons, for no one else has begotten them in Christ. For this reason, it is our duty to regard them highly." Serra had used yet another opportunity to promote the founding of missions along the Santa Barbara Channel.

Felipe de Neve was later recognized as one of California's ablest administrators, but almost from the beginning his views on certain issues were not, for Serra, consistent with the best interests of the missions. He questioned the interpretation given to concessions increasing rations for the padres. The rations were to assist the missionaries in the onerous task of feeding and clothing the converts. The number of catechumens and converts at a mission was limited by the padres' judgment of how many could be fed and clothed. Neve insisted upon following the letter of the law, which made no provision for future missions. It was immaterial that the earlier concessions would expire in 1779, less than two years away.

In the "paper war" that ensued over this and other issues, Serra's point of departure was always the Indians and their welfare. In this case he argued on the basis of the intent of the original concession: to hasten the Christianization of the natives by multiplying the number of converts and missions. Serra reasoned according to the axiom of privilege, *"Odiosa sunt restringenda privilegia sunt amplianda,"* "Restrictions should be interpreted narrowly; privileges are to be extended as widely as possible." In the back of his mind—and the minds of the other friars involved—was the consideration that these funds were not from the royal exchequer but from the Pious Fund, which had been collected from generous friends and benefactors in Mexico for the missionary apostolate.

The controversy raged on for the three long years it took to ascend the rungs of bureaucratic officialdom. Eventually, the matter was referred to Madrid, where a decision was issued in Neve's favor.

Another disagreement with Neve was over the illegal establishment of the pueblo of San José on November 29, 1777. Mission Santa Clara across the river had been founded January 12 of the same year.

In his tour of the coast, Neve had made a general survey of sites suitable for agricultural communities. His choices fell upon the plains of Los Angeles beside Río de la Pórciuncula and the Santa Clara valley, watered by Río de Guadalupe.

Provisions for such pueblos were included in the Laws of the Indies, which regulated Spain's methods of colonization. The law was explicit in upholding the rights of the Indians, both Christian and pagan: A pueblo was to be founded "in an unoccupied place and its locale not prejudicial to the Indians." Detailed legislation set forth the manner of siting a pueblo, including the distance between a pueblo, and a mission, so that they could subsist comfortably as neighbors. But the law had been conveniently overlooked in placing the pueblo of San José less than three miles from Mission Santa Clara. Naturally, conflicts arose immediately.

Adding fuel to the legal controversy (which went on for twenty years) were the differing views of Neve and Serra. The new civil governor wanted to create cities populated by *gente de razón*, "people with reason," which meant anybody but Indians, "as if" Serra commented caustically, "Indians did not have any reason." Serra argued against establishing civil colonies in California, explaining that he believed it was premature.

> Missions, Señor, missions are what this land needs and they will provide not only the principal thing, which is the light of the Holy Gospel, but also food for themselves and for the royal presidios better than these towns which have no resident priests and which lack other proper things.

Once the Indians were converted and living on mission lands, there would be plenty of unoccupied and serviceable territory that could be divided among Spaniards of good behavior.

Another source of vexation for Serra was the vice patron's decision to create Indian political officers in the rancherías near the missions. The method of colonization that Spain had developed successfully over the centuries revolved around the growth and development of the mission system. Traditionally, the plan provided that villages near the missions would gradually mature into pueblos. As these agricultural communities attained a sort of self-sufficiency, mayors and councilmen would be elected to govern local affairs. At that time, the missions would develop simultaneously into parishes and the respective bishops would appoint regular pastors from the diocesan clergy to take over the ecclesiastical administration. Meanwhile, the Franciscan apostolic missionaries would move on to new territories suitable for their specialized services. Serra and his padres were thoroughly familiar with such arrangements, comfortably attuned to all their implications. Indeed, the missions constructed by Murguía at Concá and Serra at Jalpan in the Sierra Gorda were perfect examples of how fully developed Indian parishes could be placed under the supervision of diocesan pastors.

Assuming that the Alta California missions had attained sufficient maturity, and presuming that he had the power of gubernatorial fiat, Neve issued directives to the padres at San Diego, San Carlos, San Antonio, San Gabriel, and San Luís Obispo to proceed immediately with the election in the rancherías of Indian *alcaldes*, mayor–peace officers, and *regidores*, councilmen. This was a no-nonsense order: it was to be executed within four days despite the fact that three weeks were necessary for the mail couriers to deliver the documents! The thirty-two padres along the mission chain were thrown into consterna-tion. It was bad enough that they, who had been engaged in the educ-tion of the Indians for the past seven years, had not been consulted. Even if the people were ready for self-rule, protocol, to say nothing of courtesy, demanded that the governor discuss the order with the padre presidente, who resided less than three miles from the desk where the edict originated.

The reaction of the friars was unanimously and vehemently nega-tive. Not only were the Indians unprepared for such a momentous advancement, but conditions in the local rancherías for such elections failed to comply with the Laws of the Indies. In San Diego, Fermín Lasuén and Juan Figuer, who had been enduring the most difficult hardships along El Camino Real, protested to the governor in no uncer-tain terms. In disgust, they wrote to their padre presidente that if the new policy were enforced, they would resign and ask permission to return to Mexico.

Serra's diplomacy in handling the situation is surpassed only by the compassion he displayed in seeking to console his Franciscan breth-ren. As he composed his letters, every word had to be carefully select-ed to allay their disquiet, retain their invaluable service for the mis-sions, and simultaneously assure them that their rightful autonomy would be fully respected.

Reluctantly, Junípero consented to the alcalde system, which within a year proved a complete fiasco, with the elections and management of Mission San Antonio the exception. Wearing a distinctive coat and bearing a baton or cane, the alcalde served as both village magistrate and justice of the peace. The one padre who had been somewhat sympa-thetic to the new order wrote from San Luís Obispo that not only were the regidores useless, but the mission's alcalde was taking advantage of his newfound power. Serra summarized the sentiments of all in a state-ment to the guardian, "They are so puffed up that they regard them-selves as lords."

As the months rolled by, the abuses anticipated began occurring all too soon and too readily. Baltazar, Junípero's own alcalde at San Car-los, still wearing his ordinary mission dress of loin cloth, woolen shirt, and blanket, appeared at the presidio in Monterey to complain about the restrictions of his powers by the missionaries. Shortly, thereafter, he ran away with another Indian's wife in order to take up a life shocking to the padres and scandalous to the Christian converts. At San Gabriel, the alcalde Nicolas supplied Indian women to the Spanish soldiers. Serra commented to Palóu, "The governor thinks he is in a better position to judge from his saddleseat what the abilities of these people are than we who are constantly and in the closest way in touch with them."

Neve would not admit his policy was a mistake, nor would he reply to the detailed abuses documented. In spite of Serra's serious misgivings about the plan, the alcalde system remained an institution in the California missions long after Serra's time. Some order was established out of the chaos by the careful selection of candidates for the office and the diligent supervision of the actual elections.

By all accounts Neve was more circuitous than Fages, the comandante before him. With a bureaucratic mind for meticulous detail, he would have been much more at home as a department head in some Mexico City government office. But as governor, he was responsible for carrying through the last colonization effort of Spain in the New World. Not only was he consolidating the king's grip on California, but he was slowly solving the difficulties that menaced its existence. The haphazard methods of management adopted by the missionaries irritated him. Neve felt comfortable with statistics, especially those that measured the economic growth of his jurisdiction. He required frequent reports on all that happened on paper of exact size and shape. Serra was bewildered. "I began to wonder if I had passed my whole life in a dream," Junípero wrote to Verger.

Palóu, in his biography of Serra, writes of the demanding governor:

He rather developed new ideas every day, and thought up new methods to impede the progress of the already founded missions, which were developing greatly both in spiritual and temporal matters. All these proposals, of which the diabolical enemy availed himself to harrass this fervent superior, he bore with much patience and great interior peace, despite the fact that they pierced him to the quick. They were more painful to him than any arrows which the most barbarous and cruel pagans could have shot at him.

On one occasion, Serra wrote the guardian,

[Neve] is in the habit of saying, especially to Father Fray Juan [Crespí]: "Your Reverences can see to it how they assemble and elect their *alcaldes* and *regidores* in the very same way in which the Spaniards do it. Thus in a very short time they will be organized in a corporate manner, etc."

EMBATTLED:
THE CONFIRMATION
CONTROVERSY

There is little doubt that the years 1778–1780 were among the most difficult of Serra's life. His left foot and leg were growing worse, swollen and ulcerated. In Neve, he was being forced to deal with a man who placed obstacles in his path at every turn.

The last chapter has detailed some of the conflicts between Neve and Serra over the management of the missions, but the most famous dispute was over Serra's right to confirm. Confirmation is the second step (after baptism) in the making of a Christian, and the right to administer it was usually reserved to a bishop. Because the missions were not part of a diocese, Serra applied for the right to confirm in California himself. The pope gave permission in 1774, but by the time the document wended its way through the Spanish bureaucracy, Serra received it four years later, in June 1778. Since it was good for only ten years, he had until 1784 before it expired.

With this new power invested in him, Junípero prepared to make a confirmation tour of all eight missions. He intended to travel overland to San Diego and return to San Carlos the same way, although he now dreaded the long, exhausting journey. Serra wrote to the guardian,

> My infirm flesh trembles somewhat over the thought that I will have to repeat the passage across the lands of the Santa Barbara Channel. . . . From now on, perhaps, that holy college will consider it a greater honor to have martyrs than missions in the area. The truth is that I have always found those poor pagans very lovable. The greater danger lies in the possibility of some unreasonable action on the part of the soldiers who may cause the Indians to revolt, as indeed has happened before. From whatever source such revolt comes, it is always a present danger. It may be considered, if not a miracle, then at least a special providence of God that the crossing [along the narrow channel beaches] through the midst of so many pagans is effected without any hostilities shown.

Since the *Santiago* was now anchored in Monterey Bay and soon to sail for San Diego, Serra decided to go south by sea. This would save his strength, allowing him the energy to confirm at each mission on his way north from San Diego. Embarking on August 24, the ship arrived in the harbor of San Diego on September 15, a long, fatiguing voyage due to lack of favorable winds.

But there was a problem.

When word reached Neve's ears that the padre presidente had read his confirmation authorization at Mission San Carlos on June 29 and followed its promulgation by confirming ninety-one Spaniards and Indians, the governor believed Serra had an official and formal document from the pope authorizing him to administer the sacrament. Of course, Junípero did not have the original papal brief; that had been retained at Franciscan headquarters. What Serra received was a patent from the college together with Vatican instructions concerning its implementation. The original brief had gone through all the legal formalities, including approvals by Viceroy Bucareli in Mexico City and by the council of the Indies in Madrid. However, official seals had not been stamped on the patent sent Serra, leaving the padre presidente to assume (rightly) that all the formalities had been handled by his superiors at the college.

Meanwhile, Serra was in San Diego, ready to exercise the new faculty with all the liturgical solemnity the frontier would permit. The padre presidente was pleased by the reports given him by Father Lasuén, who had been at the mission for nearly a year and was now reconciled to this difficult appointment. Not only had a new adobe church been constructed in the valley, but five hundred and fifty-one children and adults were attending services and instruction. During this year there had been one hundred sixteen baptisms, mostly of adults.

Although San Diego was still a perilous frontier, Junípero was convinced that the attitude of leniency and mercy had borne fruit. Of the five Indians who had actually killed Father Jayme, three were Christians. The forgiving padre presidente now had the unique pleasure of confirming the three reformed men. Of the two non-Christians, one had died after becoming a Christian, and the other had disappeared.

During the next few weeks, as Serra made his way north from San Diego, he confirmed over some one hundred-fifty Indians. Between San Juan Capistrano and San Gabriel, he met the couriers bringing mail from Monterey. Included was a letter for Serra from Neve. It contained the disconcerting news that the governor had suspended the double rations at the three newest missions, San Francisco, Santa Clara, and San Juan Capistrano. Serra decided not to answer Neve until he reached San Luís Obispo. From there, he wrote the governor that he would be home by Christmas and would confer with him then on the matter.

Meanwhile at San Gabriel, Serra learned that four guards and two servants had deserted, seeking asylum in the mission church. Neve ordered the military commander in the area to bring the deserters to Monterey for punishment. But not wishing to violate the right of church asylum, the officer asked Serra in writing to turn over the deserters. Serra went into the church and persuaded the men to surrender. He drew up a document asking the governor for all the clemency that the circumstances of the case permitted. On November 21, Serra informed Lasuén that he was departing for Monterey with the military group escorting the deserters. Although he had difficulty in obtaining the commander's permission to join the group, he was finally told he could go along on condition that Indians carry his baggage.

The group moved briskly through the lower San Fernando Valley and through the hill country of what is today Ventura County to the coast, where Serra so much wanted to establish the first of three missions along the Santa Barbara Channel. Then, the party took the arduous passage along the beach and the cliffs above the channel, past Point Concepción, to San Luis Obispo. No incidents along the way were recorded. Serra undoubtedly rode a mule on this trip since he was able to keep pace with the soldiers on a trip covering two hundred miles in seven days. The total number of confirmations administered by the padre presidente since being empowered was 1,897. Junípero arrived home at San Carlos on December 23, in time for Christmas.

After a four-month absence, Serra was in need of time to recuperate. "I was completely worn out during my extensive journey, but I encountered no mishap or adverse effects, thanks be to God." However, he did not realize that he was about to face the most bitter controversy of his life—a conflict so fierce and protracted that it would take a heavy toll even on a man so seemingly indestructible.

Neve had received an order from de Croix that he interpreted to mean he was to see Serra's document of authorization and after making sure it had the royal *pase* (or approval), affix his own as governor and vice-patron. But the patent Serra had in his possession was not the original papal document with embossed endorsements of the viceroy and the Council of the Indies. The original was with the college in Mexico. Neve ordered Junípero to stop confirming until he could receive further instructions from de Croix in Mexico. The governor, perhaps with a hint of triumph, explained that he did not have the slightest doubt that the patent had the approval of Viceroy Bucareli and the Council of the Indies, but as vice patron, he had to affix his own. This was the law and he would comply with it. Serra not only disagreed

Mission Dolores 1906. San Francisco Bay, in 1776, became the site of Mission San Francisco de Asis, named for the founder of the Franciscan order. It is more popularly known as Mission Dolores, from the name of the stream, Arroyo de los Dolores, which ran into the lake near the mission. Today it stands in the shadow of an imposing basilica.

with his interpretation, but felt Neve was using it for harrassment. It was obvious the issue would have to be clarified by higher authorities.

Immediately, letters were dispatched by both men to de Croix, Viceroy Bucareli, and the guardian at San Fernando. Meanwhile, Neve and Serra exchanged verbal and written arguments over the matter, Serra protesting that since a royal order endorsing his right to confirm would soon be forthcoming, he should be allowed to get on with his work of confirming. Because of Neve's intransigence, Spaniards and Indians alike were being denied religious adulthood. The vice-patron reiterated that he had no choice "without contravening the sovereign will of His Majesty." Furthermore, six months to a year was a reasonable time to wait for such a clarification, Neve continued, since in Hispanic America a full decade sometimes passed between confirmations. Junípero argued that to stop confirming suddenly would cause "scandal and wonderment" among the people, who would question why and would have to be answered either that the king forbids it or that the governor forbids it—"talk little conducive to the good of both Majesties."

Late in 1779, Serra was expected in Santa Clara and San Francisco in order to administer the sacrament of confirmation. Junípero had made his first visit to the two new missions on the San Francisco peninsula in late September 1777, after his return from the south. Reaching San Francisco on October 1, he was reunited with Palóu, and the two celebrated the feast of Saint Francis on October 4. On his visit to the presidio by the Golden Gate, Serra exclaimed: "Thanks be to God. Now Our Father Saint Francis, the crossbearer in the procession of missions, has come to the final point of the mainland of California; for in order to go farther, ships will be necessary." During the same visit he also commented to Palóu that the "procession" was disjointed; spaces between missions needed to be filled up—beginning with three missions along the Santa Barbara Channel.

Now, however, he postponed his journey north, giving his bad health as reason. The real reason was undoubtedly the conflict with Neve over his right to confirm. Later, Serra admitted that the bad state of his leg was the best excuse he could offer. Although it was valid, it would not have confined him to San Carlos without the other problem. Neve had authorized an escort only if Serra promised not to confirm.

Meanwhile, with the news that Serra could not come because of his health, the head of the expedition sent two captains and a royal surgeon to Carmel to see if the physician could improve Serra's leg. Palóu joined the small caravan as it headed south. Unknown to them, Serra had left Carmel for San Francisco the day before with a military escort. To the surprise of both parties, they met at Mission Santa Clara.

Palóu wrote:

> On October 11, we arrived at Mission Santa Clara and at the very same hour and instant the Venerable Father Junípero also arrived. He had suddenly decided to set out on the road to reach these missions in order to administer confirmation ... and to have the opportunity of meeting the gentlemen of the expedition, casting aside all thought of his affliction and placing all his trust in God. However, he arrived in such a condition that he could hardly stand. Nor could it be otherwise since he had walked twenty-seven leagues [seventy-one miles] in two days. When the officers and the surgeon saw the inflammation of the leg and the wound of the foot, they declared that it was only a miracle that he could walk. The fact is that *he did walk the entire journey*. His coming from the south and our arrival from the north at the same time by pure accident filled us with joy and surprise.

This statement is the only clear documentary evidence we have that Serra ever walked from one mission to another in California—despite popular notions to the contrary. That evening, when the surgeon offered to apply some salve to the father president's leg and foot, Serra told him it would be better to wait until he arrived in San Francisco. He feared the remedy might worsen his condition and prevent him from continuing.

The next morning, Serra began to baptize the catechumens of Mission Santa Clara de Asis. Three adult Indians were baptized, with the two naval officers and the surgeon serving as sponsors. The Spaniards were surprised that Junípero was able to stand during the lengthy ceremony, since they themselves soon grew fatigued. Palóu added that the officers "were quite moved at the devotion with which His Reverence administered the ceremonies of baptism to the adults."

The next day Serra, Palóu, and the others left Santa Clara for San Francisco, arriving at Arroyo de Los Dolores late that evening. At the mission he was asked whether he would confirm. After reflecting upon the question, Junípero answered that he would, deciding he would have to take his chances for disobeying the governor. After thanking Arteaga (the head of the expedition and an old friend) for his courtesy and thoughtfulness and congratulating him on his successful voyage of exploration, the padre presidente said, "I do not know how I can return your kindness. I should be glad to confirm as many people on shipboard as may desire it, and you may give them orders to prepare for it."

Serra, assisted by Palóu and Cambón, confirmed one hundred eighty-nine people on October 21 and 28 and November 4. One hundred one were Indians living at the mission who had been baptized during the years since the mission's founding. Virtually all the settlers and soldiers living at the presidio, as well as most of the officers and the crews of *La Princesa* and *La Favorita* were in attendance.

Nine days after Serra reached San Francisco, an overland mail courier brought the distressing news that Viceroy Bucareli had died, and that war had broken out between Spain and England. Bucareli's death was a severe blow to Serra; he had lost a greatly valued ally and friend. The frigates were ordered to return immediately to San Blas.

Before his departure, the surgeon again offered to treat Serra's chronic ailment. But Junípero again refused, saying he felt better now that he had rested. After all, he added, the phlegm in his chest, as well as the sores on his foot and leg would require time to heal. There was no use starting treatment that could not be finished. He would therefore leave the matter in the "hands of the Divine Physician."

Serra hastily wrote two letters, one to the guardian and the other to de Croix, about the confirmation issue. Referring to the fact that Neve had provided him with an escort as long as he did not confirm, Serra informed the two leaders,

I *have* confirmed and I *will* continue to confirm, since it is not in me to say, . . . that the governor has deprived me of the power to confirm or that an order came from the king forbidding me, which was the answer or excuse which the governor suggested to me to make public. The reason for my reluctance was that in lands like these such a statement would cause great scandal and become the occasion of much unfavorable talk about the sacrament or about the king, neither of which may God permit.

Junípero added that he did not know what would happen to him when Neve learned he had confirmed at San Francisco, and was about to do so at Santa Clara, as he had done at the six other missions before the suspension.

To de Croix, Serra narrated the history of his conflict with the governor. He concluded by expressing the hope that the commandant general would not take ill what he had done in confirming in the north.

Serra remained at Mission Dolores in San Francisco until November 6, then left for Santa Clara, arriving on the same day. There he confirmed one hundred sixty-six Indians and Spaniards, which, with the two he confirmed at Carmel when he arrived home in December, brought the total number of confirmations to 2,430.

But two full years would pass, years of contention and anxiety, before the padre presidente and his band of missionaries would learn what, if any, punishment was to be meted out for disobeying the orders of the governor—and hence, the king. The confirmation controversy slowly wended its way through the tangled labyrinth of the eighteenth-century Spanish bureaucracy.

On receipt of Fray Junípero's letter from San Francisco, Commandant General de Croix immediately turned the problem over to his legal adviser, who recommended that the patent Serra had in his possession should be seized by the governor and forwarded to de Croix. In addition, Serra must be forbidden under any pretext whatsoever to confirm. Acceding to the opinion, de Croix dispatched the orders to both Neve and Serra on April 20, 1780.

Meanwhile, anticipating such a ruling, Junípero had written to his superior requesting that the officially embossed documents be sent him with all possible speed. He continued to confirm, until the order from de Croix arrived in July, but did not hand over his patent, preferring to wait for the documents from the college.

According to Edwin A. Beilharz, in his scholarly biography *Felipe de Neve, First Governor of California,*

On August 14, 1780, Neve reported to de Croix what had happened. "His Reverence," he wrote, "now excuses himself from showing his papers with the pretence that he is awaiting the arrival of the ships." De Croix seems to have shared Neve's suspicion, for he wrote Serra with equal abruptness on November 29, 1780, that in spite of all protests he had offered, the order of April 20 still stood: Serra was to turn over his documents, including the

patent and all accompanying instructions he had received, to Neve, as governor of California. Neve would then send them in to Arispe for examination by de Croix.... If Serra refused to give up his papers as ordered,
Neve should "proceed with the use of his powers to take the original documents from his possession and send them in."

But Serra was determined at any cost to retain his patent, knowing
Neve would not approve it without the original documents. When the
documents finally arrived from the College of San Fernando, Neve
happened to be in Baja California on an official inspection tour. Serra
used the opportunity to return the documents, along with his patent,
and all his letters, records, and Vatican instructions pertaining to the
confirmation issue, to the guardian on the same supply ship that had
brought them.

In late December, Neve, back from his trip, asked the padre presidente for the patent and its related documents. Serra explained "in a
rather oblique fashion that the matter had already been taken care of
and that the governor must be patient." The guardian at the College
of San Fernando was sending de Croix certified copies of all the
paperwork pertaining to the papal brief and its validation by the viceroy and the Council of the Indies.

Beilharz continues,

> Neve's reactions can well be imagined. It seemed to him incredible that
> Serra really thought he could get the documents to de Croix more quickly
> via the guardian in Mexico City. If, however, Serra did still have the papers
> in his possession, trying to take them from him by force would not work
> either, for the padre presidente would have hidden them so well no one
> would ever be able to find them. "I know the unspeakable artifice and
> cleverness of this reverend father," Neve added wryly. "There is no mis-
> chief he will not attempt if exasperated. Such is his boundless unbelieveable
> pride. My politeness and moderation over more than four years have not
> been enough to turn him, and the other missionaries, from surreptitious
> conspiracies against the government and its laws.

The governor's feelings toward Junípero Serra were lacking in
charity, yet he did not wish to antagonize the missionaries, since their
assistance would soon be needed in establishing a presidio along the
Santa Barbara Channel. At a more propitious time, however, when less
was at stake, he would take Serra to task, bringing to the padre's attention in no uncertain manner the governor's authority that he had so
persistently eluded.

In early November of 1780, the guardian of the College of San
Fernando sent de Croix and Serra copies of a certified statement that
the original documents had been approved by both the viceroy and
the Council of the Indies. De Croix was satisfied (though he had still

Mission Santa Clara de Asís, 1861. Founded in 1777 and named after Saint Clare, it was later moved to higher ground because of flooding of the Rio de Guadalupe. The new church was dedicated by Serra in 1784, shortly before death. This photograph is of the fourth mission church begun in 1818 and completed in 1822, a structure which was destroyed by fire in 1926. The present University of Santa Clara chapel, the facade of which is influenced by the church pictured here, was built in 1928.

not seen the originals) and rescinded his order to Neve to seize Serra's patent.

After two years of worry, and of confirming privately only those in danger of dying, Serra received notification on August 16, 1781, that since all his documents were in order he could resume administering the sacrament of confirmation. "Serra," writes Beilharz, "though vastly weaker than his opponent, had won not only the game, but also every hand."

CHAPTER TWENTY-FIVE

THE CHANNEL MISSION

Serra sighed with relief. At long last, the confirmation question had made its tortuous way through the entangled bureaucracy of church and state.

Throughout, the padre presidente had preserved an outward calm and dignity. Not once did Junípero question the vice-patron's motives; never did he protest that the state infringed upon the church's jurisdiction. Repeatedly, he told Neve that he respectd the governor's office and appreciated his position. At times, though, he confided to the other missionaries that he felt himself unreasonably cornered and hog-tied. At the beginning of their jurisdictional merry-go-round, Serra confessed to Neve that he often pinched himself to awaken from that nightmare of unreality.

Now, with the lifting of "that secular interdict," Serra resumed the regular administration of the sacrament of confirmation at Carmel and then briefly visited Mission San Antonio to confirm several hundred Indians.

On October 7, Serra, returning to his room after offering mass, felt a moderate earthquake. Later, he learned that the tremor had been more severe in San Francisco and Santa Clara, although the only physical damage to the missions and their churches was the breaking of a flask of brandy at Santa Clara that, in Serra's words, the "poor fathers were saving for an emergency."

A week or so later, Junípero was called upon to perform a duty he had never met before: spiritually comforting a man who was about to be executed. Neve had condemned a presidio soldier to death for "breaking the seventh commandment." He must have stolen a goodly amount to merit the first sentence of death by hanging in California. Since no hangman was available, the man would face a firing squad.

Two weeks later, on October 23, 1781, Serra set out on muleback to administer confirmation at Mission Santa Clara and Mission Dolores in San Francisco. Juan Crespí, who had not been to the Golden Gate since he accompanied the Portolá expedition in 1769, asked to accompany him. Since 1772, he had remained in Carmel as Serra's faithful assistant, instructing, baptizing, marrying, and burying Indians. Now acclimatized to the cold and fog, he obediently walked to Monterey on Sundays and holy days to offer mass. A change of scenery would be good for him.

The pair arrived in San Francisco on October 26. Palóu was delighted to see, not only his one-time professor, but also his former classmate. It must have been a touching reunion for Juan and Francisco since the two had played together in the streets of Palma, started school at the same time, donned the Franciscan habit together as novices, and as students together, entered the philosophy class taught by Lector Junípero Serra.

After three days of confirmations, Serra and Crespí left Mission Dolores on November 8, hoping to return to Carmel before the rainy season set in. This would be the final reunion of the three.

At Mission Santa Clara a few days later, Serra, with all due solemnity, laid the cornerstone of a new adobe church on November 19. The ceremony, conducted by Father Murguía, was solemn and elaborate, one that pleased the padre presidente very much. Afterward, Serra and Crespí set out for Carmel. A few miles from the mission compound, Serra's mule shied and threw him to the ground "with a lively thrust." Serra, in great pain, was kept on his back by Crespí while the guard rode to nearby San José to fetch a physician. The doctor examined the padre's ribs and assured him that despite the pain no bones were broken. The following day, Serra and Crespí continued their journey, though with some difficulty, and arrived at Carmel on November 29.

Shortly after their return home, Juan became ill. Serra describes his infirmities as chest trouble and a swelling of the legs that began in the lower extremities and gradually rose higher. Since there was no physician in Monterey, the padres consulted their medical books, written by a Jesuit and published in Mexico in 1712. The remedies they applied were ineffective. On Christmas Day, Crespí was so ill he remained in bed. After receiving all the sacraments for the dying Juan Crespí died on the morning of January 1, 1782. He had lived sixty-one years, thirty of them as a missionary in the New World.

The next morning, after a requiem High Mass, during which Serra sang the church's final lullaby, Crespí's redwood coffin was lowered into a shallow grave within the sanctuary of Mission San Carlos near the main altar on the Gospel side. The first of the Majorcan triumvirate was now gone. Crespí's missionary career was not particularly colorful, although it was solid and continuous. Perhaps the most elegant tribute to him was penned by the historian Herbert E. Bolton:

> Gentle character, devout Christian, zealous missionary, faithful companion, his peculiar fame will be that of diarist. Of all the men . . . so prolific in frontier extension up the Pacific Coast . . . Crespí alone participated in all the major path-breaking expeditions: from Velicatá to San Diego; from San Diego to San Francisco Bay; from Monterey to the San Joaquin Valley; from Monterey by sea to Alaska. In distance, he out-traveled Coronado. Missionary, globe-trotter, and diarist he was; breviary, pack mule, caravel, and quill might decorate his coat of arms or his book plate.

That there was no resident physician at the presidio in Monterey was a major problem. Earlier, the one doctor assigned there had been expelled by Neve because of his professional incompetence, unsocial character traits, and general immorality, about as bad a trinity of professional defects as a medical man could have. Finding another physician for the frontier settlements and missions was of utmost concern to the civil authorities in Mexico, but it was not until 1785 that another physician came to California.

To the problems Serra was constantly facing was added a new one, in the form of taxes ordered by the king to finance the war Spain had declared against England on June 23, 1779. Since England was preoccupied with the rebellious American colonies on the Atlantic seaboard, the coast of California could bask in security, the missionaries' only participation the ordering of prayers for the success of Spanish arms.

Now, on orders from Madrid, Commandant General de Croix ordered Neve to collect taxes from all His Majesty's vassals in America. Spaniards and noblemen were to be assessed two pesos; Indians, and all others, were to donate one peso each. Serra disliked the hypocrisy and subterfuge expected of the missionaries. Without informing their converts, the padres were to pay the assessment, computed for every male over the age of eighteen, from selling of produce, from alms collected at masses, and from debts owed by soldiers.

Serra found the levy against the Indians ludicrous. The ridicule he heaped upon the assessment, perhaps the most caustic he ever penned, took the form of observations he sent to the guardian at San Fernando.

> A peso apiece has been collected as a contribution for the expenses of the war from the Indians of these missions. And this in a land where pesos have never existed and do not now exist, from Indians who do not know what a peso is. Nor could they understand why pesos are necessary to wage a war for they have had frequent wars among themselves and for them no

pesos were necessary. Much less could they understand why the king of Spain, our master, must ask them to give him a peso apiece.

By February 1782, the long, 200-mile stretch along the Santa Barbara Channel between San Gabriel and San Luís Obispo was still without a mission. Over the past twelve years, three missions had been recommended there by Gálvez, Fages, Bucareli, Rivera, and now Neve. Finally, de Croix authorized Neve to proceed. The missions were to be named San Buenaventura, Santa Barbara (the name suggested by Neve for the middle mission), and la Purísima Concepción.

The Chumash Indians were probably the most remarkable group in California. Their skill at canoe making particularly impressed early visitors. Their baskets and bowls were gracefully made. They grew crops, fished, and engaged in trade with the people of the offshore islands. Now that the missions along the channel were finally to be established, Serra recalled his most recent trip to the area (his fourth): "I saw those inhabitants, as I had always seen them, lively, agreeable, and mutely asking for the light of the Gospel."

In early March, Junípero set out from San Carlos to meet Governor Neve at Mission San Gabriel. After confirming nearly two hundred people along the way, he arrived there on the morning of March 19. Serra had spent the night at the recently founded El Pueblo de Nuestra Señora, la Reina de los Angeles del Río de Porciúncula, today's Los Angeles, his only recorded visit. He traveled to San Gabriel fasting, eager to reach the mission. Later, he told Palóu that the distance seemed greater than it really was, either because he had not eaten, or because of his great desire to reach his destination. Padres Antonio Cruzado, Miguel Sanchez, and Pedro Cambón were surprised to see him. The next morning, after celebrating High Mass, Junípero paid Neve a formal visit in order to make final plans for the channel missions. It was agreed they would leave for the area as soon as possible. On March 26, the cavalcade departed San Gabriel for the Pacific: Serra, Neve, Lieutenant Ortega, eighty soldiers and their families, Christian Indians, muleteers, cattle, and pack animals. Neve was called back to San Gabriel the first night out and the group was led forward by Ortega.

On Easter Sunday, the father president blessed the site of San Buenaventura, his ninth mission, near an Indian rancheria of five hundred inhabitants. A cross was raised, a High Mass sung, and a sermon preached by Serra, followed by the Te Deum. The mission that was to have been his third fifteen years before had finally been founded. It turned out to be his last.

That day was one of special joy. This ninth mission was named for John Fidanza, born in 1221 at Bagnarea, in Eturia, Italy. As a child, he was dying when Saint Francis restored him to health through prayer.

Mission San Buenaventura, ca. 1880. The last mission to be dedicated by Serra, Mission San Buenaventura, had long been planned by him as a vital halfway station between San Diego and Monterey. Named after Saint Bonaventure, the mission is located along Santa Barbara Channel, which was heavily populated by Indians.

When the boy rose to his feet cured, the saint exclaimed *"O buona ventura!"* "Oh what good fortune!" Thereafter the child was known as Buonaventura. He later entered the Order of Saint Francis where he rose to the dignity of Minister General and is revered as the second founder of the Order. His theological learning is so distinguished that he is hailed as the Seraphic Doctor.

The neighboring Indians had given their permission for the settlement through interpreters and were full of excitement. For the celebration feast, a young bull was slaughtered and the food distributed among everyone present. For the missionaries and military officers, a sheep was slain, since it was the Majorcan custom to eat lamb on Easter. The only apprehension Serra felt about San Buenaventura was the difficulty of transporting water from the nearby river to the mission's future grain fields and fruit trees. But he wrote to the guardian that the mission "will be second to none among those founded, and in a short time it will surpass the others."

On April 15, the caravan and pack train started north from the channel, Neve having rejoined them. Following the shoreline for about twenty-five miles, they arrived at the site of the present city of

Santa Barbara. Serra did not like the site chosen, "In my poor judgment it is not a good place for either a presidio or a mission."

This reaction of Serra's to the location of the most prominent and enduring of all the missions is surprising. He might have been disturbed by the lack of water, although he believed it possible that a dam and lengthy aqueduct could be constructed for the necessary irrigation. It is possible Serra's lack of his usual ardor was due to the strained relations between himself and Governor Neve.

On Sunday, April 21, 1782, the feast of the Patronage of Saint Joseph, the ground was blessed, the cross was raised and Padre Serra sang the High Mass. The father president then preached to the assembled congregation, upon which the ceremonies concluded with the singing of the Alabado. Thereupon, Serra prepared the usual registers for baptisms, marriages, and funerals, inscribing the title page of each with "This new Mission and Royal Presidio." There was no doubt in the Majorcan's mind that he was founding the mission as well as the presidio. Indeed, Serra tarried some weeks between the kneeling mountains and the praying sea, while he awaited the decision of the governor for the separation of the mission from the presidio. He tarried in vain. These occurrences, however, have led some to wish that Padre Junípero Serra be accredited with the actual founding of this tenth mission.

In the meantime, additional difficulties arose with Neve. At the age of sixty-eight, and with all his years of experience in the missionary field, Serra was informed by Neve that he was a poor missionary and that the College of San Fernando, founded to do such work, knew nothing about preparing missionaries or running missions. Henceforth, as governor, he would be the authority on such matters, and the mission would not be built until the presidio was finsihed. According to Palóu, Serra told Neve:

> Well, Señor, since I am not needed here, as the mission is not now to be founded, I will return to Monterey.... Meanwhile, lest so great a number of people be without Mass and priestly ministrations, I will call one of the missionaries from San Juan Capistrano here.

Saddened, Serra left Santa Barbara on May 6. Following the trail along the coast, he arrived at San Luís Obispo on May 11. The next morning, after confirming fifteen persons, he went on to San Antonio. After confirming twelve Indians there, he left for Carmel on the same day.

The next afternoon in the Salinas Valley, he encountered two mail carriers traveling south. They handed him three letters from a ship that had arrived in San Francisco. The letters were from San Fernando and were the first mail he had received from the college in two years. Unfortunately, there was bad news regarding the deployment of new missionaries. Serra had asked for six, but none were being sent. Six had indeed volunteered to go to California, but when they heard of the methods and rules imposed by Neve, they declined, with the college in full accord. The guardian and his counselors presented the viceroy with a formal statement protesting the governor's methods. Included in the mail was a copy of the protest.

Junípero arrived at Mission San Carlos on the vigil of Pentecost, May 18, refusing "remedies" for his leg and foot, which were in a terribly swollen condition. More important to him now were the problems of supplying six desperately needed men for the two new channel missions.

CHAPTER TWENTY-SIX

SERRA AND LASUÉN

After Crespí's death, Serra began to correspond at length with Fermín de Lasuén, which led to a deepening understanding, and eventual empathy, between the two. Lasuén had been dissatisfied with his assignment at Mission San Diego, the poorest and most vulnerable establishment in California, but had gradually resigned himself to his responsibility, emerging as a serious, intelligent, and mature missionary, the kind of man Serra believed was necessary at such frontier outposts. The earlier tension between the two Majorcans, engendered by Rivera, faded. In 1783, Lasuén, who was only forty-six years old, wrote:

> I am already old and entirely gray and although [to some extent] this is caused by my age, yet the difficult exercise of my position here has also brought this about. . . . This land is for apostles only and its people call for apostolic men greater than I happen to be; but, (thanks be to God) I enjoy good health and I shall try to use it to some good purpose.

The padre presidente wrote to the guardian that Lasuén "has a perfect way of handling the Indians and his influence upon them, of which he seems strangely unaware, is deeply appreciated." To Serra, it was as if Lausén's submission to suffering had somehow supplied him with a compassion and mental endowment beyond his own comprehension. With Fermín, Junípero could share his deepest misgivings about Neve and the future of the Alta California missions. "I have had [the governor] here at San Carlos for four full years," Junípero confided to Lasuén, "and now I have had a breathing spell for only three months, a vacation."

> I confide in you what I have told only Padre Palóu, namely, that at times I can scarcely bear the vice patron's presence. It is worse even than my physical

suffering. Today [I celebrated mass] with much difficulty. The nights I pass without much sleep; but the reason for this may be not so much my legs as the chief at the presidio.

At this time, a rumor began to spread at the presidio in Monterey that California was about to get a new governor. Serra wrote to Lasuén that he hoped the story was true, although he had no idea who the replacement might be. Then at last Don Felipe de Neve was promoted to the position of inspector general of the Provincias Internas; none other than Pedro Fages was assigned to replace him as governor of California.

Despite their differences, when Fages left California in 1774, Serra wrote a commendatory letter to Viceroy Bucareli asking that Fages receive credit for California's growth and development. Bucareli then assigned him to Mexico's northern frontier in Sonora, where he waged war against the Apaches for four years. Later, he was appointed commandant of arms at a presidio and rose to the position of lieutenant colonel. After a brutal massacre on the Colorado River, de Croix selected Fages to lead the punitive expedition against the Yumas. With the successful completion of the expedition, Fages was ordered to meet with Neve at Mission San Gabriel. The officer, to his astonishment, was told by Neve that he was the new governor of California.

A month later, when Fages arrived in Monterey, Serra greeted him with mixed emotions. There had been disharmony and misunderstanding in their earlier relationship. Fages, of course, could hardly have forgotten that Serra, through a personal appeal to Bucareli, had been responsible for his removal. Now, he was back with more power than ever. Serra wrote Lasuén that Fages said he wanted to be a friend of the friars, aiding them in whatever manner possible. Yet, technically speaking, Neve was the new governor's superior.

No doubt Pedro Fages wanted to begin his second term in California on a positive note and, if possible, discharge his responsibilities harmoniously. He was approaching seventy and probably wanted his remaining years to be tranquil. Serra, suspecting that Neve had issued Fages secret instructions, considered the officer little more than Neve's subordinate, rather than a full-fledged governor. "The hands indeed are the hands of Esau, but the voice is the voice of Jacob," Junípero confided to Lasuén.

There is no question Fages arrived well-primed on how to treat Serra:

Concerning the treatment, management and relationship with the Reverend Father President and the missionaries, the safest way to preserve a prudent policy is . . . to avoid all matters and occasions which could invite discord or misunderstanding. Thus, the safest procedure is *to feign igno-*

rance of everything... [and always refer] to the supreme government about those things which merit further adjudication.

In fact, the former governor had already ordered the troops accompanying Fages not to make friends with the friars or to pay any attention to their wishes or demands.

During the difficult times with Fages, the weary Serra leaned on the younger man, so different in temperament. Francis F. Guest, O.F.M., in his biography *Fermín Francisco De Lasuén,* compares the two:

> Junípero Serra and Fermín Francisco de Lasuén, in many respects, were opposites. Both were highly intelligent, yet Lasuén, gifted with a degree of perceptiveness to which Serra could not lay claim, easily surpassed him in human relations. Serra was more learned in theology, in which he had a doctor's degree; but Lasuén, though lacking the erudition of the first Father President, was endowed with greater psychological insight. Both excelled as administrators, yet, here too, Lasuén revealed a flexibility, a subtlety, a suppleness which Serra did not manifest. Both exhibited strong qualities of character, yet Lasuén suffered, for a time, from spiritual infirmities with which Serra did not have to contend. Serra was rugged, forceful, self-assertive. Lasuén was quiet, cautious, circumspect. Both were involved in controversies between the military and the religious, Serra much more so than Lasuén. And both defended the interests of the Church. But, in his encounters with the state, Lasuén was more adroit, more politic, more pacific than his predecessor in the presidency of the missions.
>
> The most important characteristic in which Serra and Lasuén differed is that, whereas Lasuén excelled as a diplomat, Serra did not. In his letters, whether to the governors, the guardians of the College of San Fernando, or the viceroys, Serra was the epitome of sincerity and candor. Frank, open, clear, direct, he came straight to the point, his scholastic training and habits of logical thinking manifesting themselves from the first line to the last. When he wanted to establish a thesis, as he often did, his letters suggest the precision of a military commander deploying his troops in advantageous positions, his paragraphs proceeding in meticulous formation like companies of infantry on the march.

Lasuén was the better psychologist, Serra, the better logician. It was Fermín Lasuén who got along more peaceably with the military commanders and governors of California. Junípero's qualities of zeal, drive, and energy were desperately needed when the Spanish settlements faced the perils of their beginnings. Jousting vigorously with his opponents, his resolve outstripped his prudence. "The truth never makes friends," he once complained to Palóu, and therefore, and unhesitantly, he challenged Pedro Fages (1770–1774) over the conflicts between the military and the missionaries; Fernando de Rivera y Moncada (1774–1777) over founding and provisioning new missions; Felipe de Neve (1777–1782) over administering the sacrament of confirmation; and again, Fages, in his second term, over a variety of minor issues, including chaplain services at the presidios.

Lasuén, soon to inherit from his predecessor the presidency of the missions, was in essence a man of peace who argued with no one. Correct in his conduct with his superiors, both ecclesiastical and civil, the gentle friar cooperated fully in all decisions arrived at by the viceroy and his counselors lest he perish in pitfalls.

Serra, by contrast, cut through red tape, winning Bucareli's support and getting the job done. He never turned back. Both padres considered themselves unsuited for the post of presidente of the missions. And yet each had implicit confidence in the other—and the College of San Fernando had confidence in them both.

CHAPTER TWENTY-SEVEN

TOWARD THE
RAMPARTS OF ETERNITY

In 1783, Governor Fages wrote twice to Neve complaining about Serra. "The opposition of Father Serra to every government measure is already manifest and has been signified not only in words but in actions and writings." "Father Serra walks roughshod over our measures, conducting himself with great despotic spirit and with total indifference."

During the two years the padre presidente and Governor Fages worked in California together, each spent a great deal of time away from the Monterey peninsula. Serra was on a second confirmation tour in southern California between the latter part of August and mid-December of 1782. He met Fages at San Gabriel as the governor returned from a tour to Baja.

After returning to Mission San Carlos at Carmel, Serra prepared for one last confirmation tour along the Camino Real, recognizing that his time was coming to an end.

In Carmel, Junípero met with two young missionaries who had recently arrived. In his conversations with Diego Nobóa and Juan Riobó, Serra explained that he saw nothing heroic in what the Franciscans were doing in the Californias. If men like themselves came and remained longer than they had to, then that was good. As for himself, he could have returned to Mexico City, or Majorca, after ten years of service. Certainly life would have been easier had he retired to the College of San Fernando. But what would be the purpose of his life if he did not give himself to those who needed him the most? No, he was not a heroic man. Perhaps a little more self-sacrificing, but that was all.

Throughout the spring of 1783, Serra suffered from severe leg and chest pains. Yet, he was determined to make one final tour of all the missions before his patent to administer confirmation expired on July 10, 1784. Because of his worsening infirmities, he decided to take advantage of the recent arrival of a supply ship in Monterey Bay and go by sea to San Diego, returning overland to Carmel. Palóu believed that Serra's health was not good enough even to travel by sea, let alone make the strenuous return journey overland. Junípero himself was painfully aware of the bad state of his health, but not even the possibility of imminent death would deter him. Before his departure, he wrote to Palóu in San Francisco, entrusting him with the affairs of the mission. Bidding him good-by, Serra finished his letter with the words, "I say all this because my return may be only a death notice, so seriously ill do I feel. Commend me to God."

Sailing on board *La Favorita*, which had returned from San Blas to patrol the California coast, Serra arrived in San Diego on September 14. There, with Fathers Lasuén and Figuer, he immediately began administering the sacrament of confirmation. That evening, he told the padres that it was the fifty-third anniversary of the day he received the habit in Palma. Now, old and dying, he could hardly walk or breathe. Yet, day after day for the next month, he confirmed. His spirit was the same, so were his eagerness and interest in everything around him. Now, in the last few months of his life, he refused to let go his love of life.

With Lasuén accompanying and caring for him as far as San Juan Capistrano, Serra baptized, married, and confirmed all those who stepped forth. Feeling much sronger than he had in a while, he was in good spirits. But when he reached Mission San Gabriel, his breathing was so bad that the missionaries sensed he was near death. One young Indian servant told Fathers Cruzado and Sánchez, "The old Father wants to die."

Although fatigued, he found the energy to continue his prayers, offer mass, confirm, and write letters to the College of San Fernando. To the guardian, he wrote:

> I tremble when I think of the more than one hundred leagues [260 miles] I still have to go in order to reach Carmel and that through much uninhabited country. But if God permits me to reach it, I shall not fail to try to go on to Santa Clara and San Francisco again to administer the last confirmations. . . . *I consider this to be my last journey.* May God be pleased to let me finish it, if it be His holy will. After that, or shortly after, Your Reverence can provide for my successor, a man of greater strength and spirit than this sinner.

Somehow, Serra managed to return to Mission San Carlos. Arriving there just before Christmas, he recuperated for four months. During that time, he confirmed an additional two hundred and seventeen. At Santa Clara, Father Murguía was finishing his new church and invited Serra to dedicate it.

On April 29, Serra left Carmel on muleback for Mission Santa Clara. There he found Fathers Murguía and de la Peña in good health. Pedro Fages and his wife, Eulalia, were also on hand. Since the structure was not quite ready to be dedicated, Serra spent the intervening days confirming two hundred and twenty-five persons, and on May 4, Junípero, in the company of the governor and his wife, set out for Mission Dolores. In San Francisco, Palóu was delighted to receive his best friend:

> For me it was an occasion of extraordinary joy to see at this mission, the farthest point attained in the conquest, my beloved and ever venerated Father Master and Lector, who nine months before had written me his farewell. . . . I wanted to enjoy his amiable companionship for some days at this mission.

Meanwhile, as Serra was confirming one hundred forty-six Indians in San Francisco, Father Murguía was running a high fever at Santa Clara. After receiving last rites on May 11, Murguía died. Still administering confirmation at San Francisco, Junípero was not present the next morning when the padre was buried in the sanctuary of the church he had constructed.

On the following Saturday, Serra went back to Santa Clara and blessed the new church in the presence of the governor, Lieutenant Moraga, Palóu, de la Peña, the colonists of San José, and the Indians. The next day it was opened for divine services. Junípero sang the High Mass, preached, and administered confirmation. Within the week, the total of his confirmations had risen to 5,275.

Palóu needed to return to Mission Dolores, but Serra detained him for some days, telling his former student that they would never see each other again. Then, in the tradition he had honored since 1750, the padre presidente made a general confession to Palóu, "shedding many tears." Palóu wrote,

> Nor did I shed fewer tears for I also feared this would be the last time we would see each other. . . . Since His Reverence was leaving for his mission and I for mine, we would be separated by forty-two leagues, territory all populated by pagans, and our desire [to be together at death] would not be easily fulfilled.

His work finished at Santa Clara and preparation made for death, Serra set out for Carmel, arriving home at Mission San Carlos on May 26.

With Murguía's death, Serra and Palóu had lost a valued friend, and the missions one of its most zealous padres. Writing about Murguía, Junípero noted, "I have grieved over and will continue to lament for a long time over the loss of a missionary who was so good that perhaps no one else can equal him."

As death approached, Serra realized that the missions he had founded and fostered under the guiding hand of San Fernando might not remain in Franciscan hands for long. There was a plan afoot to place all the missions of Baja and Alta California into the custody of the Dominicans and expel the Franciscans. Although the padre presidente could do nothing about it, he vigorously—and characteristically—expressed his opinions on the scheme.

Junípero's last written words were those found in his letter to the guardian at San Fernando on August 6, 1784, "What I appreciate above all are the prayers offered to our Most Pure Superioress that she may obtain for us effectiveness here below and after that heaven. . . . Should we lose heaven, all the rest will be of no profit."

This philosophy, so simply stated thirty-five years before when he began his apostolic career, was with him in his final month. In fact, at various stages in Serra's life, the thought of death motivated his actions. In 1743 he asked his philosophy students for only one favor in exchange for the services he had rendered as a teacher:

> I desire nothing more from you than this, that when the news of my death shall have reached your ears, I ask you to say for the benefit of my soul: "May he rest in peace." Nor shall I omit to do the same for you so that all of us will attain the goal for which we have been created.

In his farewell letter to his parents six years later, he wrote:

> A happy death, of all the things of life is our principal concern. For if we attain that, it matters little if we lose all the rest. But if we do not attain that, nothing else will be of any value.

Now, in August of 1784, during the final three weeks of his life, Junípero Serra, seventy years old, became more meditative. He had completed his last earthly journey to bestow spiritual benefits on the Indians he cared for so much, and after July 10, when his confirmation authority expired, Junípero's premonition of death was stronger than ever. He wrote to the missionaries of San Francisco, Santa Clara, San Antonio, and San Luis Obispo advising them of the arrival of a supply ship from San Blas. At the conclusion of the letter he bade them farewell until they met in eternity. He told the friars that he would be pleased if one from each mission would come north to receive one of his few personal possessions as a memento of his friendship. He especially wanted to say farewell to Father Paterna, who had arrived in Mexico with him in 1749 and was now at San Luis Obispo, and Padres Pieras and Sitjar, Majorcans stationed at San Antonio.

On August 18, Palóu arrived at San Carlos from San Francisco and was shocked by Serra's appearance. Yet, the father president was up and around. When Palóu heard Serra singing in the chapel, he was relieved. "It does not seem that the Father President is very sick," he commented to a soldier standing near him. "Father," answered the guard, "there is no basis for hope. He *is* ill. [He] is always well when it comes to praying and singing but he is nearly finished."

The next morning Junípero told Palóu that the heaviness in his chest and the swelling in his leg were worse. He asked if his friend would do him a favor. It was August 19, and for the past fourteen years Serra had celebrated a High Mass on the nineteenth of each month in honor of Saint Joseph, on whose feast day the long overdue supply ship had arrived in San Diego back in 1770, saving Alta California's first mission colony. That afternoon, Palóu celebrated High Mass, although Serra, propped up in a chair, sang the music of the mass with his converts. Later, after a small dinner of broth and vegetables, Serra returned to the church and recited the customary evening prayers with the Indians.

During the next few days, Serra and Palóu, sitting on a small bench in the warm sunshine outside the mission church, talked at length about a number of matters. Uppermost in their minds was the rumored coming of the Dominicans to replace the Franciscans. Serra naturally disliked the idea of his nine missions passing into the hands of another order, especially since the machinations of Sonora's Bishop Antonio Reyes, a fellow Franciscan, were behind the idea. Certainly the Indians would be in just as good hands with the Dominicans, but it reflected discredit on the College of San Fernando. Serra urged Palóu to return to Mexico and, if necessary, take the issue all the way to Madrid. Although Palóu called Reyes's scheme an expulsion equal to the Jesuit expulsion in Baja and a discredit to the apostolic institute of San Fernando, Junípero seemed somewhat more resigned to the blow. Treating it with calm and inner peace, Serra said that if the changes came,

> Let the holy will of God be done, for this vineyard is His and since He so orders it, doubtless these workmen are more suitable for the spiritual tillage. May the flock of holy Church increase and may the new shepherds be the most acceptable to the Lord.

Now, looking out past the mission gates to the several Indian rancherías stretching along the river in the lovely Carmel Valley, Junípero spoke about how his death would mark the closing of a period of exploration and isolation. In the fifteen years since he had led the padres along the Pacific west coast, no foreigners had ventured into the pastoral land. A few Spanish presidios and settlements had been established, and by now the colonists numbered well over a thousand, but in reality, Alta California belonged to the missions. The threat of Russian advances from the Bering Straits, the original impetus for Spain to possess and settle the territory, had now eased. But knowledge of Spain's growing weakness, due to her various European military defeats, was attracting more interest than ever to California on the part of the French, Dutch, and English. And, of course, there were the Americans, whose pioneers were beginning to be seen on the western rim of the continent.

At mid-morning on August 22, the *San Carlos* anchored in Monterey Bay. Learning of Serra's condition, the royal surgeon, Dr. Juan García, immediately rode over to Carmel to visit. He found Junípero's chest so congested that he suggested cauterizing it in order to remove the phlegm. Junípero told the physician to apply whatever remedy he chose. But García's efforts only resulted in more pain for Serra, who showed no signs of it but continued to be up and about whenever he felt he was needed.

Supplies from the ship were now carted to the mission from Monterey. Among the items were ten large rolls of cloth, which Serra ordered cut up and distributed to the Indians. On August 24, while Palóu and Serra were seated outside the mission church, an Indian woman, about eighty years old, slowly walked up and asked Serra for some cloth. Serra rose, hobbled to his cell, and returned with an old blanket. Palóu smiled and commented, probably in the Majorcan dialect, "Is she going to pay you for the chickens?" Serra chuckled, and together they recalled the time during the first days of the mission when the woman, not yet a Christian, had almost destroyed the fledgling poultry industry. At the time, Serra and Crespí had only one hen and her brood of chicks. This same woman, then almost seventy, had her nephew chase and kill the fowl so the two could have a tasty meal. Now, Serra, concluding his California labors, smiled at the wily chicken thief and handed her half of the only blanket he used at night to cover himself on his bed of wooden planks.

To recruit new missionary volunteers for California from Spain, Serra suggested that Crespí's diaries, now gathering dust in the archives of San Fernando, be published in order to publicize the possibilities for spiritual labor in the missions. But later Palóu had an even better idea. Why not publicize Junípero's own story, sending it throughout Hispanic America, Spain, and Majorca in order to stimulate interest? Thus unwittingly, Serra planted the idea of his own biography.

That same day Junípero expressed his disappointment that the missionaries from San Francisco, Santa Clara, San Antonio, and San Luís Obispo had not arrived, suggesting that perhaps the letters he had sent had been delayed at the presidio. Palóu went over to the military post to inquire and learned that the presidio had indeed forgotten to forward them. Palóu read the letters and for the first time realized that Serra had asked the padres to come for a final farewell. Without telling

Junípero, Palóu immediately dispatched the letters with a note asking the missionaries to come at once.

Serra passed a bad night and arose weaker on August 25. He told Francisco how bad he felt and said he wished to prepare himself for whatever God desired. Although he had made a confession to Palóu in Santa Clara, Serra confessed to his boyhood friend one last time, "amid many tears and with a clear mind just as if he were well." The day's long hours were filled with quiet reflection. Toward evening, Junípero drank a cup of hot broth and went to rest on his bed of planks.

Palóu continues the story of Serra's last forty hours with these words:

> As soon as morning dawned on the 27th I went to visit him and found him with breviary in his hands, since it was his custom always to commence Matins before daybreak. . . . He said he would like to receive the Most Holy Viaticum, and that for this he would go to the church. When I told him that was not necessary, that his cell could be fixed up in the best way possible and that the Divine Majesty would come to visit him, he said no, that he wanted to receive Him in church, since if he could walk there, there was no need for the Lord to come to him.

The church was more than a hundred yards away from Serra's room. In the Spanish tradition, the Blessed Sacrament would have been carried to him under a canopy, accompanied by altar boys bearing lighted candles; here, the procession was reversed. Nicolás Soler, the inspector general of presidios, and some of his soldiers, who had come over from Monterey that morning, joined the mission guard and and the Indians in a procession to the church. With a white stole over his gray habit, Serra walked unaided to the church and went directly into the sanctuary, where he knelt.

Meanwhile, Palóu vested himself in the sacristy. Then, accompanied by an altar boy carrying incense, he entered the sanctuary. When Francisco opened the tabernacle, Serra intoned the Tantum Ergo, tears filling his eyes. Palóu gave general absolution, then gave the sacred host. For some time, Serra knelt in thanksgiving after his last communion. Then, in company with the soliders and the Indians, he returned to his room.

"Some shed tears from devotion and tenderness, others out of sadness and sorrow," wrote Palóu, "because they feared that they would be left without their beloved father." After a while, Francisco went to see Junípero, but, saw him "alone in his little cell in meditation, seated on a chair next to his table. When I saw him thus absorbed, I saw no reason to enter to talk to him."

As Palóu was leaving, he encountered the presidio carpenter on his way to Serra's room. Asked his business, the man explained that Serra had called him to prepare a coffin and he needed detailed measurements and instructions. Palóu turned him away with an order to make it like the one he had made for Father Crespí. Junípero passed the rest of the day in silence, seated on his chair and drinking only a little broth for dinner.

That night Serra began to feel worse and asked for the sacrament of extreme unction. Palóu complied without delay, anointing the five senses of his superior with the consecrated oils. After the concluding prayers, Junípero and Francisco recited the Litany of All Saints and the seven penitential psalms. This was the litany chanted by their brethren while they lay prostrate on the floor of the sanctuary at their ordination to the priesthood. It had also been chanted by the villagers in Majorca wending their way to the heights of Bon Any before Serra's departure to the New World and was a familiar part of Serra's life, and now, his death.

Palóu remained the entire night with Serra, who spent most of the time on his knees, pressing his pained chest against the rough boards of his bed, which gave him some relief. When Palóu suggested that he lie down and rest, Serra replied that he felt more relieved the way he was. During the hours that followed, he became exhausted and sat on the floor supported by the arms of Indian converts who had come to see him. When Palóu asked García, the royal physician, how he was doing, the doctor shook his head, answering, "It seems to me that this blessed Father wants to die on the floor." Palóu asked Serra if he wanted to receive final absolution, and Junípero answered yes. Receiving it still kneeling, Serra seemed more comforted.

Palóu continues his narrative:

> The feast of the Doctor of the Church Saint Augustine dawned, August 28, and he appeared relieved. He did not experience so much congestion in his chest. During the whole night he had not slept or taken anything. He spent the morning seated on the rush stool, leaning against the bed. This bed consisted of some roughhewn boards covered with only a blanket, and not even a sheepskin such as was customary at our college. Along the road he used to do the same thing. He would stretch the blankets and a pillow on the ground, and he would lie down on these to get his necessary rest. He always slept with a crucifix upon his breast, in the embrace of his hands. It was about a foot in length. He had carried it with him from the time he was in the novitiate at the college, nor did he ever fail to have it with him. On all his journeys he carried it with him, together with the blanket and the pillow. At his mission and whenever he stopped, as soon as he got up from bed he placed the crucifix upon the pillow. Thus he had it on this occasion.

Around ten o'clock that morning, the officers of the *San Carlos* rode over from Monterey to see Serra. Among them were Captain José Cañizares, whom Junípero had known since 1769, and the Reverend Cristóbal Díaz, the royal chaplain from Lima, Peru, whom Serra had

Serra receives the Viaticum at Carmel Mission. This painting by Mariano Guerrero was commissioned in 1785 by Palóu, from whose hands Serra is receiving his last communion. It is now in the Museo de Historia, Castillo de Chapultepec, Mexico City.

met in San Francisco in 1779. Serra received them with warm greetings, ordering that a solemn ringing of the church bells be given in their honor. Embracing them affectionately as if nothing was bothering him, Junípero gave a special embrace to Father Díaz since, "like myself, you are a priest of Jesus Christ."

Only when the visitors were seated did Serra sit down once more on his stool, listening to stories of their voyages to Peru. After an hour or so of listening to them, Junípero smiled and said,

Well, gentlemen, I thank you that after such a long time during which we have not seen each other, and after so long making voyage, you have come from so far off to this port to throw a little earth over me.

They were surprised at his words; Serra did not look or sound like a man about to die. Attempting to be optimistic, they laughed, "No, Father, we trust that God will make you well and enable you to continue." But Serra answered, "Yes, do me this favor and work of mercy: throw a little bit of earth upon my body and I shall be greatly indebted to you."

Now, turning to Palóu, Serra said, "I desire you to bury me in the church, quite close to Fray Juan Crespí for the present; and when the stone church is built, they can put me wherever they wish." Palóu's eyes welled with tears. After a pause, he answered:

If God is pleased to call you to Himself, it will be done as Your Paternity wishes. In that case, I ask Your Paternity out of love and the special affection you have always had for me, that when you arrive in the presence of the Most Blessed Trinity, you adore the same in my name, and that you be not unmindful of me. Do not forget to pray for all the dwellers in these missions, particularly for those here present.

To this, Serra replied:

I promise, if the Lord in His infinite mercy grants me eternal happiness, which I do not deserve because of my sins and faults, that I shall pray for all and for the conversion of so many whom I leave unconverted.

Around noon, Junípero asked Francisco to sprinkle a little holy water about his cell. Palóu complied. Asked whether he felt any pain, the padre presidente said no. Suddenly, in a frightened manner, he grasped his friend saying, "A great fear has come over me. Read for me the Commendation for a Departing Soul and say it aloud so that I can hear it." Palóu reached for his ritual and began to read that prayer of faith read at every Catholic deathbed where time and circumstances permit: "Depart, O Christian soul, out of this sinful world, in the name of God, the Father Almighty ..." Palóu read the long comforting prayers in the presence of Captain Cañizares, Father Díaz, Fray Matías Noriega, and Dr. García. Sitting on his stool, Junípero answered with amens. As soon as it was over, he smiled and said, "Thanks be to God, thanks be to God, all fear has now left me. Thanks be to God, I have no more fear. So let us go outside."

Surprised and pleased at the sudden change, the group walked out of the bed chamber into a small living room. Cañizares said,

Father President, now [you] can see what my devoted Saint Anthony can do. I have asked him to make you well and I know he will. And I trust you will be able to make some more journeys for the good of these poor Indians.

Serra smiled weakly in answer. According to Palóu, "He made it very clear to us that he did not hope to get well."

In the little room, Serra sat on a chair by a table, picked up his diurnal, or daybook, containing the Little Hours, and recited his sext and none, prayers said at specific times. When he finished, it was past one o'clock. Francisco asked Junípero if he cared for a cup of broth. When it was brought, he said a prayer of thanks, drank it slowly, and whispered, "Now let us go to rest." It was siesta time and Serra had had no sleep for over thirty hours.

He walked to his little room where he had his bed, took off only his mantle and lay down over the boards, covered himself with a blanket, with his crucifix in his hands. "We all thought he was going to sleep, as during the whole night he had not slept at all."

> The gentlemen went out to eat. Since I was a little uneasy, after a short time I returned and approached his bed to see if he was sleeping. I found him just as we had left him a little before, but now asleep in the Lord, without any sign or trace of agony, his body showing no other sign of death than the cessation of breathing; on the contrary, he seemed to be sleeping. We piously believe that he went to sleep in the Lord a little before two in the afternoon, on the feast of Saint Augustine in the year 1784, and that he went to receive in heaven the reward of his apostolic labors.

Palóu closed the eyes of his friend and said the Requiescat in Pace. Fray Junípero Serra had died in the midst of his labors. He had lived seventy years, nine months, and four days. Peace and rest were finally his. Palóu was glad he had stayed in California to be with his master and friend at the end of his productive career. Palóu's record of those last days is the diary of a devoted friend and observer. No one but such a confidant could have provided such intimate details of Serra's last hours. Though the man who had coveted a martyr's crown died quietly, the closing scenes of his life have their own drama, preserved for us by Palóu.

Leaving Serra's cell, Palóu told a few Indians standing nearby to toll the church bells to announce Junípero's death. They sounded the *doble,* the signal of death that is still used to this day in Petra. The mournful ringing brought everyone to the mission. The entire population of the nearby village of converts assembled. Palóu wrote that "many Indians came weeping over the death of their beloved father who had begotten them anew in the Lord and who was more esteemed by them than if he had been their natural father." Spaniards, soldiers, and sailors joined the group viewing the body. So large was the crowding and disorder that Palóu had to close the door of the cell in order to place Serra's remains in the redwood coffin prepared the day before.

Palóu and Father Noriega removed the sandals from Junípero's feet and gave them as keepsakes to Cañizares and Díaz, who were witnessing the arrangements. Serra died wearing only his gray habit, cowl, and cord. His undertunic had been sent out to be washed. His habit now became his shroud. The body was placed in the coffin and alongside the coffin six lighted candles. Then the door was opened and the waiting mourners admitted.

Until nightfall, Indians, colonists, soldiers, and sailors entered the room, praying for the father's soul. They touched his face and hands with their rosaries and medals, whispering *"Santo Padre,"* "Holy Father," and *"Bendito Padre,"* "Blessed Father." They brought with them wreaths of yellow, pink, and purple wildflowers.

That evening a long procession accompanied Serra's remains into the church. There, the body was placed upon a table surrounded by six lighted candles. Palóu recited the De Profundis, the Miserere, and the Subvenite, each concluding with the words, "Eternal rest grant unto him, O Lord, and let the perpetual light shine upon him." When the ceremony was over, some of those present asked Palóu to leave the church open during the night so that those who wished could maintain a vigil. Palóu consented, leaving two soldiers as a guard "to prevent any kind of indiscreet piety or theft, for all desired to obtain some little thing which the deceased had used."

All through the night one group after another approached the coffin and recited Paters and Aves. Palóu promised those in the royal service that some keepsakes of the father president would be distributed after the funeral. However, during the night, a number of people, despite the two guards, cut small pieces of cloth from Serra's habit, as well as snipped some of his hair. Later, when Palóu learned these people were referring to their keepsakes as "relics," he promptly made clear the church's position on such matters. Relics, he said, could only be associated with those whom the church had beatified or proclaimed venerable.

Funeral services were held on Sunday morning, August 29. Among the mourners for the first service were all six hundred Indian converts living at Mission San Carlos in Carmel, the mission guards, the soldiers from the presidio, and the officers and most of the crew from the *San Carlos* anchored in Monterey Bay. Throughout the day, at half-hour intervals, a cannon shot was fired from the ship, answered by a volley from the cannons at the presidio. The reverberations were heard all the way to Carmel.

Within the crowded church, a vigil was sung and a solemn requiem High Mass followed, as the army and naval officers held lighted candles. Father Sitjar from Mission San Antonio led the Indian choir. After mass, the response was chanted.

Burial was deferred until late afternoon. In the meantime, some of

Serra cenotaph, Carmel Mission. This cenotaph, in the Carmel Mission Memorial Chapel, was completed in 1924 by artist-sculptor Jo Mora, and stoneworker Harold Corsini. Franciscan padres Juan Crespí (at Serra's head), Julian Lopez, and Fermín Francisco de Lasuén are represented with the padre presidente. Serra's body is buried nearby in the sanctuary of the basilica.

the people remained in the church, viewing Serra's body, praying, and touching his body with their medals and rosaries. At four o'clock, the bells called everyone together to form a procession. Led by a cross bearer and altar boys, the procession of the Indians, Spaniards, soldiers, and sailors followed, two by two, each bearing a candle. Then walked Palóu. As a last act of tribute, the military and naval officers alternated bearing Junípero's coffin on their shoulders. The procession was held in the courtyard of the mission enclosure. Four stops were made; during each a response was sung. The procession then re-entered the church, and the pall bearers placed the coffin on a table at the foot of the altar. When the final prayers were finished, Palóu read the words of consignment:

> May the angels lead thee into Paradise; may the martyrs receive thee at thy coming and lead thee into the holy city, Jerusalem; May the choirs of angels receive thee and with Lazarus, once a beggar, may you have eternal rest.

The open grave in the sanctuary was blessed and incensed. A last Requiescat was offered and the mortal remains of Junípero Serra were lowered into the opening in the floor on the Gospel side of the altar, close to the remains of Crespí. Palóu, as well as the other padres and officers, threw a little earth into the grave in token of farewell. A final response was sung, "the tears, sighs, and cries of those assisting drowning out the voices of the chanters." Then the congregation dispersed.

Seventy laborious years were now part of history.

EPILOGUE

I have been informed that (Padre Junípero Serra) died the death of the just and in such circumstances that . . . all (were) of the opinion that his happy soul went directly to heaven to enjoy the reward for thirty-four years of great and continuous labor. . . . All men said openly that that man was a saint and that his actions were those of an apostle. This has been the opinion concerning him ever since he arrived in this kingdom. This opinion has been constant and without interruption.

—Padre Sancho de la Torre, Guardian at the College of San Fernando, to the Minister Provincial of the Franciscan Province in Majorca.

After Junípero Serra's burial in the sanctuary of fog-swept Mission San Carlos Borromeo on August 29, 1784, Father Francisco Palóu temporarily assumed the presidency of the California missions, though he was reluctant to do so. Five months later, the guardian at the College of San Fernando, heeding the advice of his counselors, selected Fray Fermín Francisco de Lasuén as the permanent padre presidente.

No better selection could have been made for Serra's successor. Building economically and architecturally on his predecessor's foundation, Lasuén, before his death in 1803, founded nine more missions on the ladder: The first two completed, with San Buenaventura, the chain of three along the Santa Barbara Channel that Serra had dreamed of for so long. Santa Barbara was founded in 1786 (Serra had been present at the founding of the presidio there in 1782), and Purísima Concepción, at the north end of the channel, in 1787. In 1791 were founded Santa Cruz (on the coast west of Santa Clara) and La Soledad (inland about halfway between Carmel and San Antonio). Four missions were founded in 1797: San José, some distance from the pueblo, which had encroached on Santa Clara; San Juan Bautista, midway between Carmel and Santa Clara; San Miguel, in the mountains between San Antonio and San Luis Obispo; and San Fernando, in the valley of the same name not far north of San Gabriel. San Luís Rey, between San Juan Capistrano and San Diego, was founded in 1798.

But Serra had laid the path. He had served for fifteen years; at the time of his death, California had nine prospering missions, four presidios, and two pueblos. During his regime as president, people from at least six diverse linguistic stocks had been gathered into the missions. There had been over six thousand baptisms and over five thousand confirmations. Given the difficulties, the entire period had been characterized by phenomenal success. There is no question that it was Serra who introduced Christianity and the rudiments of European civilization to California. Even Don Felipe de Neve, who had at various times referred to him as "arrogant", "obstinate," "willfully deceitful," and "an artful contriver," said of Serra that he and his missionaries had surpassed all the king's expectations in developing Alta California's missions. He praised Serra's understanding of the character, customs, and manner of life of the Indians and said there are no other missions like his in all the world.

Even Pedro Fages, who in his confrontations with Serra was always frustrated, spoke glowingly of the progress made under the leadership of his former adversary and the Franciscan order.

> From the beginning, the founding and the spiritual as well as the temporal management of these establishments was entrusted to the religious of the College of the Propagation of the Faith of San Fernando in Mexico. It

was they who commenced the grand work amid the poverty, penury, and want which are inseparable from such undertakings in newly discovered countries. Here the difficulties were aggravated on account of the immense distances from every civilized land. Nevertheless, these religious have placed the institutions on a solid basis ... If we must do justice to all, as is obligatory, we must confess that the rapid, agreeable, and interesting progress in spiritual as well as temporal affairs which we happily observe and enjoy is the glorious effect of the apostolic zeal, activity, and indefatigable efforts of these religious.

The fruit of the labors being praised by Neve and Fages reflect not only Serra's multifarious talents but also the direction of his character. To all who encountered Junípero Serra, there was no mistaking his essential nature.

Because of his larger vision, the cross of interference by hostile secular agencies was ever his to bear. But perhaps the truth about Serra's conflicts with civil officials rests in the strong royalism of the time. The authorities in Spain were neither anti-Catholic, nor anticlerical. They merely insisted upon affirming the supremacy of the king, even in ecclesiastical affairs.

Serra, as a man of his time, accepted the position of the state as long as he believed it to be lawful, though he would never yield on certain matters of principle. Yet it was difficult for him to accept the intervention of civil functionaries in problems he saw as exclusively religious. With civil and religious interests so entangled, it was inevitable that there would be friction between the two authorities. Generally speaking, however, the men Serra dealt with were honest, properly trained, self-sacrificing officials against whom no perfidy or abuses could be alleged. The conflicts arose out of the missionaries' assertion of their rights.

However gentle and full of kindness were his heart and mind, Serra's veins did not altogether flow with milk and honey. In his last years, Junípero became more and more circumspect, even shrewd, when it came to defending his "children against the measures that seem best only to the representatives of the king". The sparkle of his mind, so often buried in routine administrative duties, would shine forth on precious reams of paper protesting "the skulduggery of greedy government officials," or the timidity of some of his own "discreet brethren."

The greatness of "el viejo," the aged one, as Serra was affectionately called, lay in his unconquerable will: he would never turn back on anything he undertook. At a time when fact was more incredible than imagination, truth on the frontier more lurid than the wildest fiction, Junípero's small, burdened physical frame marched along, climbing over every obstacle in his path. Twice he faced death at sea—at the hands of an English captain in the Mediterranean and in a storm off

Vera Cruz—and many times on land. As he once confided to the king's highest representative, he lived as close to hurtling arrows as any soldier.

And accompanying Serra on his journeys were the words of his beloved Saint Francis:

> Praise be to my Lord for our sister, the death of the body, from whom no man escapeth. Woe to him who dieth in mortal sin! Blessed are they who are found walking by His most holy will, for the second death shall have no power to do them harm.

These were his watchwords at thirty-five when he left Majorca, and they sustained him as he traveled on muleback in the fierce summer sun and the winter rain, amid pain and privation, or when he slept under stars and rode or walked over rocks and arroyos, through brambles and across shallow rivers, all the time uncertain whether the observing Indians would shoot at him or sing with him.

In mileage, the land journeys Serra made in Hispanic America between 1749 and 1784, between the ages of thirty-six and seventy, were enough to circumnavigate the globe. But the legend of *"El Gran Caminante,"* "The Great Walker" is no more amazing than reality. During his California period, he traveled 5,400 miles by sea and 5,525 by land. Despite his epithet, Junípero himself never stated in his writings that he walked between the missions, except for some thirty miles along the Santa Barbara Channel in 1777. Palóu only once explicitly describes him as walking, using there the indisputable phrase *"anduvo a pie,"* "he traveled on foot"—he was an eyewitness when Serra hiked from Monterey to Santa Clara late in 1779 in the company of a soldier (who rode). All other expressions used by either of them are indeterminate. On two occasions, Serra specifically says that he rode, not explaining the details but casually mentioning it as if it were the ordinary thing to do.

Considering that Junípero himself never stated that he walked any considerable distance in California, that Palóu only once mentions him walking, that he had to travel with a military escort he had to keep up with, that he himself twice stated casually that he rode (and implied it on another occasion), and that he suffered from a swollen and inflamed foot and leg, as well as asthma (to say nothing of advancing age), one must not conclude that he walked from one mission to another more than once.

Having taken his last earthly journey in that grim, merciless, smiting New World, Serra's life closed with his faithful friend Francisco Palóu standing by the grave next to the altar in cold Carmel Mission, saying "Farewell, Junípero, unto eternity."

Unveiling of Serra statue, Golden Gate Park, San Francisco. This statue, one of many throughout California and across the country commemorating Serra's life, was dedicated on November 17, 1907.

The *doble* that sounded Padre Serra's saintly demise in 1784 paradoxically ushered in the heyday of the mission era with the accession of Fray Fermín Francisco de Lasuén as the second Padre Presidente. The bell sounding Serra's departure, however, might rightly be regarded as the real beginning of the end of that first generation of pioneers along Spain's outpost of empire. By 1800, having completed their work for God and king, virtually the entire first generation of California pioneers had died. Junípero Serra lay at Carmel between his countryman Juan Crespí and his successor Fermín de Lasuén; Francisco Palóu slept at Querétaro, former guardians Rafael Verger and Francisco Pangua both in Mexico. Luis Jayme, bathed in his own blood, lay in peace at his mission at San Diego, and José Antonio Murguía at his, Santa Clara. Captain Juan Pérez found a watery grave in the Pacific off Big Sur. Fernando de Rivera y Moncada met a soldier's death along the Colorado River. Don Felipe de Neve died in the desert just a few weeks after Serra. The sympathetic viceroy, Antonio María Bucareli y Ursúa, was buried in the Basilica of Guadalupe. Teodora de Croix went to Peru as viceroy. Juan Bautista de Anza died in Sonora in 1788 and was buried at Arizpe. José de Gálvez died at Aranjuez, Spain, in 1787; Gaspar de Portolá died and was buried in Madrid. José Francisco Ortega died suddenly en route from his ranch near San Luís Obispo to Mission Santa Barbara in 1793; Antonio Paterna followed him to the grave at the same mission in 1797. As Serra inscribed in the register for deaths and burials when he founded Mission San Carlos at Carmel in 1770: *"Omnes morimur et quasi aqua dilabimur in terram, qua non revertuntur,"* "We all die, and like waters that return no more, we fall down into the earth."

Serra's story is a pioneer's story. Whatever was done to further the establishment of European civilization in California during his fifteen years was done because of his grand and stubborn vision. Serra's name is written on many pages of the West Coast's early history.

Today, perhaps more than any time in history, our world needs to remember a hero who also had the qualities of a saint. Serra in our midst is a great consolation. So vital in life, he projects his vitality even from the grave. And the full measure of his importance has not yet been established. This sturdy, erudite little Majorcan was surely a gentle and selfless giant among the conquistadors.

SELECTED
BIBLIOGRAPHY

I MAJOR BIOGRAPHIES

Maynard Joseph Geiger, O.F.M. (tr.) *Palóu's Life of Fray Junípero Serra.* Translated from the Spanish and Annotated. Washington, D.C.: Academy of American Franciscan History, 1955 (original edition, Francisco Palóu, O.F.M. *Relación Histórica de la Vida y Apostólicas Tareas del Venerable Padre Fray Junípero Serra,* 1787).

———. *The Life and Times of Fray Junípero Serra, O.F.M.,* Vol. 1 and 2. Washington, D.C.: Academy of American Franciscan History, 1959.

Jacinto Fernandez, O.F.M. *Summarium, Patris Juniperi Serra.* Rome, 1981; San Francisco: Serra Cause, 1984.

II OTHER IMPORTANT WORKS

Bancroft, Hubert Howe. *California Pastoral, 1769–1848.* San Francisco, 1888.

———. *History of California,* vol. 1. San Francisco, 1886.

Beilharz, Edwin A. *Felipe de Neve: First Governor of California.* San Francisco: California Historical Society, 1971.

Bledsoe, Thomas. *Poems in Praise of Fray Junípero Serra and the Missions He Founded.* Palma de Mallorca: Impr. Mossen Alcover, 1969.

Bolton, Herbert E. *Anza's California Expeditions.* 5 vols. Berkeley, 1930 (see vols. 3 and 4 containing Font's diaries).

———. *Fray Juan Crespi, Missionary Explorer of the Pacific Coast* (1769–1774). Berkeley, 1927.

———. *Historical Memoirs of New California by Fray Francisco Palóu, O.F.M.* 4 vols., Berkeley, 1926.

Bowden, Dina Moore. *Junípero Serra in His Native Isle.* Palma de Mallorca: Moore, 1976.

Culleton, Rt. Rev. James H. *Indians and Pioneers of Old Monterey.* Fresno, 1950.

Engelhardt, Zephyrin. *The Missions and Missionaries of California.* 5 vols. San Francisco: 1908–16.

———. *The Franciscans in California.* Harbor Springs, Mich., 1897.

———. *San Diego Mission.* San Francisco, 1920.

———. *San Luis Rey Mission.* San Francisco, 1921.

———. *San Juan Capistrano Mission.* Los Angeles, 1922.

———. *San Francisco or Mission Dolores.* Chicago, 1924.

———. *San Gabriel Mission and . . . Los Angeles.* San Gabriel, Calif., 1927.

———. *San Fernando Rey.* Chicago, 1927.

———. *San Antonio de Padua.* Santa Barbara, 1929.

———. *San Miguel Arcangel.* Santa Barbara, 1929.

———. *Mission N. S. de la Soledad.* Santa Barbara, 1929.

———. *San Buenaventura.* Santa Barbara, 1930.

———. *Mission la Concepción Purísima.* Santa Barbara, 1932.

———. *Mission San Carlos.* Santa Barbara, 1934.

The Founding Document of Mission San Juan Capistrano. Translated by Monsignor Vincent Lloyd-Russell. Rancho Los Cerritos, San Juan Capistrano, 1967. Los Angeles: Plantin Press, 1967.

Geiger, Maynard Joseph. *Franciscan Missionaries in Hispanic California, 1769–1848: A Biographical Dictionary.* San Marino: Huntington Library, 1969.

———. *Junípero Serra's Enduring Fame in Spain, Mexico, and California.* Santa Barbara: Serra Press, Saint Anthony's Seminary, 1960.

———. *Letter to Padre Junípero Serra.* Paterson, N. J.: Saint Anthony's Guild, 1944.

———. *The Long Road: Padre Serra's March to Saintly Honors.* Santa Barbara: The Cause of Serra, The Old Mission, 1957.

———. *Representations of Father Junípero Serra in Paintings and Woodcuts: Their History and Evaluation.* Santa Barbara: The Cause of Serra, The Old Mission, 1958.

———. *The Serra Trail in Picture and Story.* Santa Barbara: Franciscan Fathers of California, 1960.

Geiger, M. J., and Meighan, C. *As the Padres Saw Them: California Indian Life and Customs As Reported by the Franciscan Missionaries, 1813–1815.* Santa Barbara: Santa Barbara Mission Archive Library, 1976.

Guest, Francis F., O.F.M. "An Examination of the Thesis of S. F. Cook on the Forced Conversion of Indians in the California Missions." *Southern California Quarterly,* vol. LXI, no. 1, Spring 1979.

———. "Cultural Perspectives on California Mission Life." *Southern California Quarterly,* vol. LXV, no. 1, Spring 1983.

———. *Fermín Francisco de Lasuén, A Biography.* Washington, D.C.: Academy of American Franciscan History, 1973.

Kenneally, Finbar, O.F.M., ed. and trans. *Writings of Fermín Francisco de Lasuén.* 2 vols. Washington, D.C.: Academy of American Franciscan History, 1965.

Moholy, Noel Francis, O.F.M. *Our Last Chance.* Paterson, N.J.: Saint Anthony's Guild, 1952.

———. "The First Californian." *California Bicentennial.* San Francisco, 1970.

————. "The Path to Glory." *San Buenaventura*. Ventura, CA: San Buenaventura Bicentennial Committee, 1982.

————. "Miracle or Miracles?" *The Californians*. September/October, 1984.

Piette, Charles J. G. Maximin, O.F.M. "An Unpublished Diary of Fray Juan Crespí, O.F.M., from San Diego to Monterey, Apr. 17 to Nov. 11, 1770." *The Americas*, III, July–Oct. 1946 and Jan. 1947.

Teggart, Frederick J. *The Portolá Expedition of 1769–1770. Diary of Miguel Costansó*. Publications of the Academy of Pacific Coast History, vol. II. no. 4, Berkeley, Aug. 1911.

Tibesar, Antonine, O.F.M., ed. *Writings of Junípero Serra*. Washington, D.C.: Academy of American Franciscan History, 1955–1966 (see critical introduction by Eric O'Brien).

Weber, Francis. *California's Serrana Literature*. Los Angeles, 1969.

————. *Some "Fugitive" Glimpses at Fray Junípero Serra*. Los Angeles: Archdiocese of Los Angeles Archives, 1983.

INDEX